Praise for *White Too Long*

"*White Too Long* is a rich and astute reflection on the role of white churches in creating and sustaining America's system of racial caste. Robert P. Jones features his customary skillful blend of journalism, social science, and commentary, adding splashes of illuminating personal memoir, to explicate how churches perpetuated white supremacy for centuries—and still do."

—Gary Dorrien, Reinhold Niebuhr Professor of Social Ethics, Union Theological Seminary; author of *The New Abolition: W. E. B. Du Bois and the Black Social Gospel*

"Robert Jones combines the passion of a memoirist, the rigor of a social scientist, and the tenacity of a historian to produce this piercing exploration of the dark ties that bind aspects of American Christianity to the nation's original sin of racism. For anyone hoping to understand the cultural, racial, and religious fault lines that divide America today, *White Too Long* is timely, insightful and indispensable."

—Ronald Brownstein, Senior Editor, *The Atlantic*, Senior Political Analyst for CNN

"Robert Jones here makes a remarkable contribution to a growing literature in which white Christian people finally face the facts and tell the truth. His combination of historical research, data analysis, theological reflection, and personal storytelling makes this book a unique and extraordinary work. *White Too Long* is a breakthrough for Jones and a gift to his readers."

—David P. Gushee, Distinguished University Professor of Christian Ethics, Mercer University; author of *Still Christian: Following Jesus Out of American Evangelicalism*

"*White Too Long* is a work of rare courage, conviction, and analytical acuity. Part memoir, part brilliantly incisive social history, it passionately lays bare the complicity of white Christianity in America's ongoing plague of racism. Jones writes with the mind of a social scientist, the heart of a lover of humanity, and the soul of a fighter for a truly just society. *White Too Long* is a major contribution to the struggle to fully understand the forces that keep a fair and just America for all beyond our grasp."

—Obery M. Hendricks Jr., Visiting Scholar, Departments of Religion & African and African Diaspora Studies, Columbia University; author of *The Politics of Jesus: Rediscovering the True Revolutionary Nature of Jesus' Teachings and How They Have Been Corrupted*

"Jones's introspective, measured study is a revelatory unpacking of influence and history of white Christian nationalism."

—*Publisher's Weekly*

"This book is a marvel. It manages to quietly excoriate the insidious, entrenched attitudes that continue to sow racial hatred and division and to show the large and small ways that they continue. Devoid of moralizing, this powerful, heavily researched and annotated book is a must-read for religious leaders and academics."

—*Booklist* (starred review)

"A concise yet comprehensive combination of deeply documented religious history, social science research about contemporary religion, and heartfelt memoir. . . . An indispensable study of Christianity in America."

—*Kirkus Reviews* (starred review)

WHITE TOO LONG

The Legacy of
White Supremacy
in American Christianity

Robert P. Jones

Simon & Schuster

NEW YORK · LONDON · TORONTO · SYDNEY · NEW DELHI

Simon & Schuster
1230 Avenue of the Americas
New York, NY 10020

First Simon & Schuster hardcover edition July 2020

SIMON & SCHUSTER and colophon are registered trademarks
of Simon & Schuster, Inc.

For information about special discounts for bulk purchases, please contact
Simon & Schuster Special Sales at 1-866-506-1949
or business@simonandschuster.com.

The Simon & Schuster Speakers Bureau can bring authors to your
live event. For more information or to book an event, contact the
Simon & Schuster Speakers Bureau at 1-866-248-3049
or visit our website at www.simonspeakers.com.

Interior design by Paul Dippolito
Illustrations by Tim Duffy

Manufactured in the United States of America

1 3 5 7 9 10 8 6 4 2

Library of Congress Cataloging-in-Publication Data
Names: Jones, Robert P. (Robert Patrick), author.
Title: White too long : the legacy of white supremacy in
American Christianity / Robert P. Jones.
Description: First Simon & Schuster hardcover edition. | New York :
Simon & Schuster, 2020. | Includes bibliographical references and index. |
Summary: "WHITE TOO LONG draws on history, statistics, and memoir
to urge that white Christians reckon with the racism of the past and
the amnesia of the present to restore a Christian identity free of the
taint of white supremacy"—Provided by publisher.
Identifiers: LCCN 2019049393 | ISBN 9781982122867 |
ISBN 9781982122881 (ebook)
Subjects: LCSH: United States--Church history. | Christians, White—
United States—History. | Racism--Religious aspects—Christianity |
Race relations—Religious aspects—Christianity. | Racism—United States.
Classification: LCC BR515 .J66 2020 | DDC 277.30089—dc23
LC record available at https://lccn.loc.gov/2019049393

ISBN 978-1-9821-2286-7
ISBN 978-1-9821-2288-1 (ebook)

To Jodi
and
to the two First Baptist Churches of Macon, Georgia

"I will flatly say that the bulk of this country's white population impresses me, and has so impressed me for a very long time, as being beyond any conceivable hope of moral rehabilitation. They have been white, if I may so put it, too long...."

James Baldwin, *The New York Times*, February 2, 1968

Contents

– 1 –

Seeing

Our Current Moment

Introduction

The Christian denomination in which I grew up was founded on the proposition that chattel slavery could flourish alongside the gospel of Jesus Christ. Its founders believed this arrangement was not just possible but also divinely mandated.

After decades of regional tensions at the Triennial Conventions, where Baptists gathered to coordinate their church and missions work in the early eighteen hundreds, Baptists in the South brought the issue of the compatibility of slaveholding and Christianity to a head. The lead architect of these efforts was Reverend Basil Manly Sr., president of the University of Alabama, and the former pastor of the prominent First Baptist Church of Charleston, South Carolina. On November 25, 1844, Manly and a group of Alabama Baptists sent a letter to the managing board of the Triennial Convention, declaring, "Our duty at this crisis requires us to demand from the proper authorities... the distinct, explicit avowal that slaveholders are eligible, and entitled, equally with nonslaveholders [*sic*], to all the privileges and immunities of their several unions." They received a swift and blunt reply from the board: "If any one [*sic*] should offer himself as a

1

missionary, having slaves, and should insist on retaining them as his property, we could not appoint him." Leaving no doubt where they stood, they concluded, "One thing is certain: we can never be a party to any arrangement that would imply approbation of slavery."[1]

Six months later, Manly and other Baptist leaders across the South gathered in Augusta, Georgia, to form their own organization, the Southern Baptist Convention (SBC). Their "Address to the Public" declared that the goal of the new body was to direct "the energies of the entire denomination into one sacred effort, for the propagation of the gospel." By the time the SBC met in Savannah, Georgia, just one month after Confederate soldiers opened the Civil War with an attack on Fort Sumter, South Carolina, in April 1861, it was clear that its energies were also focused on supporting the Confederacy. Among other official church business that year, the SBC delegates defended the right of Southern secession and replaced references to the United States of America in the denomination's constitution with the words "the Southern States of North America."

While the South lost the war, this secessionist religion not only survived but also thrived. Its powerful role as a religious institution that sacralized white supremacy allowed the Southern Baptist Convention to spread its roots during the late nineteenth century to dominate southern culture. And by the mid-twentieth century, the SBC ultimately evolved into the single largest Christian denomination in the country, setting the tone for American Christianity overall and Christianity's influence in public life.

Moreover, while northern white Christians clashed with their southern brethren over the issue of slavery, the immediate aftermath of the Civil War revealed—to the dismay of African American abolitionist leaders like Frederick Douglass—that white Christian convictions about the evils of slavery more often than not failed to translate into strong commitments to black equality. As the dust was settling from the Civil War, this tacit shared commitment to white supremacy, and black inferiority, was a central bridge that fostered the rather swift reconciliation between southern and northern whites overall, and southern and northern white Christians specifically.

In my day job, I am the CEO and founder of Public Religion Research Institute (PRRI), a nonprofit, nonpartisan organization that conducts research on issues at the intersection of religion, culture, and politics. With training in both theology and the social sciences, I have always been fascinated by the ways in which beliefs, institutional belonging, and culture impact opinions and behaviors in public space. In our work at PRRI and generally in my research and writing, I strive to conduct research and write as an impartial observer.

But with roots from both sides of my family tree that reach back through the red clay of Twiggs and Bibb Counties, Georgia, into the mid seventeen hundreds, this book—the story of just how intractably white supremacy has become embedded in the DNA of American Christianity—is also personal. The 1815 family Bible on the top shelf of the bookcase in our home library gives witness to ancestors from middle Georgia who were Baptist preachers, slave owners, and Confederate soldiers. My family immigrated to Georgia from Virginia after receiving land grants as a reward for military service in the Revolutionary War as the government was forcibly removing Native Americans from Georgia and supporting the growth of white settlements.

I was born to Southern Baptist parents from this lineage who grew up in Jim Crow–era Macon, Georgia. I was baptized at the age of six at a Southern Baptist church in Texas, trained in Baptist Sunday school, and came of age as a leader in my Southern Baptist youth group in Jackson, Mississippi, where my family moved when I was seven. As a teenager, in addition to a raft of extracurricular clubs and activities, I was regularly at church for as many as five meetings per week: worship services on Sunday morning and evening; Baptist "Training Union" (classes on denominational polity and doctrine) and choir practice

Sunday afternoons; Monday-evening "church visitation" (outreach to potential new members and current members with low attendance levels); Tuesday-night Bible study; and Wednesday-night community supper, prayer meeting, and youth group activities. Thursday through Saturday were "Sabbath" rest days from church.

I memorized Scripture, agonized episodically over whether I was truly "saved," kept daily prayer journals, took for granted that prayer was an important part of dating (and, yes, even at times a way to get to second base), and read the Bible cover to cover over the course of a year in high school. The summer after graduation, through a connection with a former pastor, I had the opportunity to work for Billy Graham—as part of convention security, of all things—for a three-week meeting in Amsterdam for itinerant evangelists from all over the world. I received my undergraduate degree from Mississippi College—a Southern Baptist college from which my father, mother, and brother all hold degrees—and went on to complete a Master of Divinity degree from Southwestern Baptist Theological Seminary in Fort Worth, Texas.

And yet it wasn't until I was a twenty-year-old seminary student in a Baptist history class that I heard anything substantive or serious about the white supremacist roots of my Christian family tree. I generally knew that there had been a split between northern and Southern Baptists, but the narrative was vague. Baptists in the South, I was taught, were caught in larger cultural and political fights that were rending the country in the mid eighteen hundreds. And—just as I had learned from my Mississippi public school education—the true causes of the Civil War were "complicated." Slavery was not the central issue but merely one of many North-South conflicts precipitating the split.

As prominent Baptist historian Walter "Buddy" Shurden has pointed out, it wasn't until the last two decades of the twentieth century that white Baptist historians directly faced up to the proslavery, white supremacist origins of their denomination. Robert Baker, a professor at Southwestern Baptist Theological Seminary through the first half of the twentieth century, acknowledged that "the involvement of the South in the 'peculiar institution'" was a factor in the divide, but he quickly argued that there were other "strong considerations" for a separate body beyond this issue. But his student Leon McBeth—who assumed Baker's mantle as one of the leading Baptist historians of his day and in whose classroom this reality came into focus for me—gave it straight in his 1987 textbook, *The Baptist Heritage: Four Centuries of Baptist Witness*: "Slavery was the main issue that led to the 1845 schism; that is a cold historical fact."[2]

Even though I was among the first generation of seminarians who received a more honest account of Southern Baptist beginnings, the critical narrative often stopped with the causes of the Civil War. Reconstruction, if it was mentioned at all, was generally represented as a time when white southerners were victimized by vengeful occupying federal forces who supported black politicians primarily as a way of humiliating their defeated enemies. Southern whites were victims who were dishonorably treated after fighting a noble war.

It would not be until I was well into a PhD program at Emory University in my thirties that I was confronted with the brutal violence that white Christians deployed to resist black enfranchisement following the Civil War. The theologically backed assertion of the superiority of both "the white race" and Protestant Christianity undergirded a century of religiously sanctioned terrorism in the form of ritualized lynchings and other forms of public violence and intimidation. Both the informal conduits of white power, such as the White Citizens' Councils of the 1950s and 1960s, and the state and local government offices, were populated by pastors, deacons, Sunday school teachers, and other upstanding members of prominent white churches. The link between political leaders and prominent white churches was not just incidental; these religious connections served as the moral underpinning for the entire project of protecting the dominant social and political standing of whites.

This book puts forward a simple proposition: it is time—indeed, well beyond time—for white Christians in the United States to reckon with the racism of our past and the willful amnesia of our present. Underneath the glossy, self-congratulatory histories that white Christian churches have written about themselves is a thinly veiled, deeply troubling reality. White Christian churches have not just been complacent; they have not only been complicit; rather, as the dominant cultural power in America, they have been responsible for constructing and sustaining a project to protect white supremacy and resist black equality. This project has framed the entire American story.

American Christianity's theological core has been thoroughly structured by an interest in protecting white supremacy. While it may seem obvious to mainstream white Christians today that slavery, segregation, and overt declarations of white supremacy are antithetical to the teachings of Jesus, such a conviction is, in fact, recent and only partially conscious for most white American Christians and churches. The unsettling truth is that, for nearly all of American history, the Jesus conjured by most white congregations was not merely indifferent to the status quo of racial inequality; he demanded its defense and preservation as part of the natural, divinely ordained order of things.

Drawing on a mix of history, memoir, and contemporary public opinion survey data, this book reveals unsettling truths about what white Christians actually believe, what motivates their behavior, and what constitutes the core of their identity. The historical record of lived Christianity in America reveals that Christian theology and institutions have been the central cultural tent pole holding up the very idea of white supremacy. And the genetic imprint of this legacy remains present and measurable in contemporary white Christianity, not only among evangelicals in the South but also among mainline Protestants in the Midwest and Catholics in the Northeast.

The Baptist denominational history is not unique in American Christianity. Virtually all of the major white mainline Protestant denominations split over the issue of slavery. For example, Northern and Southern Methodists parted ways in 1845, the same year as the

Baptists, producing an additional spark for the tinderbox of Southern political secession. While they disagreed about slavery, both Southern and Northern Methodists agreed that black Methodists should hold a subservient place not just in society but even in Christian fellowship. Even after the southern and northern branches of Methodists reunited in 1939, they refused to integrate black Methodist churches into their existing regional jurisdictions. Instead, they segregated all black congregations into a newly created and deceptively named "Central Jurisdiction," thereby limiting their influence in the denomination for three decades until this system was finally abolished in 1968.[3] And while the national United Methodist denomination did considerable courageous work supporting the civil rights movement, most white Methodists in the pews rejected or simply ignored national denominational directives and actions. In the South, white Methodists were hardly distinguishable from white Baptists in continuing to promote white supremacy during the civil rights era.

The history of white supremacy among white Catholics is more complex. With its roots in Western Europe, Roman Catholicism has a long history of colonialism, particularly in Africa and the global South, where centuries of atrocities against and oppression of black and brown peoples were justified by convictions that white Christians were God's chosen means of "civilizing" the world. One of the first black men to set foot on North American soil, for example, was a slave, one of four Catholic Spaniards who survived a harrowing trek across what is now Florida, Arkansas, and Texas in 1536.[4] Catholics and Catholic institutions were also prominent slaveholders in states such as Maryland in the eighteenth and nineteenth centuries. In the spring of 1785, for example, John Carroll, superior of the priests working in the missions of Maryland who eventually became the first bishop and archbishop in the US, summarized the Catholic population in the newly formed state: "The Catholic population in Maryland is about 15,800. Of this number nine thousand are adult freemen, that is above twelve years of age; about three thousand are children, and the same number of slaves of all ages, come from Africa, who are called 'Negroes' because of their color."[5] In other words, about one-fifth of Catholics in late nineteenth-century Maryland were slaves owned by white Catholics or white Catholic institutions.

Racialized attitudes persisted into the twentieth century. As blacks began to pour into northern cities to escape oppression in the South as part of the "great migration" in the early nineteen hundreds, the Catholic Church responded by modifying its long-standing policy of assigning Catholics to parishes based on where they lived. In his 1970 book *Black Priest, White Church: Catholics and Racism*, Father Lawrence Lucas, a black Catholic priest, reported his experiences growing up in the 1930s and 1940s in New York's Central Harlem. As the neighborhood's racial composition shifted, whites remained assigned to their nearest parish church, but the Catholic hierarchy segregated all African Americans into St. Mark's Parish, regardless of where they lived. They also designated St. Mark's school as the destination for black children, which was put under the special direction of the Sisters of the Blessed Sacrament for the Indians and Colored People, an order of nuns founded in 1891 to work specifically with Native Americans and African Americans. White clergy rigidly enforced these lines, which protected the other eight white parishes from being integrated, sometimes violently. Father Lucas recalled one zealous priest standing on the church steps with a bullwhip to discourage any blacks from attending services. Reflecting back on his experience of these racist practices, Lucas noted dryly, "This wasn't the bad, bad South; it was the good, good North."[6]

On the other hand, Catholics faced their own serious persecution at the hands of white Protestants in late nineteenth- and early twentieth-century America. Along with African Americans and Jews, Catholics were targeted by the Ku Klux Klan as threats to a white Protestant American culture. As late as 1946, even the liberal editor of *The Christian Century*, the flagship magazine of white mainline Protestantism, could write about Catholicism as a threat to American culture, describing it as "a self-enclosed system of power resting on the broad base of the submission of its people, whose submission it is able to exploit for the gaining of yet more power in the political and cultural life of the secular community."[7]

But following the election of our first Catholic president, John F. Kennedy, in 1960, a number of forces have led to the mainstreaming of white Catholics. Kennedy's election and popularity as president served to secure Catholicism's place in a broader "Judeo-Christian" ethos. The earliest phase of the Christian Right movement didn't bridge the Protestant-Catholic divide. But when Protestant Christian Right leaders such as Jerry Falwell Sr. followed the advice of Catholic political activist Paul Weyrich to include opposition to abortion as a leading issue for the nascent movement in the late 1970s—as white Protestants were increasingly fleeing the Democratic Party over its support for civil rights—old antipathies quickly gave way to the promise of new political alliances.

By the closing decades of the twentieth century, young white Protestants could read the shifting attitudes about Catholics in the generational differences among their relatives. Grandparents thought of Catholicism as a dangerous foreign import, a papist cult that was unchristian and incompatible with democracy. Parents thought of Catholics as an outmoded but tolerable offshoot of the Christian family tree. And the youngest generation came to see them as just another "denomination" of white Christians—and one that was an important source of political reinforcement for battles being waged on two fronts: resistance to demands for black equality and opposition to the women's movement and the gay rights movement.

By the late twentieth century, Irish, Italian, French, Spanish, Polish, and other nonblack Catholics had been admitted into the ranks of white Christianity, with all the rights, privileges, and white supremacist expectations thereof. Across this bridge, the lines of cultural influence flowed in both directions. White Catholics carried abortion politics into the white conservative Protestant camp, where it was melded with antigay sentiment to create the peculiar alchemy of "family values." As I demonstrate in chapter 4, they also carried with them a particularly northern and urban brand of white supremacy. And the white Protestant Christian Right offered to legitimize their new political allies' claims to the coveted categories of whiteness and mainstream Christianity.

After centuries of complicity, the norms of white supremacy have become deeply and broadly integrated into white Christian identity, operating far below the level of consciousness. To many well-meaning white Christians today—evangelical Protestant, mainline Protestant, and Catholic—Christianity and a cultural norm of white supremacy now often feel indistinguishable, with an attack on the latter triggering a full defense of the former.

In many ways, this book is an account of my own journey of gradual personal awakening to these realities. While my seminary training in the white evangelical world and my PhD work in the (mostly) white mainline Protestant world removed some of the historical scales from my eyes, it wasn't until I was in the full swing of a career steeped in public opinion research that I realized just how fully these attitudes still haunt white Christians today.

To be sure, most white denominations, and most white Christians, have today taken pains to distance themselves from slavery, the Jim Crow laws that enforced racial segregation, and overtly racist attitudes openly espoused in the past. But in survey after survey, white Christians stand out in their negative attitudes about racial, ethnic, and religious minorities (especially Muslims), the unequal treatment of African Americans by police and the criminal justice system, their anxieties about the changing face of the country, and their longing for a past when white Protestantism was the undisputed cultural power. Whatever the explicit public proclamations of white denominations and individual Christians, the public opinion data reveal that the historical legacy of white supremacy lives on in white Christianity today.

The Importance of Our Current Moment

In the history of the nation, there are moments of extraordinary trans-formation, when the wheels of demographic, cultural, and economic change turn together. In between the old and new orders, particularly for those who are most swept up in the currents, there seems to be little direction to the flow of history. Chaos rules. The old assumptions fail. Hierarchies are turned on their heads. Common sense no longer functions. In his *Prison Notebooks*, early twentieth-century political theorist Antonio Gramsci expressed this sentiment from his cell in a Fascist prison in Italy: "The crisis consists precisely in the fact that the old is dying and the new cannot be born; in this interregnum, a great variety of morbid symptoms appear." In a recent essay, Slavoj Žižek, a contemporary philosopher and cultural critic, powerfully paraphrased the last part of Gramsci's quote in a way that captures the anxiety and fears—and real dangers—that these moments pro-duce: "Now is the time for monsters."[8]

We are living in one of these interregnum moments between an old and new order. In the last few decades, the country has under-gone tremendous demographic and cultural change, and the peaks of this emerging new landscape are gradually breaking through the surface of the public consciousness. As I documented in *The End of White Christian America*, the sun has set on the era of white Chris-tian dominance.[9] Looking just at race and ethnicity, the US Census Bureau predicts that by 2043 America will be majority nonwhite, and there are already more nonwhite than white children being born and attending the country's elementary schools. Add the lens of religion and culture, and it becomes evident that we have already crossed an important threshold. The last year that WASPs (white Anglo-Saxon Protestants) comprised a majority was 1993. In 2018, if you combined all white, non-Hispanic Christians—Protestant, Catholic, Orthodox, and other nondenominational groups—they comprised only 42 percent of the country, down from 54 percent just a decade ago in 2008.[10]

This new awareness has caused a range of reactions, with some mourning the death of the old and some pushing the new into life. More than any other factors, the demands for equality in the civil rights movement and reactions to demographic change have shaped the current contours of our two political parties. As the Democratic Party came to be identified as the party of civil rights, white Christians increasingly moved to the Republican Party—a migration that political scientists have dubbed "the great white switch."[11] Beginning with 1980 and in every national presidential election since, the voting patterns of religious Americans can be accurately described this way: majorities of white Christians—including not just evangelicals but also mainliners and Catholics—vote for Republican candidates, while majorities of all other religious groups vote for Democratic candidates. The racial divides within the Catholic Church are especially illustrative. For nearly two decades, approximately six in ten white Catholics have consistently supported Republican candidates, while approximately seven in ten Hispanic Catholics have supported Democratic candidates.[12]

In the legal arena, the Supreme Court legalized same-sex marriage in all fifty states in 2015, just eleven years after a dozen mostly southern states passed constitutional amendments prohibiting it. In politics, we elected our first African American president in 2008 and granted him a second term four years later. In the cultural arena, the #BlackLivesMatter and #TakeAKnee movements have exploded onto the scene, demanding justice for the alarming number of African Americans who are killed by police and for the disproportionate number of black men who are incarcerated. There have also been increasing calls—and some important actions—to remove Confederate battle flags and to take down a few of the thousands of Confederate monuments that dot the South's public spaces. There is even a renewed movement to have a serious conversation about economic reparations for the descendants of enslaved African Americans.

These forces have found expression, too, in the emergence of new institutions such as the recently opened Mississippi Civil Rights Museum in Jackson, and the striking National Memorial for Peace and Justice in Montgomery, Alabama. The Mississippi Civil Rights Museum—the first and only civil rights museum publicly funded by a state—unflinchingly tells the story of the brutality of white supremacy, notably including the role that white Christian churches played in justifying and enforcing segregation and resisting civil rights for African Americans. The National Memorial for Peace and Justice stands as a stark witness to the more than 4,400 African Americans who were lynched between 1877 and 1950. Notably, it is within sight of the Alabama Statehouse, where Jefferson Davis took the oath of office as president of the Confederate States of America, with Reverend Basil Manly Sr. at his side, in 1861.

Taken in isolation, these movements can appear disconnected, but they are better understood as epiphenomena, surface ripples signaling the presence of deeper currents. Like water rushing through a failing dam, this energy represents the cumulative claims to justice that have been submerged and held back by the sheer dominance of white Christian America.

Perhaps nothing has made the dynamics of our current moment clearer—including how powerfully racial divides run through American Christianity and politics—than Donald Trump's unlikely rise to power. Trump laid the groundwork for his candidacy by trolling President Barack Obama on social media and repeatedly questioning both Obama's US citizenship and religion. For example, Trump made the following unfounded claim on Fox News in 2011: "He doesn't have a birth certificate. He may have one, but there's something on that, maybe religion, maybe it says he is a Muslim." And unlike Republican presidential nominee John McCain, who actually took the microphone away from a woman who made similar claims at a town hall meeting during the 2008 campaign, Trump encouraged this line of thinking among his supporters. At a rally in New Hampshire, a supporter claimed, "We have a problem in this country. It's called Muslims. You know our current president is one. You know he's not even an American." Chuckling, Trump replied, "We need this question. This is the first question." For Trump, this was more than made-for-TV political theater; it was a successful political strategy. Even toward the end of Obama's second term in office, a September 2015 CNN/ORC poll found that 54 percent of Trump supporters, and 43 percent of all Republicans, believed Obama to be a Muslim.[13]

While Trump has been an unconventional president in many respects, one clear through line of his candidacy and presidency has been his wink-and-nod encouragement of the alt-right white supremacist movement in the United States. Trump initially refused to disavow an endorsement by former grand wizard of the KKK David Duke; refused to condemn white nationalists who marched in Charlottesville, Virginia, resulting in the death of one counterprotestor; verbally attacked black National Football League players who took a knee during the national anthem to protest the killing of African Americans by police; and has consistently avoided unequivocal condemnations of violence perpetrated by white nationalists.

There is clear evidence that we are witnessing measurable upticks in hate crimes and hate groups. The FBI reports that hate crimes increased by 30 percent in the three-year period ending in 2017;[14] the Southern Poverty Law Center reports that the number of hate groups operating across America rose to a record high of 1,020, a 30 percent increase from 2016 and the highest on record since tracking began in 1999.[15] And anti-Semitic incidents in the United States surged 57 percent in 2017, the largest rise in a single year since the Anti-Defamation League (ADL) began tracking such crimes in 1979.[16] Remarkably, the wink-and-nod behavior of the president has been so prevalent, and the resulting increase in violence so pronounced, that a 2018 PRRI survey found that a majority (54 percent) of Americans said they believe that President Trump's statements and behavior have encouraged white supremacist groups.[17]

Through it all, Trump has retained the support of white Christians. While much has been made of the strong support of white evangelical Protestants for Trump (81 percent, according to the exit polls in 2016), a Pew Research Center postelection analysis based on validated voters found that strong majorities of white Catholics (64 percent) and white mainline Protestants (57 percent) also cast their votes for Trump. By contrast, fully 96 percent of African American Protestants and 62 percent of white religiously unaffiliated voters cast their votes for the Democratic candidate, Hillary Clinton.[18]

While many have scratched their heads wondering how white Christians could support a candidate who has made white supremacy a foundation of his campaign and presidency, knowing how deeply racist attitudes persist among white Christians today makes this unorthodox political marriage less mysterious. Trump's own racism allowed him to do what other candidates couldn't: solidify the support of a majority of white Christians, not despite, but *through* appeals to white supremacy.

By activating the white supremacy sequence within white Christian DNA, which was primed for receptivity by the perceived external threat of racial and cultural change in the country, Trump was able to convert white evangelicals in the course of a single political campaign from so-called values voters to "nostalgia voters." Trump's powerful appeal to white evangelicals was not that he spoke to the culture wars around abortion or same-sex marriage, or his populist appeals to economic anxieties, but rather that he evoked powerful fears about the loss of white Christian dominance amid a rapidly changing environment.[19]

The Challenge of Seeing
White Supremacy in America

The biggest challenge for addressing the ongoing legacy of white supremacy is recovering the plain meaning of the words. For most whites, the term primarily evokes white sheets and burning crosses—extremist images, mostly from a bygone era. Eddie Glaude Jr., a distinguished university professor of African American studies at Princeton University and past president of the American Academy of Religion, describes this conceptual problem vividly in his book *Democracy in Black: How Race Still Enslaves the American Soul*:

"The phrase *white supremacy* conjures images of bad men in hooded robes who believe in white power, burn crosses, and scream the word *nigger*. But that's not quite what I mean here. On a broader level, white supremacy involves the way a society organizes itself, and what and whom it chooses to value.... And that's white supremacy without all the bluster: a set of practices informed by the fundamental belief that white people are valued more than others."[20]

Because of this radical narrowing of our understanding of white supremacy, the term paradoxically functions to soothe rather than trouble most white consciences. If white supremacy applies only to the KKK and its ilk, the logic runs, even an abstract condemnation of these extremist groups is the equivalent of a rejection of white supremacy. White responses to the problem of white supremacy too often begin with "Of course." But this inoculation of white consciences is actually as big a problem as the documented rise of fringe white supremacist groups. It creates within mainstream white Christians moral antibodies that preemptively neutralize thornier questions about the current power of white supremacy in our institutions, culture, and psyches.

If we slow down enough to reexamine the plain meaning of the phrase, its continued relevance comes clearly into view. Even rearranging the words—from "white supremacy" to "supremacy of whites"—gets us closer to a clearer meaning: the continued prevalence of the idea that white people are superior to, or more valuable than, black and other nonwhite people. And, most important, this subtle transposition gets us to what's really at stake: that white people's superior nature thus *entitles* them to hold positions of power over black and other nonwhite people.

A dizzying array of resources across multiple fields of human inquiry has been deployed to defend the idea of the supremacy of whites over other ethnic groups. By far, the strongest were theological arguments that presented white supremacy as divine mandate. Particular readings of the Bible provided the scaffolding for these arguments. Blacks, for example, were cast as descendants of Cain, whom the book of Genesis describes as being physically marked by God after killing his brother, Abel, and then lying to God about the crime. In this narrative, the original black ancestor was a criminal, and modern-day dark-skinned people continue to bear the physical mark of this ancient transgression; it did not need to be reiterated that they likely inherited not only their ancestor's physical distinctiveness but also his inferior moral character. These teachings persisted in many white evangelical Protestant circles well into the late twentieth century.

The scientific community also served to shore up the foundations of white supremacy. It spawned the nineteenth-century field of phrenology, an entire scientific movement that meticulously measured skull shapes and sizes of different people groups with the goal of providing demonstrable physical evidence for the inferior mental capacity of blacks. When this movement became discredited, some in the field of psychology took up where it left off, trading in their calipers for standardized mental capacity tests. As recently as the 1990s, psychologist Richard Herrnstein and political scientist Charles Murray argued in their controversial book *The Bell Curve: Intelligence and Class Structure in American Public Life* that black Americans' lower scores on standardized IQ tests were innately tied to race.[21]

Virtually every tool for the production of human knowledge about the world has been co-opted to justify white supremacy. The effect was a hydra-like defense of the racial hierarchy, so that with the defeat of one argument, another immediately raised its head. These justifications were so ubiquitous that they seemed to be the natural order of things, with tendrils creeping into cultural crevices big and

small, and stubbornly providing places for white supremacist arguments to take hold again, even after being dislodged elsewhere.

The Challenge of Seeing Whiteness

For most Americans who have been raised to understand themselves
as white, whiteness itself is, not surprisingly, more difficult to see than
even white supremacy. James Baldwin, writer and cultural critic, repeatedly turned to this theme as the crux of America's deepest problems in his writings and public lectures in the mid-twentieth century.
Baldwin powerfully addressed this particularly American dilemma in
an article on language and race in 1979:

> This nation is not now, never has been, and never will be, a
> white country. There is not a white person in the country, in-
> cluding the President and all his friends, who can prove he is
> white. The people who settled this country came from many
> places. It was not so elsewhere in the world. In France, they
> were French; in England, they were English; in Italy, they were
> Italian; in Greece, they were Greek; in Russia, they were Rus-
> sian. From this I want to point out a paradox: blacks, Indians,
> Chicanos, Asians, and that beleaguered handful of white peo-
> ple who understand their history are the only people who know
> who they are.[22]

I recall struggling mightily with the concept of race as a social con-
struct when I was first introduced to the idea in graduate school.
Given the virtually impenetrable black-white divide I experienced
growing up, my first reaction was skepticism. Even if race was a social invention, as far as I could tell, it would not change much in the
world I knew. But looking back now, I believe that reaction stemmed
from my assumption that this insight would be applied primarily to

understanding the constructed nature of nonwhite racial identities. And the academic deconstruction of the category "black" or "African American" seemed woefully inadequate to the task of producing any shift in black-white power relations. Even if every white person in the country became convinced of the fictional nature of blackness, it seemed unlikely to unravel the deeply held and strongly defended notions of race and racial hierarchies.

It has only gradually dawned on me—indeed, it feels like an ongoing process of understanding—that pulling back the veil on the fictional nature of *whiteness* is the necessary step. For whiteness is the mortar holding together the fortress of white supremacy, and if it crumbles, those walls will inevitably collapse. Because of its binding importance, the idea of whiteness has been, and remains today, vigilantly defended. In fact, virtually nothing has proven too costly a sacrifice on the altar of its defense: the bloodbath of the Civil War, the construction of a segregated education system, the creation of an apartheid Jim Crow system of laws enforcing segregation across all aspects of society, redlining real estate practices that divided virtually all of our major cities along racial lines, the development of a criminal justice system that disproportionately incarcerates millions of black men, and even the distortion of Christian theology. If one stops long enough to reflect on it, the ransom this fiction has demanded to sustain itself is staggering: the number of lives both white and black, the amount of money and cultural energy, and the disfigurement of some of our most precious ideals.

The project of seeing the constructed nature of whiteness, which is to say seeing ourselves more clearly for who we really are, is a particularly American responsibility, since the idea of whiteness most fully blossomed on American soil. The opportunity and the possibility of becoming white, and thereby being admitted to the privileged class, existed uniquely here; as immigrants landed on this country's shores, the real prize in the land of opportunity was not economic success but the possibility, for some, of becoming white. And this project is also a particularly Christian responsibility, since white Christian institutions and people were the primary architects and guardians of this exclusionary form of Americanness, which made full membership in the nation contingent on skin tone and religious belief.

Seeing the Role of Christianity in Sustaining White Supremacy

Speaking in 1964 on the one hundredth anniversary of the Emancipation Proclamation and in the wake of police violence against civil rights demonstrators in Birmingham, Alabama, James Baldwin flipped the script on what was then often called "the negro problem." In a talk entitled "The White Problem," Baldwin argued that the need to maintain a Christian veneer over the practice of slavery further degraded an already immoral system and distorted Christianity itself:

> The people who settled the country had a fatal flaw. They could recognize a man when they saw one. They knew he wasn't—I mean *you can tell*, they knew he wasn't—anything *else* but a man; but since they were Christian, and since they had already decided they had come here to establish a free country, the only way to justify the role that this chattel was playing in one's life was to say that he *was not* a man. For if he wasn't a man, then no crime had been committed. This is the root of the present trouble.[23]

Perhaps the most powerful role white Christianity has played in the gruesome drama of slavery, lynchings, Jim Crow, and massive resistance to racial equality is to maintain an unassailable sense of religious purity that protects white racial innocence. Through every chapter, white Christianity has been at the ready to ensure white Christians that they are alternatively—and sometimes simultaneously—the noble protagonists and the blameless victims.

And the dominant white supremacist culture that American Christianity has sustained has returned the favor by deflecting any attempt to trace the ideology to its religious source. White Christian ministers and churches can assert inerrant biblical teachings that people of African descent are, a few thousand years removed, the descendants of Cain in the Old Testament who was punished by God for disobedience with a physical mark; that the God of the universe has chosen whites to civilize and dominate the earth; and that the separation of the races, particularly white and black in this middle part of North America, is unquestionably God ordained. And when the arc of history finally reveals these Christian teachings on which so many of us were raised for what they are—that is, racist—the culture rather than Christianity takes the fall.

Conclusion

In 1990 novelist Toni Morrison gave a set of lectures at Harvard University in which she challenged a key assumption in American literature: "that traditional, canonical American literature is free of, uninformed, and unshaped by the four-hundred-year-old presence of, first, Africans and then African Americans in the United States."[24] Much of American literary criticism, she argued, approached the works of (mostly white) authors on their own terms. If a work did not thematize race, the question of how the unacknowledged presence of African Americans shaped the writing was not asked; if the text did include an African American character, analysis was largely confined to the world of the text rather than placing that world on the larger canvas of racial realities that must have informed the writer.

Morrison's insight merits quoting at length:

These speculations have led me to wonder whether the major
and championed characteristics of our national literature—
individualism, masculinity, social engagement versus historical
isolation; acute and ambiguous moral problematics; the the-
matics of innocence coupled with an obsession with figurations
of death and hell—are not in fact responses to a dark, abiding, signing African presence. It has occurred to me that the
very manner in which American literature distinguishes itself
as a coherent entity exists because of this unsettled and unsettling population. Just as the formation of the nation necessi-
tated coded language and purposeful restriction to deal with
the racial disingenuousness and moral frailty at its heart, so
too did the literature, whose founding characteristics extend
into the twentieth century, reproduce the necessity for codes
and restriction.[25]

Morrison was mostly concerned with the health of American literature, but her concerns also have particular relevance to religion.
While this perspective has received attention in the academy, most
white Christians continue to operate as if the theological world they
have inherited and continue to sustain is somehow "free of, uninformed, and unshaped by" the presence of African Americans. The
power of this mythology of pure, isolated white Christian theology
can be seen in the fact that it persists even in the face of glaring historical facts to the contrary.

For example, in the eighteenth and nineteenth centuries, as Protestant churches were springing up in newly settled territories after
Native American populations were forcibly removed, it was common
practice—observed, for example, at the Baptist church that was the
progenitor of my parents' church in Macon, Georgia—for slaveholding whites to bring their slaves to church with them. Whites sat in the
front, while enslaved blacks sat in the back or in specially constructed
galleries above. This was a norm for centuries in white slaveholding

Protestant churches, from frontier Baptists to highbrow Episcopa-
lians. And this practice wasn't limited to white Protestant churches.
Urban Catholic parishes in major cities such as New York were, as late
as the 1940s, still requiring black members to sit in the back pews and
approach the altar last to receive the bread and wine of the Eucharist,
oblivious to how this distorted the meaning of what was in theory a
sacrament of Christian unity.[26]

In these seedbeds of lived American Christianity, both Protestant
and Catholic, white Christians received instruction in the faith from
white ministers with a "dark, abiding, signing African presence" literally seated behind their backs or above their heads. While not in white
congregants' field of vision during the service, this looming presence
shaped what could be practiced (a slave master cannot share a common cup of Christian fellowship with his slaves) and preached (light
on Exodus and heavy on Paul) and how white Christians came to em-
body and understand their faith, generation after generation.

The effect of the enslaved African American presence on early
white American Christianity, and the white supremacist beliefs this
unholy arrangement conjured, was, of course, not confined to the
sanctuary. Like a distant planet whose presence is detected by its effect on the objects around it, this unacknowledged black presence
exerted a strong gravitational pull on the development of white Christianity, both inside and outside its stained glass windows.

This book illustrates the way in which the coherence of contemporary white Christian beliefs and practices are dependent on this unacknowledged African American presence. It documents the disfiguring
and intransigent legacy that a centuries-long commitment to white
supremacy has created within white Christianity and calls for an honest accounting of and reckoning with a complicated, painful, and even
shameful past.

But the book is importantly *not* an appeal to altruism. Drawing on
lessons gleaned from case studies of communities beginning to face
these challenges, it argues that contemporary white Christians must

take up this work not just because it is morally right or politically prudent but also because it is the only path that can salvage the integrity of our faith, psyches, and legacies. If we are going to understand the surging current of racism, anti-Semitism, Islamophobia, and our increasingly tribalistic politics in what the southern-born writer Flannery O'Connor dubbed our "Christ-haunted" land, we have to start here at its genesis. It's no exaggeration to say our very identities—our souls, to put it theologically—are at stake.

Remembering

Christianity as the Conductor
of White Supremacy

One of the most violent expressions of white supremacy occurred on Easter Sunday 1873 in the Baptist-dominated town of Colfax, Louisiana. The state was still reeling from defeat in the Civil War, and the 1872 election was only the second held under the auspices of the new 1868 state constitution that enfranchised black voters as part of Reconstruction. While antebellum state and local politics had been dominated by the pro-Confederate Democratic Party, the first Reconstruction election had resulted in widespread Republican victories for state and local office, including for the first time black officials such as Lieutenant Governor P. B. S. Pinchback.

Federal authorities had also reorganized the state after the war, with new towns and parishes taking on names of the Union victors. Colfax itself had been renamed in 1868. Originally called Calhoun's Landing, after a wealthy slave-owning planter, Meredith Calhoun, it now honored Schuyler Colfax, vice president under President Ulysses S. Grant. And Grant Parish, for which Colfax is the county seat, was carved out of the larger Rapides Parish and named for the president. Determined to push back these changes, including what they saw as the humiliation of federal occupation and "negro rule," whites revolted.

In Colfax, a group of armed African American Republicans, hearing of an impending attack, barricaded themselves inside the Grant Parish courthouse to defend the results of the elections and their lawful authority to assume office. Soon thereafter, a group of 150 whites surrounded the courthouse and opened fire. Leading the assault was Christopher Columbus Nash, the local sheriff and an ex-Confederate soldier who would go on to found the White League, a paramilitary organization that admonished whites in the South to organize and fight for "the maintenance of our hereditary civilization and Christianity menaced by a stupid Africanization [sic]."[1]

Nash's followers turned a small cannon on the courthouse and set fire to the roof. Nearly seventy African Americans were killed in the initial battle. When the remaining African Americans inside surrendered, thirty-seven were marched outside and publicly executed in the town square.[2] During the remainder of the day, more African Americans were rounded up and jailed, and approximately fifty more were executed that night. After the massacre, the bodies of the executed African Americans were hastily buried in trenches on the courthouse grounds, both as a terrifying symbol of what fate might await African Americans who attempted to assert political power and as an act of cruelty, since it denied their families the opportunity for proper Christian funerals and burials.[3]

Today there are two monuments to these events in Colfax, both erected by whites, which cast the occupation of the courthouse by black elected officials as a "riot" rather than what they were: a defense of the results of a lawful election that ended in a massacre by terrorists. The town cemetery is dominated by a white marble obelisk erected shortly after the event that reads: "In loving remembrance, erected to the memory of the heroes Stephen Decatur Parish, James West Hadnot, Sidney Harris who fell in the Colfax riot fighting for white supremacy." The other is an official plaque, erected in 1950 at the request of the mayor by the Louisiana State Department of Commerce and Industry, which describes the incident this way: "On this site occurred the Colfax riots, in which 3 white men and 150 black men were slain. This event, on April 13, 1873, marked the end of carpetbag misrule in the South." And although you might miss it because it is not formally marked, the "Colfax riot cannon," as it is known by most local whites, still sits in the front yard of a Colfax resident.[4]

With success in Colfax, the White League then set its sights on New Orleans and the newly elected Republican governor. In 1874 more than five thousand armed members of the Crescent City White League, constituted primarily of ex-Confederate soldiers, attacked local New Orleans and state police and drove the governor from office, occupying government buildings for three days before President Grant sent federal troops that finally forced their retreat. This conflict became known as the battle of Liberty Place, and the white citizens of New Orleans memorialized this conflict with a monument installed prominently on Canal Street in 1891. Its inscription declared that the White League's actions had overthrown the "carpetbag government, ousting the usurpers, Governor Kellogg (white) and Lieutenant-Governor Antoine (colored)." While the inscription noted that the "usurpers" were reinstated by US troops, it ended with this declaration of victory, echoing the Colfax monuments: "But the national election of November 1876 recognized white supremacy in the South and gave us our state." This monument stood in place until it was finally removed in 2017 amid threats of violence by local whites.

As the inscription notes, the period of federal protection for African American rights across the South lasted approximately two presidential election cycles. Employing what can only be called organized acts of white Christian terrorism, whites ruthlessly clawed back power in the southern states, and the federal government largely withdrew, abandoning former slaves to fend for themselves.

Southern whites felt vindicated. Mapping the experience of Civil War defeat and the resurgence of white supremacy onto Christian conceptions of crucifixion, resurrection, and salvation, they dubbed this new period "Redemption." After seizing back control of the formal political institutions, whites focused on reasserting their dominance in the cultural realm. And the means of enforcing racial dominance shifted from paramilitary clashes reminiscent of the war to the new tool of terrorism, using acts of extreme violence against individual victims to evoke widespread fear among African Americans. Their message was clear: anything but complete deference to whites could result in unspeakable forms of torture and death. For African Americans, the years immediately following the war were first elating and then devastating. W. E. B. DuBois famously described the period as one where "the slave went free; stood a brief moment in the sun; then moved back again toward slavery."[5]

One of the most chilling demonstrations of the compatibility of white Protestant Christianity with the racial violence of Redemption was the lynching of Samuel Thomas Wilkes, a black Georgia farmhand, on the third Sunday after Easter in 1899. Wilkes, who was referred to as Sam Hose or Sam Holt in contemporary news accounts, was accused of murdering Alfred Cranford, a prominent white planter, without cause as he ate dinner with his family. According to white newspaper accounts—each of which seemed motivated to outdo the other with shocking details—Wilkes snuck into the Cranford house, buried an ax deeply in Alfred Cranford's head, then tore an infant from Mattie Cranford, dashed it to the floor, and subsequently raped her multiple times in a puddle of her husband's blood.

Wilkes himself never denied killing Cranford but gave a very different account of the events. According to Wilkes, he and Cranford had a dispute after Wilkes asked to be paid for work completed and permission to go see his ailing mother. Cranford refused the request for pay and leave and told Wilkes if he pursued the matter, he would shoot him. The next day, while Wilkes was chopping wood in the yard, Cranford approached Wilkes, and they began arguing again. Cranford pulled out a revolver, and Wilkes threw his ax at Cranford, wounding him mortally in the head. He then fled directly into the woods, hiding and heading for his mother's Marshallville cabin, near which he was eventually captured. He denied assaulting Mrs. Cranford until his last breath.[6]

On April 13, a day after the alleged crime, the *Atlanta Constitution* ran the headline "Determined Mob After Hose; He Will Be Lynched If Caught." The article also included a subhead suggesting just how the lynching might proceed: "Assailant of Mrs. Cranford May Be Brought to Palmetto and Burned at the Stake." With Wilkes still at large a week later, Governor Allen Candler, a member of one of Georgia's most prominent Methodist families, offered a $500 reward for his capture. The paper put up another $500 and ran another article, declaring, "When Hose is caught he will either be lynched and his body riddled with bullets or he will be burned at the stake… the mob which is in pursuit of him is composed of determined men… wrought up to an unusual degree."[7]

The word that Wilkes had been captured and was to be lynched in the nearby town of Newnan reached Atlanta on a Sunday morning. The scene was surreal. When the city's white churches emptied from morning services, many worshippers streamed straight from church to the train station, hoping to participate in the much-anticipated lynching. To meet demand, the Atlanta and West Point Railroad put together a special run with six coaches; conductors roamed the platform, shouting, "Special train to Newnan! All aboard for the burning!" But that train was soon overwhelmed, with people hanging on to the outside of the cars and climbing onto the roofs to ensure they didn't miss the spectacle. Police had to be called in, and the railroad commissioned a second ten-car train behind the first. Packed with approximately two thousand Atlanta citizens, both trains sped toward Newnan.[8]

Meanwhile, church was also letting out in Newnan just as Wilkes was escorted off the train by his captors, who were delivering him to the jail to collect their reward. The *Atlanta Journal* noted that a spon-

taneous and solemn procession formed behind Wilkes and his captors "as church people were leaving their churches."[9] Wilkes made it
safely to the jail, but before he was locked in the cell, the crowd threw
the bailiff aside, seized the suspect, put a chain around his neck, and
brought him back outside. The scene abruptly shifted from solemn
order to enthusiastic, cheering chaos.

Before the awful carnivalesque violence erupted, there was one
moment of truth. Although there is no record of any Christian clergy
addressing the crowd, as they reached the town square and courthouse, they were confronted by two community leaders: former governor William Yates Atkinson and Judge Alvan D. Freeman. Both
had probably also just come from worship services, Atkinson from
the Presbyterian church and Freeman from the Baptist church. From
the courthouse steps, Atkinson pleaded with the crowd not to dis-
grace their state by circumventing the courts and taking the law into
their own hands. This appeal created a momentary silence, but when
someone yelled "Burn him!" mayhem ensued. Atkinson managed to
regain a hearing for one final fallback plea. Conceding that he could
not deter the mob from their plans, he pushed for a change of venue.
Atkinson threatened to testify against everyone he knew if the crowd
carried out the lynching "in the midst of our homes here in the city."[10]
With a roar of agreement, the mob lurched into action.

Given that these events occurred on a Sunday just as worshippers
were leaving church, it is striking to note the conspicuous absence
of religious opposition to the mob violence. Central Baptist Church
was a prominent, newly built structure, and its central location
provided a viewing area for many of the swirling events. Historian
Edwin Arnold noted the flow from church benedictions to the lynching processional: "members who had attended the Sunday morning
services now stood on its steps watching or joined the procession as
it passed by."[11] Certainly local clergy would have been aware of what
was happening. Yet there is no record that any clergyman addressed
the crowd.

For Atkinson's part, facing the tinderbox of imminent mob violence, he would undoubtedly have reached for the most powerful rhetorical weapon at his disposal. But just moments after a significant portion of the crowd had shared pews, observed Communion, read the Bible, sang hymns, and listened to sermons, Atkinson appealed not to Christian principles and morality but rather to the rule of law as his best strategy for dispersing the crowd. The ex-governor must have instinctively understood that white Christianity, as it was believed and practiced by his fellow townspeople, was perfectly compatible with the mob lynching of a black man.

As the throng left the town square, Wilkes was paraded through the central business district to the Central Baptist Church. There the processional changed direction, moved past the cemetery out of town, and ultimately stopped at the edge of a nearby field, which was chosen to allow a large viewing area. Along the way, at each corner, Wilkes was held aloft periodically for everyone to see, resulting in loud cheers from the crowd.

At the site, he was stripped naked, and a chain was wrapped around his body from neck to foot, locked around his chest, and attached to a tree. Tree limbs and railroad ties were laid at his feet, and young boys scavenged for additional brush to add to the pyre. Before the fire was lit, Wilkes was tortured for a half hour. His ears were cut off, his fingers removed one by one, and his genitals severed—with each held up for the approval of the cheering crowd. With Wilkes in agony but alive, he was doused with kerosene, and the pyre was lit. At that point, he screamed his last words: "Sweet Jesus!" Wilkes struggled against the flames, breaking the chain and lunging forward, at which point several whites pushed him back into the flames with large pieces of lumber and pinned him down until he died. While the intensity of the violence and suffering caused some in the crowd to look away, it also inspired expressions of religious ecstasy reminiscent of revival meetings. "Glory!" an old man in the crowd was recorded as saying. "Glory be to God!"[12]

But even Wilkes's gruesome death didn't fully satisfy the frenzied crowd. The *Atlanta Constitution* described the aftermath in vivid detail:

"A few smoldering ashes scattered about the place, a blackened stake, are all that is left to tell the story. Not even the bones of the Negro were left in the place, but were eagerly snatched by a crowd of people drawn here from all directions, who almost fought over the burning body of the man, carving it with knives and seeking souvenirs of the occurrence."[13]

This event became pivotal in W. E. B. DuBois's understanding of how embedded white supremacy was in the psyches of many white Christians, who saw no conflict with attending a lynching on the way home from church, and of the most respected white civic and religious leaders who either looked the other way or actively aided the murder. As DuBois was on his way to confront the editor of the *Atlanta Constitution* about its role in promoting Wilkes's lynching, he was stunned to see the victim's fingers and toes proudly on display in the window of the local meat market between his house and the newspaper offices.[14] The gruesome, menacing sight literally stopped him in his tracks. DuBois reversed his steps and returned to his office at Atlanta University. Realizing that facts and knowledge could not reach whites capable of such brutality in the bright light of a Sunday afternoon, he often recalled this event as one that "pulled me off my feet" and caused him to switch his career from scholar to activist. As he put it, "[I realized] one could not be a calm, cool, and detached scientist while Negroes were lynched, murdered, and starved."[15]

Much of the recorded history of slavery, segregation, and racism gives scant treatment to the integral, active role that white Christian leaders, institutions, and laypeople played in constructing, maintaining, and protecting white supremacy in their local communities. Writing in the midst of these upheavals, even historians critical of racism and

segregation often depicted white Christians as being merely complacent. They were guilty of committing sins of omission by ignoring the
post–Civil War turmoil in the eras of Reconstruction, Redemption,
Jim Crow, and the civil rights struggles of the 1950s and beyond.[16]
Even those who went further accused white churches only of complicity, of being unwitting captives of the prevailing segregationist
culture.[17] Both treatments are essentially protectionist, depicting the
struggle over black equality as external to churches and Christian
theology. More recent scholarship, however, has begun to document
the ways in which white churches, religious leaders, and members ag-
gressively defended segregation and "worked with the same enthusiasm for white supremacy inside the sanctuary as out."[18]

While charges of complacency and complicity are accurate as far
as they go, they overlook the proactive role white religious leaders
and white churches played in creating a uniquely American and dis-
tinctively Christian form of white supremacy. One of the principal
reasons white Christians fought so staunchly to ensure that their
own churches remained segregated was because they understood the
critical role these institutions played in the protection, production,
and proliferation of white supremacy. And, as I note below, while actions of white southern evangelical churches have received most of
the historical spotlight, one does not need to cast too far about to
see similar actions and shared convictions in white mainline Protestant and white Catholic churches well beyond the former states of
the Confederacy.

At a pragmatic level, white churches served as connective tissue
that brought together leaders from other social realms to coordinate
a campaign of massive resistance to black equality. But at a deeper
level, white churches were the institutions of ultimate legitimization,
where white supremacy was divinely justified via a carefully cultivated
Christian theology. White Christian churches composed the cultural
score that made white supremacy sing.

Southern Baptists and the Confederacy

Southern white Christians, particularly Baptists, played a critical role in justifying a particularly southern way of life, including what they sometimes referred to as the "peculiar institution" of slavery. Central to this story, but not widely known, are the efforts of the Reverend Dr. Basil Manly Sr. Born into a wealthy North Carolina plantation family in 1798, Manly followed his mother into the burgeoning Baptist movement in the South over the protestations of his Catholic father. Leveraging his influence as the senior pastor of prominent churches in South Carolina and Alabama, Manly became a pivotal leader in both religious and political secessionist movements. He was the chief architect of the withdrawal of Baptists in the South from cooperative fellowship with their northern brethren over the issue of slavery that established the Southern Baptist Convention; and he was instrumental in building a southern alternative to ministerial educational institutions in the North, which he perceived to be increasingly under the influence of abolitionists.

Manly was widely recognized as the leading theological apologist for slavery in his day. While some other religious leaders would defend slavery by arguing that it was not a moral but a pragmatic or political issue, Manly asserted forcefully an unapologetic theology of white supremacy, arguing that slavery was not an unfortunate necessity but rather part of the divinely ordained hierarchical order of Christian society. Manly's views were disseminated through his prolific writing, and he frequently engaged in debates with northern abolitionists. When challenged about the right of whites to own and sell African Americans as slaves during one of these exchanges, Manly delivered a vivid declaration of his unencumbered conscience, declaring, "I had no more doubt or compunction than in pocketing the price of a horse or anything else that belonged to me."[19] By the dawn of the Civil War,

Manly was acknowledged as one of the most uncompromising religious voices supporting slavery.

Manly first issued a call for a new seminary for Baptists in the South in 1835 while he was serving as pastor of Charleston Church in South Carolina. Over the next two decades, he was "the driving force" in a movement to establish the Southern Baptist Theological Seminary in May 1859.[20] Manly tapped his connections with other Southern Baptist plantation owners to make the dream a reality. Because the seminary was to be located in Greenville, South Carolina, Baptist residents of that state agreed to raise half of the necessary $200,000 in funding (equivalent to more than $6 million in 2019 dollars). Nearly all of the initial South Carolina funds were provided from the proceeds of slave labor: James P. Boyce, who subsequently became a faculty member in theology and chairman of the faculty, tapped his family's plantation fortune, which alone provided nearly $70,000; another $26,000 came from the prominent slaveholding Richard Furman family.[21] For his efforts, Manly was elected the founding president of the Southern Baptist Seminary's board of trustees, a position he held for the seminary's first critical decade leading up to and through the Civil War (1859–1868), and his son Basil Manly Jr. was named a founding faculty member in the area of the Old Testament.[22]

As important as it was to have a southern place for training Baptist ministers, establishing the seminary was just one arm of a multi-pronged campaign to protect and sustain a separate southern way of life based on a slaveholding culture and economy. Just as Manly was beginning his first term as the founding board president at Southern Baptist Seminary, he relocated from Charleston to Alabama, where he received a call to become the pastor of the First Baptist Church in Montgomery. Manly wasted no time in putting his defense of slavery and support of Southern secession to work in his new state. At the 1860 Alabama State Baptist Convention, he introduced a successful resolution declaring that Alabama Baptists believed they could "no longer hope for justice, protection, or safety" with reference "to our peculiar property recognized by the constitution."[23] The resolution concluded boldly: "Before mankind and before our God, that we hold ourselves subject to the call to proper authority in defense of the sovereignty and independence of the state of Alabama, and of her sacred right as a sovereignty to withdraw from this union."[24] Prominent nineteenth-century historian Benjamin F. Riley argued that this declaration by the most populous religion in the state did "more to precipitate the secession of Alabama than any other one cause."[25]

The following year, Manly was elected to serve as chaplain to the Alabama Secession Convention when it met in the state capitol on January 7, 1861. His opening prayer, which was published the following day on the front page of the *Montgomery Advertiser*, captured the lofty mood of the convention and the conviction that the actions being considered were of momentous civic and religious importance. He began by praising God for reserving "this fair portion of the earth so long undiscovered, unpolluted with the wars and the crimes of the old world that Thou mightest here establish a free government and a pure religion."[26] And he concluded the prayer with an appeal for divine guidance for the representatives, that they might "promote the maintenance of equal rights, of civil freedom and good government, may promote the welfare of man, and the glory of Thy name!"[27] Four days later, the Alabama convention voted to secede from the United States. Manly wrote home to his wife, Sarah, "God bless this State! You cannot conceive of the enthusiasm and feeling."[28]

Over the next few months, Manly played a key role in the formation and theological legitimation of the Confederate States of America, while simultaneously performing his roles as pastor of First Baptist Church in Montgomery and board president at Southern Baptist Seminary in Greenville. Manly helped a fellow Baptist, Jabez Lamar Monroe Curry, draft Alabama's new state constitution. When Alabama invited the other Southern states to attend a convention to form a new confederacy in February 1861, Manly was elected as the official chaplain of the Provisional Congress of the Confederate States. He offered the opening prayer, asking for divine protection and that the new Confederacy would last "as long as the sun and the moon."[29] He was in the room when the new government was organized and took credit for a preamble to the Confederate Constitution that invoked "the favor of Almighty God."[30]

But the most prominent role for Manly was yet to come. Recognizing his standing as the leading religious voice justifying slavery and calling for secession, Jefferson Davis chose him to give the invocation at his inauguration as president of the Confederacy on February 18, 1861. As eager crowds gathered along the streets of Montgomery, Manly was the only person accompanying Davis and Vice President Alexander H. Stephens in an open coach at the head of a long procession to the Alabama Statehouse. Standing on the platform next to the new president of the Confederacy, Manly implored God to "let thy special blessing rest on the engagements and issues of this day." He asked for special blessings on the Congress of the Confederate States and especially on Davis as a divine servant whose acts might be "done in thy fear, under thy guidance, with a single eye to thy glory; and crown them all with thy approbation and blessing."[31] In his diary, he concluded the entry for that day by saying, "May the blessing of God rest on this government of the Confederate States!"[32]

Within a span of nine months, then, from May 1860 to February 1861, Manly saw his strenuous efforts pay rich dividends: he delivered the first commencement address for the Southern Baptist Seminary's inaugural class as the board president; he performed his duties as the pastor of the symbolically important First Baptist Church in Montgomery; and he became the official chaplain to the Confederacy. Historian James Fuller, author of a biography of Manly, emphasized the way in which each of these efforts was working toward one end: "In Manly's eyes, the Confederacy was the culmination of God's plan for the world."[33]

Throughout the war, Manly continued these tripart duties. In service to the Confederacy, Manly was a steadfast and sought-after religious voice justifying slavery and white supremacy. As the Civil War ground on, he wrote defenses of the rebellion, offered prayers at public events, officiated at hundreds of funerals, and preached on fast days appointed by President Davis. Fuller summarized his ubiquitous presence this way: "Manly seemed always at hand to invoke the blessing of God upon the Confederacy."[34]

White Worship and Civil Rights in the South

While Manly's success and influence were perhaps unmatched during his lifetime, the broad influence he held as a religious leader was not unique. This intimate dance between white churches, culture, and politics—and perhaps more important, the personal connections among white pastors, civic leaders, and elected officials—was a familiar pattern across the South. An example from my hometown of Jackson, Mississippi, illustrates just how intact this web of power, dedicated to preserving white supremacy and resisting calls for black equality, remained more than a century later.

Jackson's influential First Baptist Church was undoubtedly the most powerful religious institution in the state during the civil rights years.[35] Sometimes referred to by locals in the know as Jackson's "Tammany Hall"—a reference to the political machine that infamously controlled New York politics in the late nineteenth century—FBC was a place where political influence and religious piety, social engineering and discipleship, white supremacy and Sunday school mixed easily. Situated across the street from the state capitol building, FBC was the single largest church of any denomination in Mississippi, boasting an 1,800-person sanctuary filled to capacity on Sunday mornings, seven assembly halls that housed a variety of programs and meetings, and a Sunday school program that enrolled 2,200 children and adults.[36]

FBC's impressive facilities were a fitting symbol of its powerful membership. It was the church home of the powerful Hederman family, who controlled Jackson's *Clarion-Ledger* and the *Jackson Daily News*, the largest newspapers in the state, along with the south Mississippi *Hattiesburg American* and, later, the Jackson television station WJTV. Multiple generations of Hedermans served as deacons at the church, wielded influence as its most generous patrons, and strongly shaped First Baptist's stance on race issues.[37] The church also counted among its prominent members Ross Barnett, Mississippi's governor from 1960 to 1964, who served as a deacon and the longstanding teacher of the men's Sunday school.[38] And FBC touted as a member Louis Hollis, the executive director of the Jackson Citizens' Council, who also served as the superintendent of the extensive Sunday school program.[39] The church provided a religious and cultural hub for these men and the organizations they represented.

In the 1950s and 1960s, the Hederman brothers, Thomas and Robert, were among the most powerful segregationist forces in the South. Two examples from the civil rights era give a taste of the reporting that Hederman-owned entities regularly generated for the Mississippi public. When the Supreme Court ruled that the all-white University of Mississippi had to admit James Meredith in 1962, the *Jackson Daily News* included a front-page story featuring a picture of a cross that had been burned outside of Meredith's assigned student housing with the headline "Greeting for Negro."[40] Similarly, the *Clarion-Ledger's* coverage of Reverend Dr. Martin Luther King Jr.'s 1963 March on Washington ran under the headline "Washington Is Clean Again with Negro Trash Removed," featuring a photo of the National Mall littered with garbage. A 1967 national review of newspaper coverage of the civil rights movement by the *Columbia Journalism Review* dubbed the *Clarion-Ledger* and the *Jackson Daily News* "quite possibly the worst metropolitan papers in the United States."[41] Hodding Carter III, a rare progressive white voice on racial issues who was managing editor at the rival *Delta Democrat-Times*, and later assistant secretary of state for public affairs in the Carter administration, was more pointed:

The Hedermans were to segregation what Joseph Goebbels was to Hitler. They were cheerleaders and chief propagandists, dishonest and racist. They helped shape as well as reflect a philosophy, which was, at its core, as undemocratic and immoral as any extant. They weren't hypocrites. They believed it. They believed blacks were the sons of Ham. The Hedermans were bone-deep racists whose religion 120 years ago decided that question.[42]

With the strong backing of the Hederman family, Ross Barnett rose to become the most powerful politician in Mississippi during the civil rights movement. He won the governorship by running an overtly segregationist campaign that appealed to religious conservatives by baptizing his white supremacist politics in Christian theology, with claims such as: "God was the original segregationist" and "The Negro is different because God made him different to punish him."[43] In addition to financing and positive media coverage from the Hedermans, Barnett received religious legitimization from the church. On the evening before his gubernatorial inauguration in 1960, for example, Reverend Dr. Douglas Hudgins, the pastor of the First Baptist Church, conducted a Christian consecration service for Barnett, presenting him with an ornate pulpit Bible in a special ceremony in the sanctuary.[44]

Barnett used Meredith's arrival at Ole Miss as a high-profile opportunity to make good on his campaign promise to prevent integration in Mississippi schools. In a widely covered speech—including front-page coverage in Hederman-owned newspapers—Barnett opened with this sweeping assertion: "There is no case in history where the Caucasian race has survived social integration." Drawing on racist hyperbole that would have been familiar to the white citizens of Mississippi, he declared defiantly, "We will not drink from the cup of genocide."[45] The next day's *Jackson Daily News* headline read, "Mississippi Mix? Ross Says 'Never!'" Just in case there was any confusion, the editorial page concluded flatly, "We support Gov. Barnett."[46]

Reverend Hudgins, the state's most prominent pastor during the civil rights era, filled the FBC pulpit from 1946 to 1969. Hudgins cast a long shadow in both religious and civic spaces. His sermons—a weekly dose of theology carefully curated to leave white supremacy undisturbed—were not only heard by the influential citizens sitting in the pews but also recorded and syndicated around the state via local radio. In addition, Hudgins held leadership positions in a number of civic groups. During his more than two-decade tenure as pastor, he served as director of the Jackson Chamber of Commerce, president of the Jackson Rotary Club, chaplain of the Mississippi Highway Safety Patrol, and a prominent member of the Masonic order.

For more than two decades, as the temperature climbed in Mississippi race relations, Reverend Hudgins built brick by brick a theological bulwark of personal and individual salvation, designed to protect white Christian power and white Christian consciences from black demands for justice. When the US Supreme Court handed down the historic *Brown v. Topeka Board of Education* decision in 1954, which ruled that state laws enforcing racial segregation in public schools were unconstitutional, the Southern Baptist Convention leadership surprisingly affirmed the decision not only as a pragmatic matter of legal concession but as consistent with Christian principles, angering many local churches. Here the SBC exhibited a trait that existed in virtually all white Christian denominations: a small group in the national leadership was considerably ahead of the regional and local church leadership. Reverend Hudgins, like many other local clergy, voiced his strong opposition to the denomination's position, both at the national convention and at home.

Then the Hedermans went to work. In addition to prominently covering Hudgins's statements, the *Jackson Daily News* carried a front-page story with extensive quotes from a number of deacons at First Baptist and included an editorial calling the SBC's affirmation of *Brown* "a deplorable action."[47] One of the most blatantly white supremacist statements came from FBC deacon and assistant to the state attorney general Alex McKeigney, who asserted that "the facts of history make it plain that the development of civilization and of Christianity itself has rested in the hands of the white race." He went on to declare that integration of any kind would ultimately result in racial intermarriage, "a course which if followed to its end will result in driving the white race from the earth forever, never to return."[48] On the editorial page of the same issue, the paper reassured its readers that Jackson's Baptist clergy and lay leaders were aligned in opposition to *Brown* and would ensure that nothing would "change the complexion of Baptist congregations in this city."[49] FBC itself maintained its official policy barring attendance by nonwhites beyond Hudgins's tenure, repealing it only in 1973.[50]

Underlying this interplay of religious, civic, and political activity was the core claim of Hudgins's theological worldview: that the cross of Christ had nothing to do with the social and political upheavals outside the walls of the church. Noted church historian Charles Marsh, who dubbed Hudgins the "theologian of the closed society," summarized Hudgins's theology this way: "Had he stated the matter more explicitly, he might have said that the cross has nothing to do with the civil rights of black Mississippians. On the other hand, the cross ought [*sic*] inspire decent white people towards the preservation of the purity of the social body. And it certainly did."[51]

In the 1950s and 1960s, First Baptist Church was a vortex of mutually reinforcing religious, social, and political influence. The Hedermans found in Ross Barnett their political champion of segregation and in Reverend Douglas Hudgins a theologian whose dignified, approving presence legitimized their power and whose sermons soothed white consciences against the mounting calls for justice outside the walls of the church. Governor Barnett found in the Hedermans patrons with nearly bottomless pockets and a media machine that lavished public praise and attention on his political life; and in Reverend Hudgins, a pastor whose approving presence signaled a divine blessing on his character. And the reverend found the church coffers full and his reputation burnished by being the pastor to such powerful men while enjoying positive and abundant personal media coverage himself. The *Jackson Daily News*, for example, lavished upon Hudgins the following praise: "Few among our theological leadership equal his power in exposition and amplification of the gospel message."[52]

This collusion by the media, politicians, and religious leaders produced a nearly impenetrable cultural bulwark. Both white evangelical and mainline Protestant churches served as cultural hubs and moral legitimizers of white supremacy, while the power of the state protected their segregated sanctuaries.

These connections weren't confined to the Baptists or even to evangelical denominations. Just a block away, Galloway Memorial United Methodist Church—a prominent congregation in the largest *mainline* Protestant denomination, the United Methodist Church—claimed Jackson's segregationist mayor, Allen Thompson, and several leaders of the Jackson Citizens' Council as prominent members in good standing.[53] Convinced that defending segregation in public institutions at the local level depended on ensuring segregation in Jackson's churches, Thompson led the city council to pass an ordinance in 1963 that made "disturbing divine worship" an offense punishable by a fine of up to $500 and up to six months in prison. He then instructed the police department that any attempt by an African American to worship at a white church qualified as a violation of this ordinance, even if the person was there peacefully or present at the invitation of a white member. The ordinance was enforced so aggressively that in several instances not only African American worshippers but also white members of the church who invited them were literally dragged from the church pews, arrested, and jailed.

The stances of white churches on the issue of integration were seen by civil rights activists and segregationists alike as the keystone holding the entire Jim Crow ediface together. In the wake of the 1954 *Brown* decision, with many national Protestant denominational offices approving the ruling, the Mississippi State Legislature moved quickly to protect the ability of local white churches to oppose their national offices and remain segregated, while still retaining their property. One of the authors of what became known as "the church property bill" argued explicitly that such a step was crucial because, he asserted, if integration came to Mississippi, "it will enter through the front door of churches."[54]

On Sunday, June 9, 1963, an integrated group of four local students organized by local civil rights activists Medgar Evers and Reverend Edwin King, a white chaplain at Tougaloo College, attempted to cross the color line at both First Baptist Church and Galloway Memorial Methodist Church, the home congregations of the governor and mayor, respectively.

Evers, field secretary of the civil rights organization the National Association for the Advancement of Colored People (NAACP), drove the students to First Baptist Church himself. As the students attempted to enter, they were met by the head deacon. Using language clearly designed to establish the basis for arrest, the deacon told the students, "In view of the tension present today, I believe your presence would disrupt the worship of all our people."[55] According to media reports, the governor arrived for worship during this confrontation but bypassed it as he entered. Finding themselves barred from the largest Baptist church in the state, the students walked one block to Galloway, the largest Mississippi Methodist church, where ushers also refused to allow them to enter.

These actions led to remarkably different responses from the two churches. While the segregationist mayor had plenty of like-minded company at Galloway, the church's senior pastor, Reverend Dr. W. B. Selah, had made his position clear to his congregation, preaching that "there can be no color bar in a Christian church." Informed in the middle of the service that Galloway's ushers had turned away the integrated group of students, Reverend Selah rose to the pulpit. After delivering a shortened sermon on "The Spirit of Christ," he pulled out a prepared statement—one he had been keeping with him for weeks

in case black worshippers were refused entry—and tendered his resignation. Reverend Jerry Furr, the associate minister, followed suit.
In stark contrast, First Baptist Church hardened its position. Meeting
the same afternoon, the board of deacons put forward a resolution en-
dorsing the church's actions, which passed without a dissenting vote.
The resolution was unambiguous, stating that FBC would "confine its
assemblies and fellowship to those other than the Negro race."[56]

The attempt to integrate the largest white Baptist and Methodist
churches in the state was the last action Medgar Evers would oversee.
Just two days after these white churches turned away black worshippers, he and King held a sparsely attended meeting at the black New
Jerusalem Baptist Church to discuss the weekend's activities and the
future of the movement. While Evers realized that most of the people
in the pews opposed integration, he had been deeply moved by the resignation of Galloway's ministers. He told King, "What they said, what
they did—refusing to preach in a segregated church—now, that has
made me feel better than anything in this whole movement in many
days."[57] King told him he would pass his sentiments on to Selah and
Furr, then said the last words he would say to his friend: "See you at
the office tomorrow, Medgar. Good night."

Evers stayed at the church to finish some work before heading
home to his wife and three young children. As Evers got out of his car
just after midnight, a gunman shot and killed him in the driveway.
The murder weapon, including a fresh fingerprint on the rifle scope,
was found in a field nearby and traced to Byron De La Beckwith
Jr., a member of the White Citizens' Council in Greenwood and an
active member of the Greenwood Episcopal Church of the Nativity.
Beckwith was well known across the Delta for his published letters
to the editor that regularly mixed Christianity and white supremacy,
with passages such as this:

"I shall oppose any person, place, or thing that opposes segregation. And further when I die I will be buried in a segregated cemetery.
When you get to heaven, you will find me in the part that has a sign

saying 'for whites only,' and if I go to Hades, I'm going to raise hell all over Hades until I get to the white section.... For the next 15 years, we here in Mississippi are going to have to do a lot of shooting to protect our wives, children, and ourselves from bad niggers."[58]

Just two years before murdering Evers, when Beckwith heard rumors that black visitors might try to attend his own church in the Mississippi delta, he had arrived early and stood on the steps with a pistol, declaring to his fellow members that he would handle things.[59] At Beckwith's first trial for Evers's murder, the Mississippi State Sovereignty Commission—an official state agency operating from 1956 to 1977 to preserve segregation—illegally investigated potential jurors to help his defense attorneys weed out Jews and blacks. Governor Ross Barnett personally appeared in the courtroom, shaking hands with Beckwith in full view of the jury. Two successive trials with all-white juries failed to reach a decision. Beckwith was not brought to justice until a third trial finally convicted him in 1994.

The influence of the Hedermans and Barnett was difficult to escape in Jackson, even for families of modest means, such as mine, who didn't run in elite social circles on the north side of town. The woods across from my childhood family home in southwest Jackson, fenced off with barbed wire and peppered with white "POSTED—No Trespassing" signs with faded red block lettering, were owned by the Hedermans to produce pulp for their sprawling printing business. And when my friends and I went water skiing or fishing, the most popular spot was the Ross Barnett Reservoir just outside town, a thirty-three-thousand-acre lake that is the state's largest source of drinking water. At Mississippi College, the dorm across the street from mine was Hederman Hall, and when I received a scholarship as outstanding freshman male student, it was the T. M. Hederman III Memorial Scholarship, established in 1964 by the Hederman family, many of whom were Mississippi College alumni.

As a public school student, I grew up singing the official state song, "Go Mississippi," which I still remember. What I did not know as a child was that the anthem took its tune from Governor Barnett's segregationist campaign jingle.[60] The original lyrics were:

Roll with Ross, roll with Ross, he's his own boss
For segregation, one hundred percent
He's not a moderate like some of the gents
He'll fight integration with forceful intent.

The new lyrics are more in line with what one might expect from a rah-rah official state song, but they retain an unmistakable note of defiance: "Go, Mississippi, keep rolling along / Go Mississippi, you cannot go wrong." The new song was officially dedicated by Barnett at the Ole Miss–University of Kentucky football game on September 29, 1962, the night before Meredith was to enroll. It was performed by the Ole Miss marching band in front of more than forty-one thousand fans.[61] Since 2000, there have been at least four bills introduced in the Mississippi legislature to replace it because of its segregationist roots; all have died in committee.[62]

Childhood Memories: Racial Desegregation in Jackson (1970s and 1980s)

Third grade was a big year for me. The year before had been an adjustment both socially and academically, as I had arrived at our neighborhood public school, Oak Forest Elementary, as a "new kid" after moving to Mississippi from Texas in 1975. But this year, I told my third-grade self, would be more fun; I had friends, and, more important, I was now old enough to ride my bike to school instead of walking or taking the bus. What I didn't know was that this would also be the year when the first African American kids would show up in significant numbers at our school.

When the "separate but equal" rationale for segregation was struck down by the US Supreme Court in the 1954 *Brown* decision, local Mississippi communities responded with more than a decade of in-action, followed by the swift erection—by both the White Citizens' Councils and white churches—of private whites-only academies, as the last delaying tactics played out and desegregation finally looked inevitable. (As of this writing, there are thirty-five such "segregation academies" remaining in Mississippi alone, schools that were founded between 1964 and 1972, and all of them have fewer than 2 percent black students enrolled today[63]).

In the largest school district in the state, Jackson Public School District (JPSD), which I attended second through twelfth grade, the complexity of the district presented opportunities for a range of eva-sive tactics. The final legal blow to these strategies of resistance did not come until a 1969 court decision. And while an integration plan was implemented in fall 1970 by JPSD, the first African American kids did not actually arrive in significant numbers at Oak Forest El-ementary School, in southwest Jackson, until 1976.

In my third-grade memory, I recall feeling more curious than tense. I did not really understand why black kids were arriving by the busful, but I still got to ride my bike, and most of my white friends from the neighborhood were still there. I didn't give it much thought then, but now I can only imagine how different the experience must have been for my new black classmates as they stepped off the bus in our all-white neighborhood for the first time.

School integration did have the ripple effect of at least partially in-tegrating related institutions such as sports leagues, which often drew upon school groups to form teams. While my elementary-school-age soccer teams were mostly white, we typically had two or three African American players. But there were clear episodic reminders that while my fellow black students attended the same schools and had the same teachers, we still lived in strikingly segregated social worlds, and that when those worlds overlapped, my black classmates and friends were tenuous guests in a world of white dominance.

We played many of our games at Battlefield Park, a public park commemorating the battle of Jackson, where Confederate forces resisted but lost a decisive battle to General Ulysses S. Grant's Union forces as they pushed their way to Vicksburg, Mississippi. On at least one occasion, I recall seeing Ku Klux Klan members in full white regalia, handing out white supremacist pamphlets and collecting donations at the red light while we were waiting to turn into the park for a game. From my perch in the back seat of our gold Chevy Impala, I remember being struck by the fact that their hoods were pushed back to reveal their faces openly and that one of the men was holding his son, also robed, who was a few years younger than me. The boldness of the event was unusual enough to stick out in my memory, but also unsurprising enough to spark only a short conversation with my parents, who explained matter-of-factly that these people held negative views about black people and that we disagreed with them. As I recall, the game proceeded as planned, without any acknowledgment of my black teammates, who also had to drive past this threatening display of white power on their way to enjoy a sunny, crisp fall Saturday morning at the soccer field.

While my schools and sports teams became integrated, one place that remained strictly segregated was my Southern Baptist church, Woodville Heights Baptist Church, which cast a watchful eye on the neighborhood from its place on a hill a few blocks from my house. For most of my childhood and adolescence, I understood church segregation in benign terms, as the result of cultural preferences for different styles of worship. Neither group would be happy with racial mixing, the argument went, because each race naturally preferred its own type of preaching and music.

The first black person I recall seeing in the church sanctuary during a service was a man named Sheldon Gooch, an inmate from the notorious Mississippi State Penitentiary in Parchman, usually just called

"Parchman Farm." As part of a prison-approved temporary leave program, Gooch, a young man of about thirty, was making the rounds at
a number of white churches to sing and testify about how finding God
in prison had saved him from a dysfunctional childhood in inner-city
Detroit and a life of violent crime as a young man in Mississippi.

I remember that Sunday-evening service as unusual, and certainly out of the comfort zone for my congregation, but I don't recall
anyone experiencing it as threatening. Our regular Sunday-evening
service was always less formal and, from time to time, featured outside preachers, speakers, or performers. As the service began, our
pastor rose to the pulpit, explained that we had a special guest, and
introduced Sheldon Gooch. He did not introduce the other conspicuous guest: a prison guard who was required to accompany Gooch and
ensure his return after the service. Both were easy to identify. Gooch
was a muscular, dark-skinned African American man, and the white
guard carried a sidearm; both wore uniforms: the easily identifiable
blue pants with a darker blue stripe on the outside of the leg and
matching denim button-up shirt for the inmate, and an ill-fitting tan
and brown ensemble for the guard.

As our pastor took his seat and Gooch ascended the half dozen
steps to the royal-blue carpeted stage, a silent and nervous anticipa-
tion filled the sanctuary. Knowing the curiosity and probable anxiety
in his audience, he calmly grabbed the microphone, planted himself
stage left of the pulpit, and went straight to his story. He opened by
describing his childhood.[64] "I grew up in the streets of Detroit, and
I was living in a tough situation. I came up in a single-parent home
with four brothers. We were on food stamps and welfare and the
whole thing—just a typical ghetto statistic. And it was tough." He then
told of running with the wrong crowd, being strung out on crack and
heroin by fifteen, and landing in prison for the first time at seventeen.

After being paroled, he moved to Meridian, Mississippi, where his
mother had relocated, opened a school of self-defense, and seemed to
be on a better path. But he slowly became involved again with drugs

and found himself back in prison, facing a new sentence of life plus sixty years for three counts of armed robbery. A major influence on him was Wendy Hatcher, a five-foot-tall white prison chaplain who was originally from England. As Gooch told it, "Early each day, she would say, 'Oh, good morning, Sheldon, the Lord loves you and has a plan for your life, and I hope you have a good day and God bless you,' with that British accent. I'd see her coming in the gym in the morning, and I'd run and hide. And here I am, one of the most feared guys in this penitentiary, and I'm scared of this little bitty old white woman. But the spirit in me was on the run from the spirit in her."

His prison work detail was in the gymnasium, and one day Gooch was assigned to set up for a church service Hatcher had organized. There, as he sat through the service involuntarily, he heard the message that he said changed his life. "I heard them say, 'Jesus Christ can set you free no matter where you are.' And I said, 'Man, you know what, if anybody needs to be free, it's me. Let me just listen.' At that point, I knew I needed Jesus, and he was there to save me. And on that night, November 18, 1982, in Parchman Prison, I gave my life to Jesus Christ." After a long, dramatic pause to emphasize the paradox, he wrapped up his testimony, saying, "Life plus sixty years, but I found freedom from the slavery and bondage of sin."

Despite the more colorful aspects of his story, most of us gradually, if unconsciously, exhaled as his narrative assumed a familiar arc of evangelical testimony: lost but now found, sinful but now redeemed, captive but now free. Similarly, while his vocal performance contained flourishes and repetitions that were more at home in the black gospel tradition, on the whole he covered renditions of hymns and contemporary Christian songs that were familiar. More than the music, what stood out to me most was the central theme of Gooch's testimony, which he drove home in his signature closing song, "I'm Free," which he composed shortly after his conversion experience. The last minute of the five-minute song is an instrumental filled only with plaintive repetitions of the two-word phrase "I'm free… I'm free… I'm free…"

Although I wasn't conscious of it at the time, in retrospect, I real-ize that Gooch's easy acceptance hinged on the fact that his testimony reinforced a complex choreography of white supremacy. The power-fully built black man wore his prison-issued clothes and performed under the watchful eye of an armed white prison guard who would escort him back to prison after the service. His personal narrative evoked stereotypes of black inner-city ghettos and dangerous black male bodies that needed to be subdued and disciplined by white au-thorities before surrendering and submitting to a Jesus introduced to him by a white European woman. And the central point of Gooch's testimony subtly evoked a common trope of Old South white ideol-ogy: the happy slave who finds his true purpose in the service of a white master, where he is better off than before his enslavement.

But it was another sanctuary visit that exposed just how rigorously the color line continued to be patrolled at church. My large church youth group, numbering more than a hundred, was known in south-west Jackson as a vibrant and safe place for teenagers to socialize. In addition to the typical Bible studies and Sunday school, we had a young, charismatic female youth minister (an anomaly in the male-dominated Baptist world) who scheduled regular activities, organized events, and turned part of the church educational space into a youth room—with couches and a pool table—that functioned as a social hub and kind of community center. These popular extrachurch events were intended as outreach and attracted kids from the neighborhood and area schools. And from time to time, the participants were not all white.

This occasional participation by a few black teens in the outside activities may have raised some individual eyebrows, but it never gen-erated any public conversation of which I was aware. But in my junior year of high school, one of our African American friends—I'll call him Michael—attended one of the Sunday-morning services. Since he had participated in an all-night "lock-in" event at the church gymnasium the night before, and everyone from that event was sitting together in the first three pews in the church, as was youth group tradition, I don't think any of our friends gave it much thought.

But among the older members of the church, our friend Michael's Sunday-morning visit generated a buzz of anxious conversation. It was one thing to allow black kids to participate in extracurricular church activities, but it was another to allow them to attend worship or Sunday school. His presence among us raised a frenzy of anxious questions. What if he wanted to join the church as a member? What if, in an era in which African American and white children sharing community pools was still uncomfortable to most whites in the South, he wanted to be baptized by full immersion in the sanctuary's baptismal pool installed so visibly above the choir loft? What if his entire family wanted to join the church? And, God forbid, what if Michael became an active member of the youth group and wanted to date one of our white teenage girls?

The anxious need to be prepared for, and possibly intervene in, these potential eventualities resulted in an emergency deacons' meeting the following week. I don't know what happened at that meeting, and the issue quickly dissipated, as our friend had simply wanted to visit and had no interest in joining the church. But the events stayed with me and pushed an uncomfortable fact into my consciousness: that a black kid sitting in the pews among us was perceived as a much greater threat than a black prison inmate performing on our church stage.

The White Christian Shuffle: Contemporary Efforts to Address White Supremacy Among Southern Baptists

White Christians, and even my own childhood home denomination, are gradually beginning to face the bare fact that white supremacy has played a role in shaping American Christianity. But they have been too quick to see laments and apologies as the end, rather than the beginning, of a process. They also remain full of contradictions and too quickly avert their gaze when the weighty implications of history require concrete, sustained action in the present.

At a 1995 meeting in Atlanta that commemorated the 150th anniversary of its founding, the Southern Baptist Convention finally got around to apologizing for its perpetuation of racism, its role in defending slavery and Jim Crow, and its failure to support the civil rights movement. The messengers at the convention voted to pass a formal resolution that repudiated "historic acts of evil such as slavery from which we continue to reap a bitter harvest." They also acknowledged that SBC churches "failed, in many cases, to support, and in some cases opposed, legitimate initiatives to secure the civil rights of African-Americans" and issued an apology "to all African-Americans for condoning and/or perpetuating individual and systemic racism in our lifetime."[65]

The 1995 convention also saw Reverend Gary Frost of Youngstown, Ohio, elected to second vice president, making him the first African American to reach that level of leadership. Shortly after the resolution passed with only twelve minutes of discussion, Frost rose to the podium to play out a piece of contrived cultural theater that seemed to imply that a kind of magical reconciliation had instantaneously occurred. Frost issued a brief declaration: "On behalf of my black brothers and sisters, we accept your apology, and we extend to you our forgiveness in the name of our Lord and savior, Jesus Christ." Enthusiastic applause erupted from the overwhelmingly white delegates. In less than fifteen minutes, 150 years of Southern Baptist white supremacy was seemingly absolved.

Given the SBC's white supremacist legacy, this resolution received widespread attention, including front-page coverage in the *New York Times*.[66] But while some black religious leaders welcomed the move, many others, such as Reverend Arlee Griffin Jr., pastor of the four-thousand-member Berean Missionary Baptist Church in Brooklyn and historian for the historically African American Progressive Na-

tional Baptist Convention, were more skeptical. Citing the denomination's long legacy of racism, Griffin replied, "It is only when one's
request for forgiveness is reflected in a change of attitude and actions
that the victim can then believe that the request for forgiveness is au-
thentic."[67]

Twenty-five years later, the SBC is still wrestling with the legacy of
white supremacy and still attempting to step straight from confession to absolution without pausing seriously over the question of
restitution or repair. The trajectory of two prominent white denominational leaders who were a part of the 1995 working group that produced the apology demonstrates just how difficult real changes of
attitude and actions are, just how deep the defensive impulses live,
even when there is an explicit attempt to move away from a racist
past.

In spring 2012 Richard Land—the director of the SBC's Ethics and
Religious Liberty Commission and one of the chief architects of the
denomination's racial reconciliation efforts—made incendiary com-
ments on his radio show about the killing in Florida of Trayvon Martin, an unarmed black teenager, by a self-appointed neighborhood
vigilante. Land asserted that President Obama had "poured gasoline
on the racialist [sic] fires" and that Reverend Jesse Jackson and Reverend Al Sharpton were "race hustlers" who were using the case "to try
to gin up the black vote for an African American president who is in
deep, deep, deep trouble for reelection."[68] After a public outcry, Land
lost his radio show, was forced to apologize publicly twice, and by the
end of the year had stepped down from the position he had held for
twenty-five years.[69]

The second key figure is Al Mohler, president of Southern Baptist Seminary—the oldest SBC seminary, which was founded in 1859
in Greenville, South Carolina, but relocated to Louisville, Kentucky,
after the Civil War. Mohler presents a case study in the limitations of

how far even well-intentioned white evangelicals are willing to go to reckon with their white supremacist past. On the one hand, Mohler has a long history of working to address the denomination's racist history. In 2015, twenty years after his work on the SBC apology on slavery, a self-described white supremacist named Dylann Roof murdered nine worshippers at a historic black South Carolina church. Mohler responded by posting an article on the seminary's website addressing the legacy of "white superiority" in the theology of the seminary's founders. And, most prominently, in 2018 he led Southern Baptist Seminary to create a report documenting and lamenting the institution's support of slavery, racism, and Jim Crow.

But Mohler's approach represents what I've dubbed "the white Christian shuffle," a subtle two-steps-forward-one-step-back pattern of lamenting past sins in great detail, even admitting that they have had pernicious effects, but then ultimately denying that their legacy requires reparative or costly actions in the present. It's a sophisticated rhetorical strategy that emphasizes lament and apology, expects absolution and reconciliation, but gives scant attention to questions of justice, repair, or accountability. A careful reading of Mohler's 2015 language helps illuminate the inner workings of this strategy.

After the 2015 South Carolina church shooting, Mohler posted his boldly titled response: "The Heresy of Racial Superiority—Confronting the Past, and Confronting the Truth." The piece began strongly. Defining *heresy* as an error "so important that those who believe it . . . must be considered to have abandoned the faith," Mohler flatly named the idea of "racial superiority" as a Christian heresy. And he declared that Roof's actions were "a hideous demonstration of the deadly power of this heresy." Mohler also declared directly that "one cannot simultaneously hold to an ideology of racial superiority and rightly present the gospel of Jesus Christ" or "defend the faith once for all delivered to the saints."[70] And he directly connected the dots between the white superiority that animated the SBC's founding and contemporary racial violence:

"The Southern Baptist Convention was not only founded by slave-holders; it was founded by men who held to an ideology of racial superiority and who bathed that ideology in scandalous theological argument. . . . We bear the burden of that history to this day. Racial superiority is a sin as old as Genesis and as contemporary as the killings in Emanuel AME Church in Charleston. The ideology of racial superiority is not only sinful, it is deadly."[71]

And in 2018 the seminary's report on the legacy of *Slavery and Racism in the History of the Southern Baptist Theological Seminary*, which Mohler had commissioned, noted:

"The founding faculty of this school—all four of them—were deeply involved in slavery and deeply complicit in the defense of slavery. Many of their successors on this faculty, throughout the period of Reconstruction and well into the twentieth century, advocated segregation, the inferiority of African Americans, and openly embraced the ideology of the Lost Cause of southern slavery. What we knew in generalities, we now know in detail."[72]

The report is fairly thorough in its treatment of the white supremacist views of the four founding faculty of the seminary, noting that all owned significant numbers of slaves, some on multiple plantations in multiple states. It notes that one of them, James P. Boyce, who served as the seminary's first president, was a chaplain to the Confederate army who described himself in a letter to his brother-in-law as "an ultra proslavery man." It highlights John Broadus's leadership in drafting and presenting articles at the 1863 Southern Baptist Convention pledging the denomination's support for the Confederacy. (It does fail to fully represent Broadus's judgments about the capabilities of African Americans: "the great mass of them belong to a very low grade of humanity.") The report documents the white supremacist views of Basil Manly Jr., son of the seminary's founding president, and his desire to reestablish white political control during Reconstruction. Writing to his wife, Sarah, after the Civil War, for example, Manly Jr. declared that the presence of freed slaves was an "incubus and plague" upon Greenville, and that it "might become a desirable place of residence" if it "could be cleared of negroes and establish a system of free schools." And the report notes that in an 1866 interview with a New York newspaper after the close of the war, the fourth founder, William Williams, declared that even though slavery was abolished, "we still maintain that slaveholding is morally right."[73]

Mohler even asks the right ultimate question in his cover letter to the seminary report:

"Eventually, the questions come home. How could our founders, James P. Boyce, John Broadus, Basil Manly Jr., and William Williams, serve as such defenders of biblical truth, the gospel of Jesus Christ, and the confessional convictions of this Seminary, and at the same time own human beings as slaves—based on an ideology of race—and defend American slavery as an institution?"

So far, so good. But while in each case Mohler's logic would seem to have painted the seminary into a corner of accountability, he consistently finds a way out, interspersing indictments with a quick two-step of qualifications and evasions. In the 2015 online article, Mohler declared, "I gladly stand with the founders of the Southern Baptist Convention and the Southern Baptist Theological Seminary," and lauds them as "titans of the faith once for all delivered to the saints."[74] But how can these men be both saints and heretics?

Follow the footwork. Although Mohler notes that both Boyce and Broadus served as chaplains for the Confederate army, he also defends them as "consummate Christian gentlemen, given the culture of their day." He also makes the outlandish assertion that each of these men "would have been horrified, I am certain, by any act of violence against any person." This is plainly false, since the Manlys were known to have theologically defended, tolerated, and on occasion ordered their slaves be beaten.

Beyond even all of this rhetorical maneuvering, however, is a strategy of marginalizing the central character: the Reverend Dr. Basil Manly Sr. Mohler omits any mention of the senior Manly in his 2015 article. While there is a longer treatment of Manly buried in the body of the 2018 report, Mohler makes no mention of him in his three-page cover letter, nor is there any reference to Manly in the report's four-page, thirteen-bullet executive summary. Instead, both focus the critical spotlight on the four founding *faculty* members, leaving the seminary's founding institutional architect and board president in the murky shadows.

By all reasonable applications of Mohler's own criteria, the inescapable verdict should be that the founders of the SBC and the seminary, including the pivotal Basil Manly Sr., were indeed slaveholding, theological apologists of white supremacy and therefore heretics. Yet Mohler ultimately absolves them of responsibility and accountability—along with himself and contemporary Southern Baptists—by citing mitigating circumstances and continuing to hold on to a theology, cultivated and passed down by these very founders, that frees contemporary white Christians from any responsibility beyond lament and apology. Finally, Mohler makes a sweeping excuse that is simply absurd: "So far as I can tell, no one ever confronted the founders of the Southern Baptist Convention and the Southern Baptist Theological Seminary with the brutal reality of what they were doing, believing, and teaching in this regard."[75] Yet Basil Manly Sr., for example, was deeply involved in the abolitionist debates, and came to prominence precisely because, in the face of public challenges to his views, he was an unflinching religious defender of chattel slavery—including theological defenses of brutal practices such as whipping slaves and selling slaves even if it broke up families.

In his 2015 article, Mohler declared, "We must repent and seek to confront and remove every strain of racial superiority that remains." Yet in the cover letter to the report, he distances himself from current action required by this past with the following theological flourish: "We must repent of our own sins, we cannot repent for the dead." One foot forward, shuffle back.

Notably, following the release of the 2018 report, Mohler and

Southern Seminary have taken no consequential steps to act on their own weighty conclusions. While both the 2015 article and the full 2018 report are available on the seminary's website, there has been no attempt to update the biographical entries of these four founding faculty members with these new revelations on the regular pages of the site. The biographical page describing Broadus, for example, makes only a passing reference to the Civil War, no references to his support for slavery, and closes with this summary: "Broadus dedicated his life to teaching Southern Baptist ministers how to have a passion for biblical, doctrinal, and vibrant preaching in order to bring glory to the name of Christ."[76]

This inaction is also visible on the seminary grounds. Today the Southern Baptist Seminary campus features older buildings named for these founders, such as the James P. Boyce Centennial Library and Manly Hall, a dormitory. But it also contains newer buildings dedicated to their legacies by Mohler himself just a handful of years after the historic SBC apology: Boyce College, which opened in 1998, grants undergraduate degrees in biblical studies; and Broadus Chapel, which opened in 1999, serves as a two-hundred-seat venue that is used for worship, weddings, lectures, and a preaching lab.

In his 2015 article, Mohler says three separate times that he will not consider removing the names of these men who are honored on the seminary's buildings but will "stand without apology with the founders and their affirmation of Baptist orthodoxy." And his cover letter accompanying the 2018 Southern Baptist Seminary report doubles down on his intention to preserve these names on the school's buildings:

> In light of the burdens of history, some schools hasten to remove names, announce plans, and declare moral superiority. That is not what I intend to do, nor do I believe that to be what the Southern Baptist Convention or our Board of Trustees would have us to do. We do not evaluate our Christian forebears from a position of our own moral innocence. Christians

know that there is no such innocence. But we must judge, even as we will be judged, by the unchanging Word of God and the deposit of biblical truth. Consistent with our theology and the demands of truth, we will not attempt to rewrite the past, nor can we unwrite the past. Instead, we will write the truth as best we can know it. We will tell the story in full, and not hide. By God's grace, we will hold without compromise to the faith once for all delivered to the saints.

In May 2019 Mohler's response to a petition from a coalition of black and white local ministers in Louisville demonstrated the limits of Southern's conception of repentance. Prompted by the seminary's report lamenting its slaveholding and white supremacist roots, the group suggested that Southern could "make an act of repentance and repair to descendants of American slavery for its leading role in crafting a moral and biblical defense of slavery." Specifically, they suggested that Southern could gift a biblical tithe (10 percent) of its nearly $1 billion endowment to Simmons College of Kentucky, a nearby historically black Christian college. Mohler's response was unyielding. "We do not believe that financial reparations are the appropriate response."[77]

I've highlighted these responses—and nonresponses—to the legacy of racism and white supremacy by Southern Baptists not because they are extraordinary but because they are typical of a self-protectionist rhetorical strategy that white Christians deploy too often to give the appearance of accountability while shoring up the status quo of white supremacy.

Understanding White Supremacy's Presence
Beyond Southern Evangelicalism

White evangelicals have captured most of the historical spotlight because of their overt support for slavery, Jim Crow laws, and segregation, and because of their concentration in the former states of the Confederacy. And it is true that white mainline Protestants and white Catholics—due to both geographic and theological divergences from white evangelicalism—do have different historical stories they can tell about their relationships to white supremacy and black claims to equality in America. But these differences at the national institutional level hide similarities among white Christians at the congregational level.

White mainline Protestants were the first to publish Martin Luther King Jr.'s "Letter from Birmingham Jail"—one of the most eloquent and enduring examples of public theology in the twentieth century—in their flagship magazine *The Christian Century*. The National Council of Churches (NCC) lobbied strongly for civil rights legislation, and the United Methodist Building on Capitol Hill served as a staging area for King's 1963 March on Washington for Jobs and Freedom. In a 1957 address at the NCC annual meeting, Reverend King himself acknowledged the Council's consistent support for civil rights, stating, "This great body, the National Council of Churches, has condemned segregation over and over again and has requested its constituent denominations to do likewise."[78]

There were prominent Catholic religious and political leaders who were strongly supportive of the civil rights movement, such as Archbishop Patrick O'Boyle of Washington and Archbishop Joseph E. Ritter of St. Louis, who desegregated their cities' churches and parochial schools years before the *Brown* decision.[79] And at their 1958 national gathering, the US bishops released a major statement titled "Racial Discrimination and the Christian Conscience," which declared that "enforced segregation" could not "be reconciled with the Christian view of our fellow man."[80] President John F. Kennedy, who first introduced comprehensive civil rights legislation in 1963 that would not be passed until after his death, was, of course, Catholic. And white Catholic churches were at times the exception to the rule of white segregated churches that turned away black worshippers in the Deep South.

However, the pro–civil rights orientation of white mainline Prot-estant and white Catholic leaders is not an accurate barometer of the influence of white supremacy among white Christians sitting in the pews. Declarations on racial justice by national institutions and hierarchies were more often than not ignored or actively flouted by local clergy and their congregations. For example, in late 1940s Los Angeles, Reverend W. Clarence Wright, the pastor of Wilshire Pres-byterian Church, headed the fight to keep the well-to-do Wilshire district all white. When an African American war veteran moved into the elite, Waspy neighborhood, the clergyman personally sued to evict him. Wright lost the case. In one of the few early cases where courts held that racially restrictive neighborhood covenants were un-constitutional, the judge issued a sharp rebuke to the pastor, declar-ing that there was "no more reprehensible un-American activity than to attempt to deprive persons of their own homes on a 'master race' theory."[81]

Despite this local victory, racially restrictive housing covenants remained common practice in cities across the country until they were finally struck down nationally by the Supreme Court in *Shel-ley v. Kraemer* in 1948. In this landmark case, based on an attempt by whites to prevent a black couple from buying a house in their St. Louis neighborhood, white mainline Christians were on the wrong side of history. J. D. and Ethel Shelley had moved from Mississippi to St. Louis to escape the oppressive racial atmosphere of the Deep South. They saved and purchased a house, only to have the transac-tion challenged in court by a white neighbor, Louis Kraemer, because the original deed to the house specified that no "people of the Negro or Mongolian Race" could purchase the house.[82] The court sided with the Shelleys in a broad ruling. Because deeds barring sales to non-whites require judicial enforcement, the court found, they could not be construed as merely private discrimination but rather violated the Fourteenth Amendment, which prohibits state governments from participating in segregation.[83]

This important case is widely studied by law students as a turning point in dismantling decades of segregationist practices not only by the federal, state, and local governments but also by developers, real estate agents, and neighborhood associations. With a single stroke, it opened all neighborhoods to all people. It was argued and won by NAACP attorney and future Supreme Court justice Thurgood Marshall, and it has the distinction of being a rare unanimous decision that was determined by a 6–0 vote. Three of the justices had to recuse themselves after finding that their own houses were entangled in racially restrictive neighborhood covenants.[84] Today the modest Shelley House has been designated a National Historic Landmark.

But few law students are taught that the restrictive covenants in the neighborhood had been organized by the Marcus Avenue Improvement Association, a white home owners' association that was sponsored by the Cote Brilliante Presbyterian Church. Kraemer's legal attempt to evict the Shelleys was funded from the church's coffers, an action officially approved by the congregation's trustees. Waggoner Place Methodist Episcopal Church South, another nearby mainline Protestant church, was also a signatory of the restrictive covenant. Six years earlier, its pastor had defended it in court in a case the association brought to prevent a local distinguished black attorney from purchasing a home in the neighborhood.[85] And few took notice of the actions of the white church members following the court decision that opened their neighborhood to African Americans. In less than a decade after the Shelleys moved in, most of the white church members had moved out of the neighborhood and abandoned the church: the white congregation held its last Communion service on May 27, 1956.[86]

Perhaps the most glaring example of the chasm between national denominational positions and local sentiment among white mainline Protestants occurred in 1963. Six years after Reverend King praised the National Council of Churches for its leadership on civil rights, and in the same year that the *Christian Century* published his "Letter from Birmingham Jail," Atlanta's Lovett School, affiliated with the New York–based Episcopal Church, notified Reverend and Mrs. King that their six-year-old son, Martin Luther King III, was being denied admission on the basis of his race.

For their part, white Catholics also resisted, sometimes violently, influxes of African Americans into their own ethnic neighborhoods in the industrial cities of the Midwest and Northeast.[87] The widespread opposition to racial equality by the US Catholic Church led W. E. B. DuBois to single it out for particular criticism. In a 1925 letter to Reverend Joseph B. Glenn, a priest in charge of St. Joseph's mission in Richmond, Virginia, a parish established in 1884 specifically for black Catholics, DuBois wrote a stinging indictment of the church's relationship to African Americans:

> The Catholic Church in America stands for color separation and discrimination to a degree equaled by no other church in America, and that is saying a great deal…. The white parochial schools even in the North exclude colored children, the Catholic high schools will not admit them, the Catholic University at Washington invites them elsewhere, and scarcely a Catholic seminary in the country will train a Negro priest. This is not a case of blaming the Catholic Church for not doing all it might— it is blaming it for being absolutely and fundamentally wrong today and in the United States on the basic demands of human brotherhood across the color line.[88]

Catholic clergy, churches, and laity were also active in policing neighborhood boundaries in major cities across the country. When the United States entered World War II in 1941, the government commissioned a new bomber plant in Willow Run, a suburban area of Detroit. The Federal Works Agency (FWA) was put in charge of building temporary housing for workers, and included a segregated housing project for African Americans, designated as the Sojourner Truth

Housing Project. After considerable controversy following the objections of white elected officials, which resulted in the firing of the FWA director who had proposed the project, it was nonetheless eventually greenlighted. When blacks began to move in, whites in the nearby neighborhoods rioted. The clash between whites and their new African American neighbors resulted in more than a hundred arrests and thirty-eight hospitalizations, almost all of which were among African Americans.[89]

The riot made national news. A less acknowledged fact was that this violent white resistance was organized by a home owners' association that was headquartered in a local church, the St. Louis the King Catholic Church. When the association appealed to the Federal Housing Administration (FHA) to cancel the project, their spokesperson was the church's priest, Reverend Constantine Dzink, who gave the following testimony: "Construction of a low-cost housing project in the vicinity ... for the colored people ... would mean utter ruin for many people who have mortgaged their homes to the FHA, and not only that, but it would jeopardize the safety of many of our white girls." His closing remarks also contained a thinly veiled warning about how far his own church members and fellow white community members were willing to go to resist the housing project: "It is the sentiment of all people residing within the vicinity to object against this project in order to stop race riots in the future."[90]

In New York, the response of the Roman Catholic Church, in many instances, was to facilitate the flight from historically Irish and Italian inner-city neighborhoods out to the suburbs, where new churches and schools were built. While the bishops often did not immediately close the original parish churches and schools, now populated by black Catholics, they did shift resources away from them to the new white parishes. Reflecting on his personal experience with these dynamics in 1970, Father Lawrence Lucas, a black Catholic priest, described how these actions left many black Catholics angry and hurt, feeling forsaken by a white Jesus and a white church:

When blacks appeared on the scene, the white Christ, after fighting like hell to keep them out, fled and abandoned their buildings to the niggers as one step better than blowing them up. In
the cities, the abandoned edifices of this white Jesus' love are
allowed to die a slow death from lack of upkeep and support....
When the white Jesus ran away from the invading niggers he
did not put his buildings—churches, schools, hospitals—in his
pocket or put a match to them. No, he was in such a hurry that
he just left them behind and appointed some "heroic" white lieu-
tenants to keep the niggers from utterly destroying his invest-
ments while feigning a response to their needs.[91]

The first meeting of the National Black Catholic Clergy Caucus in 1968
opened with a sharply worded statement: "The Catholic Church in the
United States is primarily a white racist institution, has addressed itself primarily to white society and is definitely a part of that society."[92]
On January 8, 1969, a group of twenty mostly white Catholic priests
similarly called out the Archdiocese of Newark, New Jersey, for neglecting the needs of more than a half million African Americans in
the archdiocese's inner city. They issued a public statement, covered
in the *New York Times*, that read in part: "For a decade, the drama
and urgency of the desperate need of the inner city has been ignored
by the official Church in Newark. The official Church is apathetic. It is
racist."[93] Less than four years later, with none of the initial demands
addressed by the archdiocese, seven of the twenty priests who filed
the original complaint had left the ministry, including the two leading spokesmen and the only black priest in the archdiocese. Four of
the original priests who remained in their posts, all in their thirties,
lodged an additional complaint in 1972. Reverend Michael Linder reiterated the charge in an interview with the *New York Times*: "They
were very much racist and they still are, if you define racism as not allowing black and Spanish-speaking people to project themselves into
leadership positions in the Archdiocese."[94]

In *The Color of Law: A Forgotten History of How Our Government Segregated America*, Richard Rothstein summarizes how prevalent white Christian support for enforcing neighborhood segregation was:

> Church involvement and leadership were commonplace in property owners' associations that were organized to maintain neighborhood segregation. In North Philadelphia in 1942, a priest spearheaded a campaign to prevent African Americans from living in the neighborhood. The same year, a priest in a Polish American parish in Buffalo, New York, directed the campaign to deny public housing for African American war workers, stalling a proposed project for two years. Just south of the city, 600 units in the federally managed project for whites went vacant, while African American war workers could not find adequate housing.[95]

We could easily continue to pile up examples, but a pattern is clear: white Christians and their institutions, especially at the local level, were not just passively complicit with but also broadly and actively resistant to black Americans' claims of equality. This massive religious resistance was happening even as white Protestant mainline denominational offices and the American Catholic bishops, at the national level, were issuing statements calling for their constituents to support aspects of the civil rights movement. In the same 1957 speech in which Reverend King praised the NCC for its consistency as a national body in supporting civil rights, he also had this to say:

"All of these things are marvelous and deserve our highest praise. But we must admit that these courageous stands from the churches are still far too few. The sublime statements of the major denominations on the question of human relations move all too slowly to the local churches and actual practice. All too many ministers are still silent while evil rages."[96]

The US Catholic bishops followed up their initial 1958 statement a decade later with a 1968 statement titled "The National Race Crisis," which noted, "Now—ten years later—it is evident that we did not do enough; we have much more to do.... It became clear that we failed to change the attitudes of many believers."[97] Yet another decade later, in 1979, the bishops issued a statement titled "Brothers and Sisters to Us," which declared, "Racism is an evil that endures in our society and in our church. Despite apparent advances and even significant changes in the last two decades, the reality of racism remains."[98] The statement went on to conclude that "too often what has happened has been only a covering over, not a fundamental change."[99]

On the tenth anniversary of "Brothers and Sisters to Us" in 1989, the Bishops' Committee on Black Catholics conducted a survey of the impact of the statement and issued a sharply worded conclusion: "The promulgation of the pastoral on racism was soon forgotten by all but a few. A survey... revealed a pathetic, anemic response from archdioceses and dioceses around the country. The pastoral on racism had made little or no impact on the majority of Catholics in the United States."[100]

At the twenty-fifth anniversary of the statement in 2004, the bishops again conducted a survey to assess its impact. They found that only 18 percent of US bishops had issued statements condemning racism as a sin. Moreover, Bryan Massingale, a priest and author of *Racial Justice and the Catholic Church*, notes that "most of these statements were written by only a handful of bishops" and that few move beyond personal attitudes to deal with systemic racism. Most tellingly, the study found that nearly two-thirds (64 percent) of Catholics reported that they had not heard a single sermon on racism or racial justice over the entire three-year cycle of the lectionary.[101] In other words, even while working through the entire text of the Bible over that period, the overwhelming majority of priests did not find a single occasion to preach on racial justice issues.

To be sure, there are important questions about the ultimate resolve of the leadership of the National Council of Churches, the mainline Protestant denominations, and the US Catholic hierarchy to connect their declarations with discipleship at the local church level. But this disconnect between official positions of church leaders and the attitudes of their flocks is also testimony to the entrenched power of white supremacy in American Christianity, built up over centuries. As I noted in chapter 1, this massive white Christian resistance was happening, to echo Father Lucas, not just in the "bad, bad" South but in the "good, good" North.[102]

While white evangelicals were providing Christian legitimization of the Confederate Lost Cause, white mainline Protestants in the pews were protecting their long-claimed title to the throne of white Anglo-Saxon Protestant dominance. For their part, Catholics seized the moment to transform the terms of the conflict. Amid the turmoil, they ceased to perceive the fight as one between Irish and black or Italian and black ethnic groups. Rather, the flight out of their old parishes in the wake of black encroachment was the critical moment when the Irish and Italian and other European Catholics—who each had long thought of themselves as an immigrant group with a distinct ethnic heritage from a specific country of origin—discovered that they could be white.

Conclusion

A moment of reckoning is upon us, and it's time that we white Christians do better, to see what is plainly in front of us and to wrestle with the unsettling implications. What if the racist views of historical "titans of the faith" infected the entire theological project contemporary white Christians have inherited from top to bottom? If white supremacy was an unquestionable cultural assumption in America, what does it mean that Christian doctrines by necessity had to develop in ways that were compatible with that worldview? What if, for example, Christian conceptions of marriage and family, the doctrine of biblical inerrancy, or even the concept of having a personal relationship with Jesus developed as they did because they were useful tools for reinforcing white dominance? Is it possible that the white supremacy heresy is so integrated into white Christian DNA that it eludes even sincere efforts to excise it?

White Christianity has been many things for America. But whatever else it has been—and the country is indebted to it for a good many things—it has also been the primary institution legitimizing and propagating white power and dominance. Is such a system, built and maintained not just to save souls but also to secure white supremacy, flawed beyond redemption? If we're even going to begin to answer these questions, we need to take a deeper dive into the inner logic of white Christian theology.

– 3 –

Believing

The Theology of White Supremacy

Growing up inside Southern Baptist churches in Texas and Mississippi, I never once wrestled seriously with our denomination's troubled racist past. Staring at those words on the page now, it seems impossible that I can write that sentence. But it's true. And it seems that understanding just how this could be—that I and so many of my fellow white Christians were never challenged to face Christianity's deep entanglement with white supremacy—will help explain why we still have such limited capacities to hear black calls for equality.

The most powerful thing about my childhood experience in church was its ability to generate a palpable feeling of living under a protective sacred and social canopy. Physically gathering for multiple meetings per week at the church tucked into the southeast corner of our neighborhood generated a strong sense of community. A vibrant weekly Sunday school program, for both children and adults, provided space for thinking through Christian beliefs in the context of everyday life; and, at least from my childhood perspective from the 1970s and 1980s, these discussions focused mostly on our personal lives—and not a small amount of gossip—mostly steering clear of national politics.

Even in my average-sized church of about three hundred people, there were committees for everything—including a "committee on committees," the job of which was to ensure that the rest of the committees were chaired and filled. If people were sick or in the hospital, the visitation committee ensured they were called, prescriptions were picked up, and company was kept. When babies were born and people moved into the community, the hospitality committee organized showers and welcome baskets to be left on front porches. When someone died, the bereavement committee organized a food brigade to help families feed the influx of far-flung relatives and to avoid the need to cook while grieving after the funeral.

There were also social functions specific to our working-class, economically aspiring community. When someone lost a job, members were alerted to look for other opportunities in their networks. And when my friends and I graduated from high school and college, recognition banquets were organized, our names were printed in the church bulletins for special worship services at which the community ceremonially sent us out into the world, and our accomplishments were celebrated in the congregational newsletter. At church, I learned how to sing, write, date, give a persuasive public speech, and run an efficient meeting using *Robert's Rules of Order.*

But I didn't learn much about how my religious tradition, which had undeniably done so much good for so many people, including me, had also been simultaneously entangled in justifying unspeakable racial violence, bigotry, and ongoing indifference to African Americans' claims to equality and justice. I believe the key to understanding this paradox is embodied in two words: *protection* and *purity.*

My church succeeded in generating a culture of protection for most of us in our white, working-class corner of southwest Jackson. One of the earliest Bible verses I was urged to memorize—and I can still quote it by heart, including chapter and verse—was Romans 8:28: "For we know that all things work together for good for those who love God and to those who are called according to his purposes."[1] And for most of my childhood and youth, this promise was a source of great comfort to me. I heard it cited in general conversations during lean economic times, preached at funerals, and my fellow teenagers and I certainly leaned on it after painful romantic breakups or when our adolescent hopes were dashed by parents or other powers beyond our control. I still believe there is something beautiful, admirable, and healthy here. This sensibility—that both God and the community had our backs—instilled in me a resiliency that has stayed with me throughout my adult life.

I think the fact that white churches produced such a strong sense of safety and security for those of us who were inside the institution is why it is so hard for white Christians to see the harm it did to those who were outside it, particularly African Americans, and the other kinds of damage it did to us, numbing our own moral sensibilities and limiting our religious development. The problem was not that the community functioned to enhance the lives of those within it; all good communities do that. Rather, the problem was that it had developed in such a way that its main goal was protecting and improving white Christians' lives within an unjust social status quo, which is to say a context of extreme racial inequality and injustice.

Because of the existing conditions of inequality, late twentieth-century white Christian theology didn't necessarily need to actively work against African American civil rights (although it did this too). Rather, its most powerful tool was its ability to constrict radically the scope of whites' moral vision. Martin Luther King Jr. singled out this dynamic in his "Letter from Birmingham Jail," when he looked in vain for white Christian support for the civil rights movement in Birmingham, Alabama. He lamented that white Christians "have remained silent behind the anesthetizing security of stained glass windows."[2] As I discuss in this chapter, white Christian theology has developed to play this role powerfully: to render black claims to justice invisible while protecting white economic and social interests, all the while assuring them of their own moral purity.

While white Christianity was protecting the interests and consciences of those under its canopy, white Christians were also staunchly defending the purity and innocence of the religion itself. They accomplished this principally by projecting an idealized form of white Christianity as somehow independent of the failings of actual white Christians or institutions. The mythology—really, the lie—that white Christians tell ourselves, on the few occasions we face our history, is that Christianity has been a force for unambiguous good in the world. No matter what evil Christians commit or what violence Christian institutions justify, an idealized conception of Christianity remains unscathed. This conviction is so deep that evidence to the contrary is simply dismissed.

The problem with this defensive posture is that it prevents us from seeing areas where the religion may have gone off course; where new bearings are needed. In *Democracy in Black*, theologian Eddie Glaude Jr. laid out the stakes clearly:

> When Communists declare that Stalinism wasn't really communism, or when Christians and Muslims claim that the horrific things some Christians and Muslims have done in the name of their religion isn't really Christianity or Islam, what are they doing? They are protecting their ideology or the religion from the terrible things that occur in its name. They claim only the good stuff. What gets lost in all of this is that the bad stuff may very well tell us something important about communism, Christianity, or Islam—that there may be something in the ideology and in the traditions themselves that gives rise to the ugly and horrific things some people do in its name.[3]

One recent expression of Christian protectionism can be seen in the $400 million, 430,000-square-foot Museum of the Bible, which opened on November 17, 2017, two blocks from the National Mall in Washington, DC. The massive project was supported primarily by the Green family, the white evangelical owners of the corporate giant Hobby Lobby.[4]

When the museum was formed as a legal entity in 2010, it declared its mission was "to bring to life the living word of God, to tell its compelling story of preservation, and to inspire confidence in the absolute authority and reliability of the Bible." By 2012, that mission had been scrubbed to read, "We exist to invite people to engage with the Bible through our four primary activities: traveling exhibits, scholarship, building of a permanent museum in DC, and developing elective high school curriculum." But this shift seemed to reflect more of a public relations move than a real change in mission. For example, even as late as the museum's opening, all members of the board of directors were required to sign a statement of Christian faith.[5] And despite its self-proclaimed nonsectarian approach, the museum is unmistakably presenting the Bible as the cultural object it is in the Protestant imagination—as an unmitigated force for good in human history.

Overall, the museum's approach is to defend the Bible as an artifact that is responsible for the achievement of Western civilization and its virtues. For example, there's abundant information on the Bible's influence on William Wilberforce, the British evangelical abolitionist, including a staging of the Broadway musical *Amazing Grace* in the museum's state-of-the-art 472-seat World Stage Theater. But the much wider influence the Bible had justifying European colonialism, chattel slavery, and white supremacy gets scant treatment.

To its credit, the museum added an exhibit featuring a "slave Bible" in November 2018, which is on loan from Fisk University in Nashville. The title page reads, "Parts of the Holy Bible, selected for the use of the Negro Slaves, in the British West-India Islands." The slave Bible, one of only three known still to exist, was constructed specifically to help white Christian missionaries emphasize passages demanding obedience to masters and to exclude passages suggesting equality or liberation. As a large wall display notes, the slave Bible excludes 90 percent of the Old Testament and about half of the New Testament. For example, the revised book of Exodus, which is named for the liberation of the Israelites from Egyptian servitude, contains the story of their enslavement and of Moses receiving the Ten Commandments, but it excises the story of the Israelites finding their freedom. While the existence of this display is important, nestled within the massive museum, it is the exception that proves the rule of the Bible as "the good book." It shows the way a mutilated Bible could reinforce slavery, but it fails to cast light on the evil that an intact Bible could foster among whites.

After its opening, biblical scholars Candida Moss, Edward Cadbury Professor of Theology at England's University of Birmingham, and Joel Baden, professor of Hebrew Bible at Yale Divinity School, toured the gleaming facilities and interviewed museum founder and Hobby Lobby president Steve Green and museum president Cary Summers. While they noted that the museum founder and leadership seem earnest and well intentioned, they also concluded that they betrayed "an interpretive naiveté" about the white Protestant assumptions they are importing into the museum and its collections.[6] Baden summarized his central concerns this way:

> The most troubling aspect is their seeming inability to distinguish between the Bible and American Protestantism. Their three-minute promo is a fascinating demonstration of this problem. At least half of it is a reenactment of American history which has no bearing on the Bible—the signing of [the] Declaration of Independence, for example, or the Revolutionary War. The worry is that the museum portrays a story of the Bible that culminates in Protestantism and America.[7]

Moss concurred, saying, "It's not really a museum of the Bible, it's a museum of American Protestantism. Their whole purpose is to show this country as a Christian country governed by Christian morality."[8] Ultimately, the museum is a monument to the Bible as cultural talisman, a fixed object of Christian purity that protects the positive story of a triumphant white Protestantism. The Greens are known as savvy business leaders, and their $400 million investment aims to pay large dividends. The museum attempts to shore up the reputation of the Bible at a time when old assumptions are slipping, and this white-washed presentation of the Bible in turn provides something virtually priceless: the plausibility of white Christian innocence set against a backdrop of divinely ordained progress.

The concerted effort to protect the purity of Christianity is not just operative among Christian elites. This vigilance is also dramatically illustrated in a 2015 national survey conducted by PRRI.[9] Respondents were asked the following question: "When people claim to be Christian and commit acts of violence in the name of Christianity, do you believe they really are Christian, or not?" Overall, 75 percent of Americans answered "no," they did not believe such perpetrators were authentically Christian. Not surprisingly, high numbers of white Christians also rejected the possibility of real Christians committing violence, including 87 percent of white evangelical Protestants, 77 percent of white mainline Protestants, and 75 percent of white Catholics.

These sentiments were not just generally proreligion but also specifically about the necessary moral innocence of Christianity. When respondents were asked an identical question about self-proclaimed Muslims committing violence in the name of Islam, only 50 percent of Americans said they did not think such perpetrators were authentically Muslim. Fewer than half of white evangelical Protestants (44 percent) and white mainline Protestants (41 percent) said they did not think such violent actors were really Muslim; Catholics were more consistent across questions, with a majority (54 percent) of white Catholics saying they did not believe violent actors were authentically Muslim, but even here there was a 20 percentage point difference in their evaluations of the religious authenticity of self-proclaimed Christians and Muslims who kill in the name of their respective religion. Overall, white Christians are between 20 and 40 percentage points more likely to protect their own religion's reputation from being marred by the bad actions of its members.

This double standard exists despite evidence that white suprema-cists account for far greater numbers of domestic terrorism than any other group and a growing proportion of extremist violence worldwide. A 2018 Anti-Defamation League report, for example, shows that 2018 was the fourth most violent year for domestic terrorism since 1970 and that nearly eight in ten of these attacks were motivated by white supremacy. And white supremacy, as it has developed historically in the United States, is typically tied to a concept of the superiority of Protestant Christian culture, motivating attacks not just on African Americans and immigrants but also on Jews, Muslims, Sikhs, and other non-Christian religious minorities.[10] Looking at global trends, the *New York Times* found that attacks by white extremists were growing and now represent nearly one in ten attacks worldwide. While certainly not all white supremacists identify as Christian, the analysis found that these extremists often included in their worldview the lost dominance of western Christendom. Experts described the typical profile of these attackers as men "who identify as white, Christian, and culturally European" and who feel their privileged position in the West is threatened "by immigrants, Muslims, and other religious and racial minorities."[11]

The result of this double standard is that for Islam, particular examples of violence may offset literally billions of peaceful counterexamples. But with Christianity, centuries of dedication to the forceful preservation of white supremacy, and growing white Christian extremism today, aren't enough to demand serious moral concern about the religion. The right-wing assertion that Islam is "not a religion" but a violent ideology could easily find traction if turned around and applied equally and honestly to Christianity. Even when it is no longer deniable that Christian theology underwrote and justified the white supremacist right to "[wring] their bread from the sweat of other men's faces," as Abraham Lincoln put it, and thereafter the right to segregate African Americans into a permanent underclass by the force of law and lynching, white Christians point to a corrupt culture rather than a compromised Christianity.

Blame can be deflected virtually anywhere else, but the question of whether Christian theology and culture are implicated cannot be asked. Christian theological purity and innocence must be maintained at all costs. But if we white Christians are going to get any critical leverage on our past, and the distortions this past has brought into our present, we have to let go of both the quest for self-protection—that is to say, the advantages we hoard at unjust costs to others—and the insistence on our racial and religious innocence.

This chapter is an invitation to that journey. It describes the historical roots of the theological world of white Christianity, illustrating how white supremacy not only drove the actions of white Christian leaders, churches, and denominations, but also how white Christian theology was diligently constructed to protect and justify it. While white Christian theology evolved in response to the changing environment, it responded primarily by shifting from more overt to more subtle expressions of white supremacy rather than a wholesale reexamination of its racist roots. A close examination of key theological doctrines such as the Christian worldview of slaveholders, sin, and salvation, the centrality of a personal relationship with Jesus, and the use of the Bible reveals how each was tailored to resist black equality and protect white superiority, and how this legacy dramatically limits the moral and religious vision of white Christians today.

Slavery and Christian Theology: Two Conflicting Conceptions

Rev. Basil Manly Sr. and the Compatibility of Slavery and the White Christian Worldview

One window into the worldview of Christian white supremacy is the ardent defense of slavery and the Confederacy that was proffered by Reverend Basil Manly Sr. As founder of Southern Baptist Seminary and chaplain to the Confederacy, Manly was one of the most prolific and tireless Christian defenders of slavery. While Manly was one of the most prominent purveyors of white supremacist theology, he was not unique among Southern Baptists, and he had counterparts in the southern branches of the other major Protestant denominations, such as William Capers, a Methodist, and James Henley Thornwell, a Presbyterian. Like his fellow defenders of slavery, Manly grounded his arguments with generous citations from the Bible.[12]

Manly's most systematic defense of slavery was encapsulated in one of eight "Sermons on Duty," a series he honed and preached at various venues across the South. Notably, his discussion of slavery was embedded in a larger theological framework of the patriarchal family, which he saw as central to God's plan for human society. Different members of the family have divinely ordained differentiated roles, he argued, and the practice of slavery should be understood within this hierarchical context. Thus, the divine order for accomplishing social needs "naturally lead to different occupations—some to labor, some to plan, and to direct the labor of others."[13] Like a symbiotic ecosystem, genders and races had their roles to play, and when all parts functioned as designed, the ecosystem thrived, and individual members—whatever their lot—were content, since they were fulfilling their created purpose.

Having established the principles of social hierarchy and role differentiation as divine mandates, Manly then turned to other sources, such as history and science, to drive home his point. The history of human civilizations, he argued, made God's intentions clear: "In all times, in all countries not excepting his own," the African "race has been in a state of servitude."[14] Drawing on new entomological studies, Manly developed a popular "Lecture on Ants," in which he marveled at a species of slave-making ants that "have become tired of the drudgery of their own labor, it seems, and by a strange and astonishing instinct, resort to violence to obtain laborers of a difference species than their own."[15]

Manly sees two lessons to be gleaned from the ants. First, they demonstrate a benevolent paternalism, since the smaller ants, who are enslaved by the larger ants, "are scarcely equal to their own protection against any other troop that chose to attack them." Furthermore, Manly notes the wisdom of their instinctive tactics: the ant slave-master species, which is "wiser than the African kings," steals eggs and hatches them in its own nest rather than capturing adults. Manly concludes, "So they grow up with an affection for their captors, when otherwise they would have shared in all the instinctive horror, and hatred for the slaveholders which reigns throughout the separate nest of negroes."[16] He concluded with a message for his northern listeners: "It surely ought to comfort the abolitionists to know that although the ants do hold slaves, the masters are humane and gentle, and the slaves are contented, industrious, and happy."[17]

The implications of these examples, of course, were clear to his readers: that in all times, in all countries, whites have been *naturally* in a state of dominance fulfilling their God-given role to direct the labor of others. As the superior human species, whites are protecting blacks from likely worse fates by enslaving them in a benevolent environment. Finally, at least one major source of resentment among enslaved Africans in America was the result of a purely tactical error that could be corrected: that the slave traders made the mistake of abducting teenagers and adults rather than small children and babies who would not recall a previous state of freedom.

But Manly had admonishments for his fellow white Christians as well. Within this hierarchical worldview, those at the top have their own duties and responsibilities. Just as fathers had a duty to govern their families with benevolence, masters had a similar duty toward their slaves. In a sermon entitled "Duties of Masters and Servants," Manly admonished slave owners, "God has made you their masters—placed them under your protection, made you their guardians, the conservators of their lives and happiness."[18] While Manly admitted that current slave owners did not meet this ideal, he was convinced that Christianity and the Christian churches were the key to achieving it.

In Manly's reading of history, the frequent downfall of slave-owning societies was that masters did not heed their duties to treat their slaves well. Christianity, Manly argued, was the perfectly calibrated religion, and southern American culture was the ideal setting, to bring the natural system of slavery into sustainable balance. Given that many Africans were destined for enslavement, being enslaved by Christian nations "meliorated the condition of a portion of them."[19] Therefore, even enslaved Africans could be grateful for American slavery, since the benevolence of Christianity moderated the cruelty of the institution. Operating in this harmonious way, Manly argued, both masters and slaves would see that "mutual advantage and satisfaction arises out of the relation, and the proper discharge of its duties." Moreover, following these duties would put masters and slaves alike on the path to "possessing in common, the inheritance and dwelling place of Heaven."[20] Manly conjured a powerful depiction of a harmonious hierarchical system where knowing one's place and doing one's duty lead to an idyllic social life and mutually advantageous individual rewards, not just in this life but also for eternity.

It was an impressive theological achievement. Manly spread this gospel of white supremacy in his own pulpit, writings, public forums, and other speaking engagements. In the 1850s, the newly formed Southern Baptist denomination also sponsored essay contests for clergy and laypeople alike "on the duties of Xtn [*sic*] masters," for which Manly served as a judge.

Frederick Douglass and the Confounding Influence of Christianity on White Supremacy

The idyllic portrait painted by Manly, however, was at serious odds with the experience of white Christianity by enslaved people themselves. In the same year the Southern Baptist Convention was founded under Manly's leadership, Frederick Douglass published the first of his three autobiographies, *Narrative of the Life of Frederick Douglass, An American Slave.*[21] Written when Douglass was in his late twenties, the book gained a wide American and transatlantic audience and served as an important spark to the growing abolitionist movement and to Douglass's prominence as a leader. At the end of the book, Douglass has an entire appendix dedicated to a scathing description of his experience of American Christianity. This passage, which has not received as much public attention as it deserves, is worth quoting at length:

I am filled with unutterable loathing when I contemplate the religious pomp and show, together with the horrible inconsistencies, which every where [*sic*] surround me. We have men-stealers for ministers, women-whippers for missionaries, and cradle-plunderers for church members. The man who wields the blood-clotted cowskin during the week fills the pulpit on Sunday, and claims to be a minister of the meek and lowly Jesus. The man who robs me of my earnings at the end of each week meets me as a class-leader on Sunday morning, to show me the way of life, and the path of salvation. He who sells my sister, for purposes of prostitution, stands forth as the pious advocate of purity. He who proclaims it a religious duty to read the Bible denies me the right of learning to read the name of the God who made me. He who is the religious advocate of marriage robs whole millions of its sacred influence, and leaves them to the ravages of wholesale pollution. The warm defender of the sacredness of the family relation is the same that scatters whole families—sundering husbands and wives, parents and children, sisters and brothers, leaving the hut vacant, and the hearth desolate. We see the thief preaching against theft, and the adulterer against adultery. We have men sold to build churches, women sold to support the gospel, and babes sold to purchase Bibles for the *poor heathen! All for the glory of God and the good of souls!* The slave auctioneer's bell and the church-going bell chime in with each other, and the bitter cries of the heart-broken slave are drowned in the religious shouts of his pious master. Revivals of religion and revivals in the slave-trade go hand in hand to-gether. The slave prison and the church stand near each other. The clanking of fetters and the rattling of chains in the prison, and the pious psalm and solemn prayer in the church, may be heard at the same time. The dealers in the bodies and souls of men erect their stand in the presence of the pulpit, and they mutually help each other. The dealer gives his blood-stained gold to support the pulpit, and the pulpit, in return, covers his infernal business with the garb of Christianity. Here we have religion and robbery the allies of each other—devils dressed in angels' robes, and hell presenting the semblance of paradise.[22]

Not only was Douglass incensed at the deep hypocrisy within white Christianity but also his own lived experience had convinced him that Christianity's central contribution to chattel slavery was to make it *less*, not more, humane. When Douglass came to live with his owner Thomas Auld at St. Michaels, Maryland, in 1832, he described him as a man without religion and without kindness. He was arbitrary in his demands, quick to punish, and, worst of all, he and his wife did not provide his slaves with enough to eat despite the presence of abundant food in the household. The couple was, as Douglass put it bluntly, "well matched, being equally mean and cruel."[23] In the fall of that year, Auld attended one of the many Methodist camp meetings that were common rural events of the period and had a conversion experience. He became a zealous Christian, praying three times a day, and soon became a Sunday school class leader and an "exhorter" at revival meetings, where, Douglass reports, "he proved himself an instrument in the hands of the church in converting many souls."[24]

His home even evolved to become known as "the preacher's house," where itinerant ministers would regularly visit as they made their rounds.

Douglass notes that he initially welcomed the news of Auld's conversion with some "faint hope" that these newfound Christian beliefs would lead his master to emancipate him and his fellow slaves or at least to treat them more humanely. But Douglass was quickly disappointed, finding that the addition of Christian faith into the household actually made conditions worse; for what Auld found in Christianity was not a prick of conscience leading to moderation or benevolence but rather sturdier support for his cruelty. Douglass saw this perverse dynamic clearly: "Prior to his conversion, he relied upon his own depravity to shield and sustain him in his savage barbarity; but after his conversion, he found religious sanction and support for his slaveholding cruelty."[25]

Douglass notes that a frequent target of Auld's Christian-infused cruelty was a young woman and fellow slave named Henny, who had been disabled after falling into a fire as a young child and suffering massive burns. As Douglass perceived it, Auld singled her out because of her inability to work and her general helplessness. Douglass described the scene as follows:

> I have seen him tie up a lame young woman, and whip her with a heavy cowskin upon her naked shoulders, causing the warm red blood to drip; and, in justification of the bloody deed, he would quote this passage of Scripture—"He that knoweth his master's will, and doeth it not, shall be beaten with many stripes." Master would keep this lacerated young woman tied up in this horrid situation four or five hours at a time. I have known him to tie her up early in the morning, and whip her before breakfast; leave her, go to his store, return at dinner, and whip her again, cutting her in the places already made raw with his cruel lash.[26]

Douglass is also clear that his experience of the impact of Christian piety on Auld was not an exception but rather the rule among slaveholders. When Auld found Douglass to be insufficiently servile, he was sent as punishment to live with Edward Covey, who was known in the area for two things: as the area's "nigger breaker" and as "a professor of religion—a pious soul—a member and a class-leader in the Methodist church." A frequent visitor to Auld's house was Reverend Rigby Hopkins, an ordained minister in the Reformed Methodist Church, who boasted frequently of his slave management tactic of issuing regular, preemptive whippings of his slaves. He had such a fierce reputation that his household was known among slaves as the worst in the area. Yet, as Douglass notes, "there was not a man any where round [sic], who made higher professions of religion, or was more active in revivals—more attentive to the class, love-feast, prayer and preaching meetings, or more devotional in his family—that prayed earlier, later, louder, and longer—than this same reverend slave-driver, Rigby Hopkins."[27]

Reflecting back across his life, Douglass concluded solemnly: "Were I to be again reduced to the chains of slavery, next to that enslavement, I should regard being the slave of a religious master the greatest calamity that could befall me. For of all slaveholders with whom I have ever met, religious slaveholders are the worst. I have ever found them the meanest and basest, the most cruel and cowardly, of all others."[28]

In his first piece of public writing, Douglass eloquently cut to the heart of the problem with white Christianity. The "garb of Christianity" and the church covered the injustices of slavery in the social realm, and Christian theology gave "religious sanction" to punishment and cruelty in the personal realm. The churches conferred respectability, and even elevated esteem, on white Christian slaveholders; and the theological blessing of slavery paradoxically lobotomized white Christian consciences, severing what natural moral impulses there may have been limiting violence and cruelty.

The Religion of the Lost Cause

Manly's theology was developed in the heady days of Southern seces-
sionism and optimism that victory in the war, a vindication of God's
favor, would be swift. After the South's military defeat, and the dis-
solution of the slaveholding system on which his wealth depended,
Manly, too, was a defeated and ailing man. In September 1865 he took
an oath of loyalty to the Union and received a pardon signed personally by President Andrew Johnson. Despite his offer to pay them for
their labor, most of his nearly forty slaves—whom he had thought of
as members of the family under his paternalistic rule—left his Alabama plantation, and he was forced to suspend operations and auc-
tion off the farm implements.[29] This defeat also chastened Manly's
theology. Although he never abandoned his racial paternalism or his
conviction that slavery was neither morally nor religiously wrong, in
a sermon delivered late in his life, entitled "Our Brother in Black," he
conceded pragmatically, the "only way ... to deal with the black man
whom we find in America—is to *give him his rights.*"[30]

But as Manly was attempting to make peace with a disappearing
world in the closing chapter of his life, the next generation of church
leaders was struggling to shore up the tottering white Christian
worldview in the face of decisive military defeat. As noted southern
historian Samuel S. Hill summarized it: "Many southern whites have
regarded their culture as God's most favored. To a greater degree than
any other, theirs approximates the ideals the Almighty has in mind
for mankind everywhere."[31] Even after the war, this fundamental conviction was questioned by few. The central question was a theodicy
dilemma: how to square the ideas of providential power and white
Christians as God's chosen people with military defeat. Finding Confederate political ambitions foreclosed, the new battle was transposed
from the political arena, where disputes were settled with military
violence, to the cultural arena.

This new cultural project has become widely recognized by scholars as "the religion of the Lost Cause," a term derived from an 1866 book with this name by a Richmond editor named Edward Pollard, who called explicitly for a "war of ideas" to sustain southern identity.[32] All cultural movements need a core organizing idea. Ideally, this idea is widely shared, legitimized by authoritative institutions, grounded in a moral worldview, and connected to other values and interests. And if it is seen to be under threat and in need of urgent defense, all the better. The Confederate political project may have run aground, but its animating core commitment to white supremacy survived and fit these criteria well.

From its beginning, the Lost Cause was more than the plain meaning of those words might indicate. To white southerners, it did not imply a fatalistic embrace of defeat. Refracted through the prism of their Christian theology, through "Amazing Grace," the lost could be found, and resurrection meant that even physical death was not the final chapter in the story. White southerners solved their theodicy dilemma a number of ways. Some accepted that they had not lived up to their duties as benevolent slave owners and that defeat was a punishment for this shortcoming. Toward the end of the war in 1865, as Confederate armies were experiencing a series of crushing defeats, the editor of the *Christian Index*, for example, admitted that the losses in "this unjust and cruel war" might be connected to southerners neglecting their "parental obligations" toward their slaves.[33]

Others attempted to disconnect the outcome of the war from divine judgment, arguing that military victory is not necessarily connected to righteousness. Speaking more than thirty years after the war before a Nashville church service connected to the yearly Confederate Veterans' Reunion in 1897, Presbyterian minister Reverend James I. Vance told those gathered, "Truth is truth, whether it have a conquering army at its back or wear the chains of imprisonment, like Paul in his cell at Rome.... His enemies could nail Christ to the cross, but they could not quench the ideals he embodied. He seemed to be a lost cause as the darkness fell on the great tragedy at Calvary, but out of what seemed Golgotha's irretrievable defeat has come the cause whose mission it is to save that which is lost."[34]

Reverend Vance and countless other white ministers helped their audiences map Confederate defeat in the Civil War onto the New Testament stories of the wrongful imprisonment of an apostle and even the crucifixion of the Messiah. The future implication is clear: just as Jesus was resurrected from the dead and will ultimately come again to rule the earth in righteousness, there will yet be a time when the noble ideals of the Confederacy, even if not the practice of chattel slavery itself, will rise again.

The religion of the Lost Cause proved to be a powerful form of cultural civil religion. Charles Reagan Wilson, in his classic text, *Baptized in Blood: The Religion of the Lost Cause, 1865-1920*, summarized the connection to white Christianity and church leaders:

"... Christian clergymen were the prime celebrants of the religion of the Lost Cause. They were honored figures at the center of Southern community, and most of them had in some way been touched by the Confederate experience.... These ministers saw little difference between their religious and cultural values, and they promoted the link by constructing Lost Cause ritualistic forms that celebrated their regional mythological and theological beliefs."[35]

Notably, this new theological move allowed white Christian leaders to reenlist the support of many who had been active in the abolitionist cause. Though it strains contemporary moral sensibilities, many white Christian abolitionists could simultaneously oppose the specific practice of chattel slavery while still maintaining core white supremacist attitudes. As Michael Emerson and Christian Smith point out in their landmark book *Divided by Faith: Evangelical Religion and the Problem of Race in America*, even the leading evangelical revivalist Charles Finney, who was a moderate abolitionist during the war, nonetheless defended segregation and race-based prejudice. He made this distinction in a letter reprimanding a close friend who

was supporting integrated seating in their church: "You err in sup-
posing the principle of abolition and amalgamation are identical.
Abolition is a question of flagrant and unblushing wrong. A direct
and outrageous violation of fundamental right. The other is a question of prejudice that does not necessarily deprive any man of any
positive right."[36] Thus, with the question of slavery off the table, the
distance between many southern and northern white Christians actually closed, bridged by the continued shared commitment to white
supremacy and segregation.

Through impressive growth from the late nineteenth through the
mid-twentieth centuries, evangelical Christianity, although anchored
in the South, became the dominant, most dynamic expression of
American Christianity. Leading church historian Charles Marsden
estimates that in the late nineteenth century, over half of the general population and more than eight in ten Protestants were evangelical.[37] When southern Methodists rejoined their northern brethren
in denominational reunification in the late 1930s, they brought their
Lost Cause theology with them into what was at the time the largest
Protestant denomination. By the second half of the twentieth century,
Southern Baptists had become the largest single denomination in the
country, claiming more than sixteen million followers at their apex.
And beginning in the late 1970s, white Catholics received a powerful
infusion of this theology through their involvement with the Christian
right movement, which fortified their own existing streams of colonialist theology. As I show in chapter 5, even though white evangelical
Protestants have begun to shrink as a proportion of the population in
the last decade, the diffusion of their theology into white Christianity generally has meant that their particular cultural worldview, built
to defend their peculiar institution, holds influence far beyond their
ranks today.

Eschatology: Shifting Conceptions of History and Human Responsibility

The Lost Cause shift from politics to culture held major implications for evangelical eschatology, particularly thinking related to the idea of the millennium, a thousand-year reign by Christ that is referenced in the book of Revelation. While the shift did not happen overnight, white evangelicals' new cultural situation created the conditions for a theological sea change, with profound implications for evangelical ethics.

Prior to the Civil War, it was generally popular for white Christians to be what theologians call postmillennialist: to believe that Christ will return for this victorious period only when society has advanced sufficiently toward the ideal of a Christian civilization. The role of Christians, in this model, is to work for the salvation of souls and to participate in reform efforts to help build this model society. The optimism and enthusiasm expressed by Manly and others at the inauguration of Jefferson Davis, for example, tapped this sensibility. The establishment of the Confederacy represented progress toward God's ideal for human society.

After a humiliating and decisive Civil War defeat, however, such an optimistic vision of imminent political realization of Christian ideals held less attraction. By the late nineteenth century, the Lost Cause generation began to adopt a premillennialist theology that held the opposite: the present world represents the work of a sinful and fallen humanity, it will continue to decline, and it will be redeemed only by the second coming of Christ. This view was widely spread by the publication of the *Scofield Reference Bible*, which Reverend C. I. Scofield, a Confederate war veteran from Tennessee, first published with Oxford University Press in 1909.[38] By the end of World War II, the *Scofield Reference Bible* had sold two million copies. Today it has been in print for more than a hundred years.[39]

The most significant outcome of this shift is that the logic of premillennial theology undercuts calls to social justice, since it proceeds from the presumption that the world is evil and in continual decline. The presence of injustice is the unsurprising outcome of a fallen world, not a call for action. Major human intervention is futile, since the world is beyond anything but divine redemption. In due time, Christ will return and set things right. In the meantime, rather than reforming the world, Christians should focus on spirituality and the care of souls: deeper Christian discipleship for themselves and salvation for others who are not "saved."

The reorientation of religious faithfulness, with its radical contraction of human social responsibility, has been a hallmark of white evangelical theology ever since, influencing white evangelical thought not just on race but on other social problems as well. In a 2014 PRRI survey focused on climate change, for example, this correlation between this premillennial end-time thinking and lower support for human intervention in social problems was striking. More than three-quarters of white evangelicals, compared with less than half of Americans overall, agreed that the severity of recent natural disasters was a sign that we were living in "the end times." And while approximately six in ten Americans overall believed climate change was a major problem or a crisis to be addressed, only 44 percent of white evangelicals agreed.[40]

Sociologists Michael Emerson and Christian Smith noted a striking example of the social apathy this theological worldview evoked even in white evangelical leaders who were racial moderates. When Billy Graham was asked about Martin Luther King Jr.'s 1963 "I Have a Dream" speech, in which he evoked a vision of his children playing with white children, Graham replied with resignation: "Only when Christ comes again will little white children of Alabama walk hand in hand with little black children."[41]

Sin and Salvation Through a Personal Relationship with Jesus

Sin and salvation were ever-present in the white Christian world in which I grew up. If there was a Bible verse I knew as well as Romans 8:28, it was Romans 3:23: "For all have sinned and fallen short of the glory of God."[42] Every church service, both Sunday morning and Sunday night, ended with an "altar call." Although Baptists officially eschewed liturgy, the invitation was a highly choreographed ritual with an order and set of expectations that rivaled a Latin Mass. As the worship service closed, the pastor would come down the three steps of the stage and stand below the pulpit in front of the center aisle, typically with outstretched arms. He would then issue "the invitation" for anyone present to walk down to the front of the church to give his or her life to Christ. The pastor would emphasize the universal tendencies toward sin and the need for forgiveness through a personal relationship with Jesus, all in more conversational and hushed tones than he used with the sermon.

The music minister would signal the congregation to rise and sing one of the informally designated invitation hymns, usually one with a slow, repetitive stanza cycle designed to enhance contemplation and to give the Holy Spirit time to bring a sense of conviction in individual hearts. "Just as I am" was a favorite selection. The choir would sway gently to the swelling organ accompaniment as they led the congregational singing: "Just as I am without one plea, / but that thy blood was shed for me. / And that thou bidst me come to Thee, / Oh Lamb of God, I come. I come."

Despite my participating in this ritual thousands of times growing up, its power was not fully impressed upon me until my seminary days. During spring break one year, I accepted an appointment to preach a set of five "revival" services at a small church in rural southern Illinois. I was greeted by an enthusiastic pastor who was splitting his time among multiple churches in the small towns that dotted the area's cornfields. When he picked me up from the airport, I noticed he had taken the initiative to blow up my seminary yearbook picture to fill a grainy 8" x 10" black-and-white page, which he had prominently taped to both the left and right backseat car windows, complete with the words "Robert Jones—Evangelist."

I knew the liturgical formula—I had been trained on "issuing the invitation" in homiletics (preaching) classes in seminary—but when I saw that the revival service was attended by only a dozen regular members, all seemingly over the age of seventy, I felt justified in skipping the invitation at the end of the service. As I greeted the members who filed out of the back door of the church after the service, several politely commented that they had missed the invitation and hoped I would consider issuing one the next night. The pastor was more admonishing, telling me, "You never know what the Lord will do." For the next four nights, I dutifully issued the invitation to these same attendees to ask forgiveness for their sins and enter into a personal relationship with Jesus. No one responded, but everyone was content that the familiar formula for individual repentance of sin and acceptance of salvation had been followed.

It's nothing short of astonishing that a religious tradition with this relentless emphasis on salvation and one so hyperattuned to personal sin can simultaneously maintain such blindness to social sins swirling about it, such as slavery and race-based segregation and bigotry. African American observers of white Christianity, from Frederick Douglass to Martin Luther King Jr., have been utterly mystified at this paradox. As I noted above, Douglass raged against the "horrible inconsistencies" of a religion that had "men-stealers for ministers, women-whippers for missionaries, and cradle-plunderers for church members."[43] Nearly 120 years later, King issued a similar exasperated lament from a Birmingham jail cell:

On sweltering summer days and crisp autumn mornings, I have looked at the South's beautiful churches with their lofty

spires pointing heavenward. I have beheld the impressive out-
lines of her massive religious education buildings. Over and
over, I have found myself asking: "What kind of people worship
here? Who is their God? Where were their voices when the lips
of Governor Barnett dripped with words of interposition and
nullification? Where were they when Governor [George] Wallace gave a clarion call for defiance and hatred? Where were
their voices of support when bruised and weary Negro men and
women decided to rise from the dark dungeons of complacency
to the bright hills of creative protest?"[44]

This confounding contradiction points to the remarkable power of
white Christian culture and the theology that undergirds it. As soci-
ologist Ann Swidler has noted, all groups have what can be thought
of as a kind of "cultural tool kit": a repertoire of shared ideas and behaviors that allow them to organize and interpret reality.[45] This tool
kit necessarily acts like a filter, allowing some things to come sharply
into focus while blurring other things into an indistinguishable background field. Through the workings of this cultural filtering, some
things seem like common sense, while others are less comprehendible
or appear obviously nonsensical.

In a groundbreaking 2000 study, Michael Emerson and Christian
Smith applied these insights to the results of thousands of quantitative and qualitative interviews with black and white Christians.
Particularly on questions related to race, they found that white evangelicals' cultural tool kit consisted of tools that restricted their moral
vision to the personal and interpersonal realms, while screening out
institutional or structural issues. Specifically, Emerson and Smith discovered that the white evangelical cultural tool kit contained three
main tools that are all interconnected by theology: freewill individualism, relationalism, and antistructuralism.[46]

Spelled out, freewill individualism means that, for white evangelicals, "individuals exist independent of structures and institutions,

have freewill, and are individually accountable for their own actions."[47] Relationalism means that white evangelicals tend to see the root of all problems in poor relationships between individuals rather than in unfair laws or institutional behavior. Finally, antistructuralism denotes the deep suspicion with which white evangelicals view institutional explanations for social problems, principally because they believe invoking social structures shifts blame from where it belongs: with sinful individuals.[48]

Emerson and Smith summarized the blind spots this cultural tool kit creates for white evangelicals as follows: "Absent from their accounts is the idea that poor relationships might be shaped by social structures, such as laws, the ways institutions operate, or forms of segregation.... As carpenters are limited to building with the tools in their kits (hammers encourage the use of nails, drills encourage the use of screws), so white evangelicals are severely constrained by their religio-cultural tools."[49] Moreover, the broader premillennialist theological context in which these individualistic conceptions of sin and salvation are embedded further reinforces this constriction of moral vision, both in terms of perceived problems and solutions.

Over the last two decades, there is increasing evidence that this cultural tool kit, developed primarily in the context of white evangelicalism, has become embedded across white Christianity more generally. In a follow-up study published a dozen years later, in 2012, for example, Emerson and coauthor Jason Shelton found stark differences between African American Protestants on the one hand and *both* white evangelical Protestants and white mainline Protestants—the latter group that historically embraced a more structuralist theology—on the other.[50]

For example, when asked about the underlying causes of racial inequality in jobs, income, and housing, only about four in ten black Protestants agreed that these inequalities exist because "African Americans just don't have the motivation or willpower to pull themselves up out of poverty." By contrast, nearly six in ten (59 percent) white evangelicals agreed, as did half of white mainline Protestants.[51] When asked about structural solutions, while 71 percent of black Protestants agreed that the government should do more to help minorities increase their standard of living, a mere 32 percent of white evangelicals and only 38 percent of white mainline Protestants agreed.[52]

Overall, the pattern Shelton and Emerson identified was that while differences were greater between black Protestants and white evangelical Protestants (registering major differences on ten of twenty-one racial identity politics items measured), there were also significant differences between black Protestants and white mainline Protestants on seven of twenty-one items. Notably, there were significantly fewer differences (four of twenty-one) between black and white *non*-Protestants.[53]

So, these findings indicate that there are still significant differences of degree between white evangelical and white mainline Protestants. This makes cultural sense. White mainline Protestants historically received a strong dose of theological structuralism via the social gospel movement and the social justice work of the National Council of Churches. For example, white mainline Protestantism's magazine *Christian Century* has steadily focused on social justice and was the place where King's "Letter from Birmingham Jail" was originally published.

Given this divergent institutional history, however, we would expect larger differences between the evangelical and mainline expressions of white Christianity. Instead, we see that white Protestant affiliation generally is correlated with an individualist rather than structuralist cultural tool kit. In other words, the cultural tool kits of white mainline Protestants increasingly contain the individualist tools of their white evangelical cousins. Although Shelton and Emerson's 2012 analysis was limited to Protestants, as I'll demonstrate in chapter 5, more recent research from PRRI confirms these findings but also reveals that this cultural creep has now extended even into the theological world of white Catholics. Through the twin pathways of white racial identity and the increasing relevance of Republican partisanship in each of these groups, the freewill individualism of white evangelicals has been diffused throughout white American Christianity.

Finally, these cultural tools—freewill individualism, relationalism, and antistructuralism—coalesce powerfully in white evangelical Christology, which centers on having a personal relationship with Jesus. The personal Jesus paradigm represents, in compressed form, the entire conceptual model for white evangelicals' individualist cultural tool kit.

Jesus is conceived of as a savior figure because he does what individual humans cannot: he reconciles human beings to God by sacrificing his life to atone for human sin. So, the only way to human salvation is through this connection between a person and Jesus. And this relationship is understood to have been initiated two millennia ago by Jesus through his death on the cross. Hence, the logic of the model begins with an invitation to a relationship already in motion, a point expressed in hundreds of hymns, such as this popular one: "I will sing the wondrous story / Of the Christ who died for me, / How He left His home in glory / For the cross of Calvary."

In the personal Jesus paradigm, Jesus did not die for a cause or for humankind writ large but for each individual person.[54] Responding positively to this invitation, entering into this relationship, is an intimate decision that must be made freely by each person as an accountable act of the will. In popular language, this act of human agency is articulated as answering a "knock at the door," "letting Jesus come into your heart," and as reciprocating a gift, such as "giving your life to Jesus." Because the most fundamental religious act is one that takes place in the interiority of an individual's emotional, psychological, and spiritual life, it naturally fuels an antistructuralist mind-set. There's nothing in this conceptual model to provide a toehold for thinking about the way institutions or culture shape, promote, or limit human decisions or well-being.

And, notably, in the white evangelical conception of Jesus, though not often interrogated, Jesus is white, or, as in the late nineteenth-century racial classifications, an Aryan Caucasian.[55] There are no descriptions of Jesus's physical characteristics in the gospels, and what we do know—that he was Jewish and from the Middle East—easily makes nonsense of any claims that Jesus shared with white American Christians a European heritage. But from the white European point of view, shot through with colonialist assumptions about racial hierarchies and white supremacy, there was no other possible conclusion. The story of human salvation had to find expression in a divinely ordained, hierarchical universe. As the exemplar of what it meant to be perfectly human, Jesus by definition had to be white. Whites simply couldn't conceive of owing their salvation to a representative of what they considered an inferior race. And a nonwhite Jesus would render impossible the intimate relationalism necessary for the evangelical paradigm to function: no proper white Christian would let a brown man come into their hearts or submit themselves to be a disciple of a swarthy Semite.

The Bible and the Social Status Quo

White evangelicals have generally claimed that their worldview and theology are derived directly from a straightforward reading of an inerrant Bible, and thus, by extension, a direct reflection of God's will. But the evidence suggests that it is more accurate to say that white evangelicals, like everyone who engages the text, read their worldview back into the Bible. In human hands, the Bible is as much a screen as a projector.

While their fellow black Christians were reading liberation stories from Exodus and prophets such as Amos and Hosea who were calling for social and economic justice, white evangelicals stayed focused more narrowly on the gospels and the writings of Paul to early Christian churches, which were interpreted more easily to be about salvation, right relationships, maintaining order, and keeping the peace. In the hands of clergy committed to white supremacy, cultural selectivity was as effective as the actual redactions in the slave Bible on display at the Museum of the Bible. This piecemeal approach—which might as well have been captioned with the parallel inscription "Parts of the Holy Bible, selected for the use of the slave owners, in the United States"—had the effect of neutralizing calls for racial justice and social change. White Christian selectivity harnessed the Bible in service of maintaining the current status quo, which, conveniently, was structured to maintain white supremacy.

Even as social norms gradually changed in favor of recognizing greater rights and equality for black Americans, white evangelicals called on this individualist reading of the Bible to distance themselves from fully embracing these changes. During the debates over the morality of slavery, its white evangelical defenders typically held the upper hand when debates were restricted to biblical arguments; they could straightforwardly outquote the abolitionists, citing examples of explicit support for slavery and numerous places where the Bible notes the existence of the practice and fails to condemn it. And more fundamentally, they pointed to verses that they claimed legitimized the racial supremacy of whites over blacks as the divinely ordained form of relationships between the races.

Abolitionists had a more complicated task. At the most basic level, they concentrated on drawing awareness to the brutality of slavery as it was practiced. This allowed them to avoid direct biblical debates by distinguishing between what were perhaps more benign instances of slavery in the Bible and harsher contemporary realities. If they went further, and many did not, they had to make more general arguments about the centrality of principles of love and equality to Christianity; and then argue further that these principles should apply to social and political life as well as personal life. But white evangelicals, with their individualist tool kits, were primed and well equipped to reject both lines of argument. The brutality of slavery they dismissed as acts of particular individuals rather than broad patterns; and the broad application of love and equality was denigrated as a move that illegitimately brought "politics"—by which they meant anything social or structural—into religion.

A century later, during the civil rights movement, this template was still functioning. When Reverend Martin Luther King Jr. began to gain traction on American consciences by citing the prophetic tradition of the Bible, praying with the prophet Amos that God would "let justice roll down like waters and righteousness like a mighty stream," white evangelical leaders tried to undermine his work as illegitimate. Just weeks after "Bloody Sunday" in Selma, Alabama, in 1965, the Reverend Jerry Falwell gave this response in a sermon:

"Believing the Bible as I do, I would find it impossible to stop preaching the pure saving gospel of Jesus Christ and begin doing anything else—including the fighting of Communism, or participating in the civil rights reform.... Preachers are not called to be politicians, but to be soul winners."[56]

Of course, Falwell eventually reversed himself, founding his own political organization, the Moral Majority, in 1979 and becoming a major player on the political right. The precipitating event that changed his tune? Falwell was enraged that Bob Jones University, a conservative white Christian institution, had lost its tax-exempt status in 1976 because it refused to rescind its racially discriminatory policies.[57] Shortly after that decision, Falwell preached: "The idea that religion and politics don't mix was invented by the devil to keep Christians from running their own country."[58]

While this sentiment is a complete repudiation of his former declaration, the about-face is consistent if it's understood as a mere tactical change to an underlying commitment, defending a white supremacist status quo. When white supremacy was still safely ensconced in the wider culture, white evangelicals argued that the Bible mandated a privatized religion. This was a powerful way of delegitimizing the work of black ministers working for black equality. But as these forces gained power, white evangelicals discovered a biblical mandate for political organizing and resistance.

The historical contradictions between the various confident declarations about biblical teachings on race by white Christians are head spinning. As a social consensus coalesced around the immorality and sinfulness of slavery following the Civil War, white evangelicals retreated from the previously unflinching claims of biblical support for slavery. And only just recently, as Americans are beginning to name white supremacy as a social sin, white evangelicals have also repudiated their previous, and equally confident, claims that the separation of the races was an obvious biblical dictate. Having reluctantly conceded these points, with concessions coming only after they have become socially untenable, white evangelicals, incredibly, continue to assert that their current theological conclusions are derived directly from an inerrant Bible.

There is stronger evidence that it is the other way around: that white Christians' cultural worldview, with an unacknowledged white supremacy sleeping at its core, has been read back into the Bible. And if this is true, a deeper interrogation of our entire theological worldview, including our understanding and use of the Bible and even core theological doctrines of a personal relationship with Jesus, is in order. Until we find the courage to face these appalling errors of our recent past, white Christians should probably avoid any further proclamations about what "the Bible teaches" or what "the biblical worldview" demands.

Conclusion

This theological worldview—Lost Cause theology, premillennialism, an individualist view of sin, an emphasis on a personal relationship with Jesus, and the Bible as the protector of the status quo—has created a mutually reinforcing, closed habit of thought among white evangelicals. The system protects white Christian interests on the one hand and white consciences on the other. In return, white Christians defend the system from external critique, relying on the cultural tool kit it provides.

Lost Cause theology, with its underlying commitment to preserving white supremacy, has proven remarkably durable, even as it has adapted to new times. Its main contours are still discernible in dynamics driving our politics today. Paul Harvey, historian at University of Colorado at Colorado Springs, summarized the Lost Cause narrative this way: "Ultimately... white spiritual leaders preached that a sanctified, purified white South would rise from the ashes to serve as God's 'last and only hope' in a modernizing and secularizing nation."[59] Writing in the mid-1960s, cultural anthropologist Anthony Wallace described Lost Cause religion as a revivalist movement aiming "to restore a golden age believed to have existed in the society's past," terms eerily close to contemporary calls by President Donald Trump to "Make America great again."[60] It is true that old-school Lost Cause theology is rarely aired in mainstream white churches today. But its direct descendant, the individualist theology that insists that Christianity has little to say about social injustice—created to shield white consciences from the evils and continued legacy of slavery and segregation—lives on, not just in white evangelical churches but also increasingly in white mainline and white Catholic churches as well.

To be sure, this theological worldview has done great damage to those living outside the white Christian canopy. But what has been overlooked by most white Christian leaders is the damage this legacy has done to white Christians themselves. To put it succinctly, it has often put white Christians in the curious position of arguing that their religion and their God require them to aim lower than the highest human values of love, justice, equality, and compassion. As antebellum Presbyterian preacher Donald Frazer argued emphatically, many abolitionists had the shoe on the wrong foot by pretending to be "more humane than God."[61] It was God's law, not human conscience, that set the limits on the treatment of blacks by whites, he argued. Moral discomfort, even moral horror or outrage, has no place in this theological worldview. But surely it should give white Christians pause to continue to pledge allegiance to a theological system that contracts rather than expands our moral vision; that anesthetizes rather than livens up our moral sensitivities.

These contradictions are not just theoretical. Increasing anxieties around the perceived decline of white identity and white Christian culture are driving right-wing extremism both at home and abroad. What these movements get right is that those who have assembled under the banner of whiteness have lost something vital in this centuries-long struggle for power. Their hope is that they will regain a secure identity by reenthroning white Christian dominance through xenophobic politics and a culture war based on violence and terrorism. But there is a better, more realistic path forward. Confronting a theology built for white supremacy would be a critical first step for white Christians who want to recover a connection not just to our fellow African American Christians but also to our own identity and, more importantly, our humanity.

– 4 –

Marking

Monuments to White Supremacy

The largest post–Civil War gathering to honor the Confederacy occurred not in the nineteenth century, but on June 3, 1907—more than four decades after General Robert E. Lee surrendered the last major Confederate army to Ulysses S. Grant at Appomattox Courthouse in Virginia. An estimated two hundred thousand people—including eighteen thousand former Confederate soldiers—gathered in Richmond, Virginia, the former capital of the Confederacy, to witness the dedication of an elaborate monument to Jefferson Davis, the former Confederate president, on what would have been his ninety-ninth birthday. The five-day celebration included the annual reunion of the United Confederate Veterans and a convergence of numerous southern women's associations, most prominently the United Daughters of the Confederacy (UDC), the driving force behind the Confederate monument movement.

On the evening of Wednesday, May 29, there was a reception of the allied men's and ladies' Confederate groups to kick off the celebration. On Thursday and Friday, May 30 and 31, there were joint business meetings of the UDC and other related women's groups, which were hosted at the Second Baptist Church, followed on Friday evening by a reception at Richmond's Confederate Museum and a ball. Saturday,

June 1, activities included a visit to veteran residents of the nearby Robert E. Lee Camp Confederate Soldiers' Home and a formal reception with the Virginia governor and first lady at the executive mansion. Sunday, June 2, was left free for the Sabbath, to allow worship at local churches.

All of this built up to the day of the monument dedication on Monday, June 3. The ceremonies were drenched in the white Christian theology of the Lost Cause. The official program for the event noted that there would be "special services in all Richmond churches" in the morning before the main unveiling event and "special services in city churches and sacred concert at the Horse-Show Building" in the evening.[1] Even the business meetings and other less ceremonious events kicked off with prayer by a local pastor or by the well-known Southern Baptist Reverend Dr. J. William Jones, a Virginian and the chaplain-general for the United Confederate Veterans, whom historian Charles Reagan Wilson dubbed "the evangelist of the Lost Cause."[2] Jones, who had personally helped raise $10,000 for the Davis monument, was also popular for rousing prayers that began with invocations of the "God of Abraham, Isaac, and Jacob, God of Israel, God of the centuries, God of our fathers, God of Jefferson Davis, Robert Edward Lee, and Stonewall Jackson, Lord of hosts and King of kings."[3]

After the morning church services, the town reassembled for an elaborate parade to the memorial site. As the surviving Confederate veterans led the processional forward, a band played "Dixie" and other Confederate favorites such as "My Maryland!" While "My Maryland!" is less known today, it was a Confederate favorite because it paid tribute to a state that, while officially a part of the Union, was nevertheless a slave state situated south of the Mason-Dixon Line and home to many Southern sympathizers. Set to the tune of "O Tannenbaum," the song was penned in 1861 by James Ryder Randall, a Georgian living in Baltimore, as a tribute to what became known as the Pratt Street Riot, in which Southern sympathizers attacked Union soldiers as they marched through Baltimore en route to Washington.[4] In contrast to the rose-colored nostalgia of "Dixie," the lyrics of "My Maryland!" are more bellicose:

> *Thou wilt not yield the vandal toll, Maryland, my Maryland!*
> *Thou wilt not crook to his control, Maryland, my Maryland!*
> *Better the fire upon thee roll,*
> *Better the blade, the shot, the bowl,*
> *Than crucifixion of the soul,*
> *Maryland! My Maryland!*
> *I hear the distant thunder-hum, Maryland, my Maryland!*
> *The Old Line's bugle, fife, and drum, Maryland, my Maryland!*
> *She is not dead, nor deaf, nor dumb—*
> *Huzza! She spurns the Northern scum!*
> *She breathes! She burns! She'll come! She'll come!*
> *Maryland! My Maryland!*[5]

After the veteran columns, leading members of the UDC marched, followed by a group of white children, dressed in the colors of the Confederacy, who pulled the veiled monument through the streets on a wheeled platform to its final resting place.[6] Present on the platform were various descendants of de facto Confederate royalty, such as Mary Anna Jackson, General Stonewall Jackson's widow, and Mary Lee, the daughter of the late Robert E. Lee.[7] After an opening prayer, the crowd was addressed first by Virginia governor Claude Swanson and then by the orator of the day, Clement Evans, a revered former Confederate general turned influential Methodist minister. Finally, Margaret Howell Jefferson Hayes, the only surviving child of Jefferson Davis, and her two sons, pulled ropes to unveil the monument to thunderous applause punctuated by rebel yells.[8]

The monument to Jefferson Davis had been delayed for nearly two decades after his death, mostly because the UDC members wanted to make the monument to the president of the Confederacy, especially in the former capital of the Confederacy, grand. They didn't disappoint. The final structure, which carried a price tag of $50,000 (approximately $1.4 million today), featured at its center a bronze statue of Davis, "of heroic size," standing atop a twelve-foot pedestal. He is speaking with outstretched arm, designed to depict his farewell speech to the US Senate before joining the Confederacy after Mississippi seceded from the Union. The text of that speech wraps around the curving base of thirteen Doric columns, which represent the states of the Confederacy (eleven official states plus two border states that sent delegates to the Confederate Congress). Behind the Davis statue is a massive column topped with a female statue that UDC materials describe as "an allegorical bronze figure" whose "right hand points to heaven." The combined measurements of the monument are fifty feet wide by thirty feet deep, and sixty-seven feet tall, or approximately the height of a five-story building.

The UDC's official printed program for the unveiling featured prominently, on the inside cover, an explanation of the figure at the top of the tallest column in the monument:

"Symbolized in the *Vindicatrix* which crowns the shaft of the monument erected by the Jefferson Davis Monument Association, the emblem of Southern womanhood, fitly stands, the immortal spirit of her land shining unquenched within her eyes, and her hand uplifted in an eternal appeal to the God of justice and of truth."[9]

Bold bronze lettering beneath this female figure is emblazoned with the motto of the Confederacy, "Deo Vindice," or "With God as our Defender." The UDC left no doubts that this monument was more than a memorial. It was a defiant declaration of vindication that looked both to the past and the future.

The Davis monument was the crowning achievement establishing Richmond's Monument Avenue as a living testimony for the Lost Cause that began with the placement of an initial monument to Robert E. Lee in 1890. By the turn of the century, Richmond leaders had planned an elaborate westward expansion of the city focused around a striking new avenue. Its construction would include a broad, green, tree-lined linear park running its full length that divided the east-bound and westbound traffic. At major cross streets, the greenways would terminate at traffic circles, which would host monuments to the leaders of the Confederacy.

By 1919, with the addition of a monument to General Stonewall Jackson, Richmond supporters of the Lost Cause had completed an homage to the recognized trinity of Confederate leaders: Generals Lee and Jackson, plus a tribute to Confederate general J. E. B. Stuart (dedicated with less fanfare the same day as the Davis monument), who died defending Richmond during the war. Wealthy white Richmonders flocked to the new development, building elaborate houses on what quickly became, in the first few decades of the twentieth century, the most enviable street address in the city.

By 1930, Richmond's white aristocracy had also uprooted seven of its prominent churches, replanting them in the shadows of the Confederate monuments. When west Richmond construction crews weren't erecting Confederate monuments, they were relocating white Christian churches. Walking west on Monument Avenue, just ahead of Stuart Circle, is St. James's Episcopal Church, built in 1912. Continuing on, two churches flank opposite sides of Stuart Circle, each facing the J. E. B. Stuart Monument: First English Evangelical Lutheran Church (built in 1911) and St. John's United Church of Christ (1928). Farther west, near the Lee Monument, is Grace Covenant Presbyterian Church (1923). Between the Lee and Davis Monuments sits First Church of Christ, Scientist (1929). Finally, the massive First Baptist Church (built 1929), taking up an entire city block, directly faces the Stonewall Jackson Monument, and St. Mark's Episcopal Church (1922) stands just around the corner.

Monument Avenue, with its blend of monuments to Confederate leaders, leading churches of the major white Christian denominations, and imposing homes, was carefully designed to serve both as a living civic tribute to the Confederacy for Richmond's white elite and as a Lost Cause pilgrimage site for whites across the South. This vision was largely successful. A century later, it remains a leafy, upper-class, mostly white neighborhood dotted with tall-steepled churches and massive granite and bronze tributes to the Confederacy. As an official National Historic Landmark district, it still serves as a tourist magnet. And it continues to make its cultural statement. As historian Charles Reagan Wilson noted: "Richmond was the Mecca of the Lost Cause, and Monument Boulevard was the sacred road to it."[10]

The Force Behind the Monuments: The United Daughters of the Confederacy

The monument to the former president of the Confederacy was one of the most elaborate, and its unveiling generated the largest single postwar gathering of Lost Cause celebrants. But the work of the UDC extended well beyond monuments. It included a multipronged effort to defend and promote Confederate culture with a particular aim of vindicating these values nationally while passing them on to the next generation of southern white children.

As the work of the United Daughters of the Confederacy expanded, their elaborate performances of Lost Cause values were repeated in local monument unveilings across the South. Notably, children became central to these rituals, for both symbolic and strategic reasons. Children were involved even in raising money, such as a challenge launched in Moultrie, Georgia, for them to gather "a mile of pennies" to be presented at a monument's dedication.[11] Processionals often featured thirteen young girls, representing the purity and innocence of the Lost Cause, who were dressed in white, their sashes emblazoned with the name of a Confederate state and two supportive border states. And unveilings frequently featured children's choirs, which rehearsed songs ahead of the event in their local churches and public schools.

Most of the time, these were fairly straightforward performances, but they could also be elaborate spectacles. For example, at a 1911 dedication of a monument to Jefferson Davis in New Orleans, 576 white public school students were dismissed for the day to participate in the ceremonies. Dressed in red for the background, blue for the bars, and white hats for the stars, they were arranged to form a living Confederate flag. They sang not only "Dixie" but also "America" and popular hymns, a practice designed to declare that Confederate values were not those of traitors but were instead noble, patriotic, and Christian. As historian Karen Cox notes, "For white southerners, monument unveilings were at once a public expression of regional devotion and a means of reclaiming their identity as patriotic Americans. . . . They saw no contradiction in singing 'America' along with 'Dixie,' or waving flags of the Confederacy with that of the United States."[12]

Even the placement of the monuments in prominent public places was done with the next generation in mind. After dedicating a monument to Confederate soldiers in 1899 on the county courthouse grounds in Franklin, Tennessee, UDC leaders celebrated its educational value; that children "might know by daily observation of this monument" the values for which their ancestors fought. This message, obviously, was meant for white children and conveyed quite a different message—the continued assertion of white supremacy—to the African American children and adults in the community.[13]

In addition to the massive monument-raising effort, the UDC engaged in a broad range of other actions, all aimed at its explicitly stated goal to achieve "the vindication of the men of the Confederacy."[14] The May 1932 issue of *Confederate Veteran*, the popular official monthly magazine of the United Confederate Veterans, the United Daughters of the Confederacy and other Confederate veterans groups, contained this report from a UDC affiliate in Virginia about activities in local schools:

> The Greenville Chapter, at Emporia, has presented to the Emporia High School Library over one hundred books on Southern Literature, reference books, biographies, with Confederate

book plate in each volume. It has also presented every white school in Greenville County copies of Horton's History, a Confederate flag, and several copies each of Dr. Lyon G. Tyler's Confederate Catechism; and in all of these schools, essays have been written on both the Catechism and Horton's History.... For three years, a prize has been offered in the Colored High School for the best essay on "Causes Leading to the War between the States," based on Horton's History. There were splendid results each year.[15]

Across the South, in large cities and small towns, UDC women preserved oral histories and Confederate relics; policed public school history textbooks for anti-South bias and produced their own alternatives, such as a white supremacist primer for schoolchildren entitled *The Ku Klux Klan or Invisible Empire*, which was written in 1914 by UDC historian-general Laura Martin Rose and subsequently adopted by the state of Mississippi as a supplemental text for public schools; placed thousands of portraits of Robert E. Lee and Jefferson Davis in public schools, where they could be displayed next to existing portraits of George Washington; and secured Confederate Memorial Day as a public school holiday so that schoolchildren could attend celebrations and help place miniature Confederate flags on the graves of soldiers.

World War I provided an opportunity for a new vindication strategy for the United Daughters of the Confederacy: from defensive defiance to a more cooperative strategy to achieve national acceptance on their own terms. Seeing the overseas conflict as an opportunity to prove their patriotism without having to abandon their assertions that the Confederate cause was just, they threw themselves into the war effort. They established cooperative efforts with other mainstream organizations and also spearheaded projects that provided relief while supporting their goals of unconditional reconciliation.

One of the most illustrative examples of the UDC's reach was the partnership between it and an American military hospital in Neuilly,

France, which was seeking supplemental funds as the carnage piled up in the war. The UDC struck a deal with the hospital, committing to sponsor up to seventy beds, at a cost of $600 per year, if they could attach a brass plaque to the bed memorializing a Confederate veteran. The tribute on the first "endowed bed" read: "The United Daughters of the Confederacy—A Tribute of Honor and Devotion to Jefferson Davis."[16]

The organization finally began to lose steam in the decades after World War I, which had brought North and South together again against a common enemy, and as the last of the Confederate generation died off. After the First World War, the UDC did not return to its monument-building fervor, but in just twenty-five years of work since its founding in 1894, its main goal—the vindication of the Confederate cause—had largely been accomplished. These female Lost Cause crusaders had literally staked their white supremacist claims in public spaces across the South and had contributed significantly to the ideological victories fought in postwar national literary and historical circles.

As historian Melvin Urofsky observes in his history of the Virginia Historical Society, by the end of the nineteenth century, "nearly all northern historians adopted the southern view on race in general and the inferiority of African Americans in particular."[17] For example, even Albert Bushnell Hart, a progressive historian who was the descendant of abolitionists and himself a proponent of black advancement, could write, "Race, measured by race, the Negro is inferior, and his past history in Africa, and in America, leads to the belief that he will remain inferior."[18] In a 1918 presidential update published in *Confederate Veteran*, UDC president Mary Poppenheim declared the UDC's cultural vindication mission largely accomplished, adding with satisfaction that their successes had been achieved "without sacrificing a single principle."[19]

While the organization is a shell of its former self today, its legacy remains—not just in granite and bronze, but also in the ways its past educational efforts continue to shape American culture and religion, limiting white vision and hindering black equality. Karen Cox closed her important study of the UDC, *Dixie's Daughters: The United Daughters of the Confederacy and the Preservation of Confederate Culture*, with this summary:

> National reconciliation had been achieved effectively on the South's terms, and certainly on the Daughters' terms. The North had accepted the Lost Cause narrative as fact, which was an essential element of reunion. That narrative, perpetuated most vigorously by the UDC, was, at its core, about preserving white supremacy. Reconciliation had allowed white southerners to return to the American fold as patriots, not traitors, one of the desired results of the Daughters' work. For African Americans, however, the results of this reunion would add decades onto their journey for freedom.[20]

Growing Up Amid the Confederacy

Like tendrils reaching forward from the past, these pervasive features of white southern culture creeped quietly into my own consciousness during my youth. Though born in Atlanta, I grew up mostly in Jackson, Mississippi, a city founded in 1821 and named after General Andrew Jackson, a slaveholding Presbyterian from South Carolina who became a hero during the War of 1812 and, eventually, the seventh president of the United States. In 1970s and 1980s Jackson, I experienced the immediate aftermath of desegregation and was aware of the subdued but simmering racial anxieties it produced among whites. But as a white kid, I also subconsciously absorbed from the culture around me many tenets of the cult of the Lost Cause.

My public high school was awash in Confederate symbols and rituals. Forest Hill High School—which at the time of my attendance in the early 1980s was integrated and divided evenly between white and black students—was a historically white school in the working-class southwest quadrant of Jackson. Even after the school was integrated in the early 1970s, it retained "the Rebels" as the school name and "Colonel Reb" as the mascot. When our majority-black football team scored a touchdown during Friday-night home games, a white male cheerleader ran down the length of the sideline with a bedsheet-sized Confederate flag as the band played "Dixie" for the cheering crowd. While this dissonance was mostly lost on the white students, including me, it clearly sent the message to the African American students who arrived mostly on buses from other parts of town that they were second-class citizens of a white-dominant school.

While Jackson has its share of Confederate monuments, the one that had the greatest impression on me as a kid was the massive carving of Davis, Lee, and Jackson on the side of Stone Mountain just outside Atlanta. My family made the drive down Interstate 20 from Jackson, Mississippi, to Macon, Georgia, a couple of times a year, which required a right turn at Atlanta. From time to time, we'd stop to see a Braves baseball game or go to local sites. On one trip in early high school, we stopped to visit the famous mountain.

What I didn't realize visiting as a kid, or really even in my twenties, is that this carving represented the largest tribute to the Lost Cause ever produced. The sculptures, which took nearly five decades to complete, comprise the largest bas-relief carving in the world, larger than Mount Rushmore; they rise four hundred feet off the ground and cover 1.6 acres of the mountain's face. The project was begun in 1916 at the behest of the president of the United Daughters of the Confederacy, C. Helen Plane, who was from Georgia and had a summer home at the base of the mountain. Besides being a unique geological feature, the mountain had cultural significance as a meeting place for the Ku Klux Klan, which was granted an explicit right to continue ceremonies there undeterred during the construction. Although it didn't make it into the final design, Plane made an early suggestion to the sculptor that the KKK be included, explaining, "I feel it is due to the Klan[,] which saved us from Negro dominations and carpetbag rule, that it be immortalized on Stone Mountain. Why not represent a small group of them in their nightly uniform approaching in the distance?"[21] The park finally opened on April 14, 1965, on the exact one hundredth anniversary of the assassination of President Lincoln. Today Stone Mountain Park is Georgia's most popular attraction, receiving more than four million visitors each year.

In retrospect, the most remarkable thing about my growing up in the Deep South is how massive contradictions somehow evaded serious moral or religious interrogation. From fall 1983 to spring 1986, the two institutions that most shaped my life, my school and my church, were dominated by Confederate symbols on the one hand and Christian symbols on the other. Monday through Friday, I navigated school grounds and events saturated with Confederate imagery and rituals; and twice on Sunday as well as on Monday through Wednesday evenings, I was surrounded by Christian imagery and participated in Christian worship and discipleship. For most of high school, I had a regular morning devotional prayer and reflective journaling practice, and I read my Bible daily.

This juxtaposition produced virtually no cognitive dissonance. Neither I nor my white friends thought of ourselves as racists or white supremacists or even in racial terms. And virtually all of my friends took their Christian faith seriously. To the best of my memory, my conscience was never significantly challenged as I participated in varsity soccer and cross country with black teammates, cheered at pep rallies, served as senior class president, or even as I sported a Confederate battle flag license plate on the front of my 1967 Chevy El Camino pickup truck as a symbol of school spirit. When we visited Stone Mountain, we weren't thinking about it as a monument to the Confederacy and white supremacy; neither the significance of those figures nor the presence of the four flags of the Confederacy at the head of the hiking trail raised an eyebrow or pricked our consciences. It is a testimony to their power, and to the success of groups such as the United Daughters of the Confederacy, that as late as the 1980s, these symbols could escape Christian or moral interrogation.

The Legacy of Confederate Monuments Today

At its apex, toward the end of World War I, the United Daughters of the Confederacy was a formidable national organization, boasting a membership of more than 100,000 women. To put this reach in perspective, the more mainstream Women's Christian Temperance Union claimed a southern states' membership of only 6,500 at the turn of the century. In addition to a strong mission that channeled Lost Cause sentiments into action, they crafted an organizational structure with a low bar for establishing local affiliate groups. The national UDC bylaws allowed for a chapter to be formed whenever there were at least seven white female descendants of Confederate army or navy veterans, permitting chapters to quickly sprout not just in hamlets all over the South but also among Confederate diaspora in far-flung states such as California, New York, and Illinois.[22]

According to a comprehensive Southern Poverty Law Center (SPLC) report, as of July 2019, there were 1,747 documented Confederate monuments, place names, holidays, and other symbols still in public spaces. Among this number were 780 monuments to the Confederacy, 300 of which were in the three states of Georgia, North Carolina, and Virginia alone.[23] And these astounding totals remained *after* more than 100 of these symbols had been removed since the 2015 massacre at Charleston's Emanuel AME Church. Most of these monuments were installed, either wholly or in part, by the United Daughters of the Confederacy. The prevalence of these markers within the states that constituted the Confederacy—and this is only a count of symbols on *public* property—is astonishing.

In contemporary debates, the primary argument for preserving

Confederate monuments rests on the assumption that these symbols are simply surviving markers that date from the time of the old Confederacy and therefore should be preserved as history. But the comprehensive database compiled by the SPLC, illustrated in Figure 4.1 on the next page, confirms that few Confederate monuments in public spaces were put in place in the immediate aftermath of the Civil War. Rather, more than nine in ten of the public monuments were erected after 1895. Fully half of them were erected between the turn of the twentieth century and the 1920s, with another boomlet of intense activity between 1955 and 1970.[24] In other words, the Confederate monument phenomenon was no innocent movement to memorialize the dead; it was primarily a twentieth-century declaration of Lost Cause values designed to vindicate white supremacy and bolster white power against black claims to equality and justice. These Confederate monuments, strategically placed in public spaces, are deposits left by the high tide of white supremacy.

Placed in historical context, the spikes in monument construction are clearly correlated with periods of white reassertions of political and cultural power. The SPLC report summarized these patterns as follows:

The first [spike] began around 1900, as southern states were enacting Jim Crow laws to disenfranchise African Americans and resegregate society after several decades of integration that followed Reconstruction. It lasted well into the 1920s, a period that also saw a strong revival of the Ku Klux Klan. Many of these monuments were sponsored by the United Daughters of the Confederacy. The second period began in the mid-1950s and lasted until the late 1960s, the period encompassing the modern civil rights movement.[25]

The UDC's most visible accomplishment—and the one that may prove to be the most difficult to reverse—is the sheer number of Confederate monuments entrenched on public land. The organization was

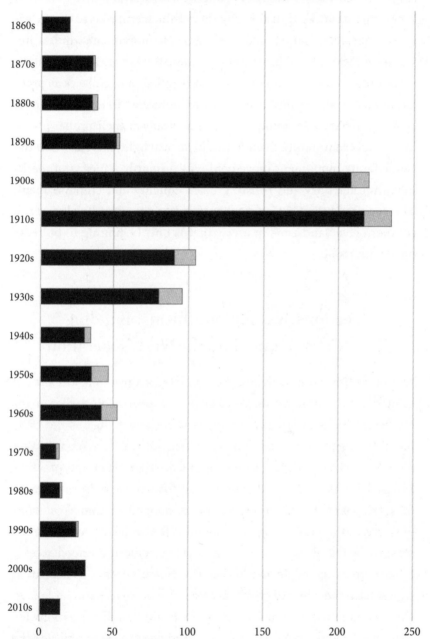

FIGURE 4.1 Installation of Confederate Monuments in Public Spaces, by Decade

Note: This chart does not include monuments or other symbols for which the dedication dates are unknown. Gray bars indicate symbols that have now been removed from public spaces.

Source: Data from "Whose Heritage? 153 Years of Confederate Iconography," Southern Poverty Law Center, 2018.

singlehandedly responsible for changing the cultural practices of Civil
War remembrances, transforming them from memorials to Confederate soldiers placed largely among the dead, to monuments vindicating
southern ideals placed prominently among the living. They sought to
place Confederate monuments in well-traveled public places as proclamations of white supremacy that were intended to teach their own
children about and remind African Americans of their proper places
in the local community. Seen in this historical light, it is clear that the
Confederate monument movement was primarily a means of marking white territory and resisting black equality and empowerment.
The success of the UDC and other allied groups literally altered the
southern civic landscape in a way that is only beginning to be reck-
oned with today.

Lectionaries and Catechisms: Building
Lost Cause Values into the Next Generation

Mirroring this work in civic space, the UDC set out to instill a set of
Confederate "truths" within the next generation, building what might
be thought of as internal monuments of the heart. Just as the UDC
blended Confederate and American patriotism, the organization
also overlaid Confederate rituals onto Christian belief and practice.
Mildred Lewis Rutherford, who served for five years in the powerful UDC position of historian general, developed an annual calendar
of suggested monthly program emphases for local chapters. Like the
seasons of the church calendar and the specific prescribed weekly
biblical readings of denominational lectionaries, this coordination
would have the effect of creating a stronger sense of national fellowship, as members in scattered chapters could imagine a nationwide
sisterhood, along with their children, studying the same topics at the
same time. These synchronized, seasonal activities also provided educational recommendations around developing Lost Cause holy days,

such as Confederate leaders' birthdays, Confederate Memorial Day, and "Christmas in the Old South." For example, the program for the winter and spring of 1915 included the following topics, as summarized by historian Karen Cox:

"In January children studied Robert E. Lee and Stonewall Jackson, whose birthdays were commemorated that month. For February, the subject was 'secession and the result.' March featured the study of 'our leaders' and singing 'Dixie.' Memorial Day was studied and commemorated in April, while in May Jefferson Davis and Abraham Lincoln were to be compared by asking the question, 'Which violated the Constitution?'"[26]

Consistent with their mission, the UDC also included monthly topics dedicated to the role of women in the Confederacy. In July, for example, children were asked to interview their grandmothers and write an essay on the topic "The Life of Ole Mis' on the Old Plantation."[27]

In addition to seasonally coordinated communal practices, UDC leaders also developed educational materials for children that were explicitly modeled after, and intended to complement, familiar religious practices, such as the *UDC Catechism for Children*.[28] Catechisms have been used by a wide array of Christian traditions for centuries as a means of religious instruction, especially for children. They are typically the backbone of Confirmation classes, in which youngsters demonstrate adequate knowledge of the faith before being accepted as full members of the church. For example, the catechism used in the Methodist Episcopal Church in the second half of the nineteenth century begins with five basic questions about God, followed by orthodox Christian answers:[29]

(1) Who made you?

God.

(2) Who is God?

The Creator of all things.

(3) What is God?

An uncreated Spirit.

(4) Where is God?

God is everywhere.

(5) What does God know?

God is all-wise; he knoweth all things, even the thoughts of our hearts.

The UDC's Confederate catechism follows this form and was designed, as church catechisms were, for recitation in meetings as UDC leaders worked with children. It contains no fewer than sixty-four questions for children to master in order to demonstrate their grasp of Lost Cause orthodoxy. Here are the first five items from the *UDC Catechism for Children*:[30]

(1) What causes led to the war between the States, from 1861 to 1865?

The disregard, on the part of States of the North, for the rights of the Southern or slave-holding States.

(2) How was this shown?

By the passage of laws in the Northern States annulling the rights of the people of the South—rights that were given to them by the Constitution of the United States.

(3) What were these rights?

The rights to regulate their own affairs and to hold slaves as property.

(4) Were the Southern States alone responsible for the existence of slavery?

No; slavery was introduced into the country in colonial times by the political authorities of Great Britain, Spain, France and the Dutch merchants, and in 1776—at the time of the Declaration of Independence—slavery existed in all of the thirteen colonies.

(5) How many of the colonies held slaves when the federal constitution was adopted, in 1787?

All except one.

In addition to the questions above, the catechism contains numerous questions on the most sensitive subject: slavery. Orthodox answers point out that General Grant himself was a slave owner and that southerners had not supported slavery "as a principle" but as an economic necessity. And it advanced the following cornerstones of southern slaveholding orthodoxy:[31]

(13) How were the slaves treated?

With great kindness and care in nearly all cases, a cruel master being rare, and lost the respect of his neighbors if he treated his slaves badly. Self interest [*sic*] would have prompted good treatment if a higher feeling of humanity had not.

(14) What was the feeling of the slaves towards their masters?

They were faithful and devoted and were always ready and willing to serve them.

By design, a white Christian child growing up with the parallel rituals in civic and religious spaces would have experienced white supremacist and Christian values as seamlessly interwoven. It would not have been unusual to have teachers leading children in recitation of one catechism on Saturday at a UDC Children of the Confederacy gathering and recitations of the other the next day at Sunday school. And the liturgical rhythm of the year would reinforce these connections. Both Easter and Confederate Memorial Day—which remains an official state holiday in Alabama, Mississippi, and South Carolina—are celebrated in the spring within weeks of each other, and the Christian theological emphasis on resurrection during this liturgical season strongly reinforces the Lost Cause hopes of a defeated white South flowering into new life.

The Lost Cause in Stained Glass

Over time, Robert E. Lee, Stonewall Jackson, and Jefferson Davis in particular evolved into Confederate Christian saints who were treated as religious icons. In addition to the public monuments, groups such as the United Daughters of the Confederacy, and many upper-class southern whites in general, worked to incorporate images of this Confederate trinity in sacred spaces, principally through stained glass installations in churches and other public buildings. By creating these figures in the medium of sacred art, and displaying their images alongside—or even as—Jesus, the New Testament apostles, and the Old Testament biblical patriarchs, Lost Cause supporters elevated these figures above history into Christian sainthood while elevating the white South as God's chosen people, despite military defeat.

Of the post–Civil War heroes, historian Reagan Wilson describes Robert E. Lee as "the apex of the Lost Cause pantheon." Lee was described as a gentle and virtuous crusading Christian knight, often depicted as Moses leading his people to the promised land or as a Christ figure. It would not be lost on congregational members that both were tragic yet hopeful analogies: Moses never made it to the promised land and Jesus was crucified; but Moses pointed the way to the Jewish people's ultimate arrival in the promised land, and Jesus rose from the dead.

Although Davis outlived the war by nearly twenty-five years, his arrest and subsequent imprisonment in irons by Northern troops at the end of the Civil War became the defining event for his identity in the developing Lost Cause mythology. Davis came to function as a Christian martyr, whose life and treatment immediately after the war symbolized the South's broader mistreatment and humiliation. As is true of most heroes, his esteem and mythos grew significantly after his death in 1889, and the UDC helped install more church stained glass windows featuring Davis than Lee after 1900.

By contrast, Stonewall Jackson represented "a stern Old Testament prophet-warrior." Praised for his intense Protestant faith, manliness, and fierceness in battle, Jackson was portrayed as an embodiment of God's wrath.[32] In the face of the emasculating experience of defeat, Jackson's image evoked courage, valor, and an unflinching sense of the righteousness of the cause.

These stained glass portrayals appeared not just in tall-steeple symbolic churches directly connected with these icons. Smaller congregations were also mining the raw materials of the Bible to fashion new meaning from their experience of defeat in the Civil War. Some of the earliest stained glass depictions installed following the war were fairly straightforward adaptations of biblical stories to postwar grief and less concerned with iconography related to these leaders. In Portsmouth, Virginia, for example, a window in Trinity Church, set in place while federal troops were still occupying the city in April 1868, depicts the biblical scene of Rachel weeping at a tomb, on which are inscribed the names of church members who had died during the war.[33] The choice of Rachel is fitting; in the Bible, Rachel, the wife of the patriarch Jacob, is often evoked as an embodiment of deep grief expressed in the wake of tragedy but with hopes of a potential restoration of God's chosen people.

Churches that were more directly connected to these Confederate leaders developed a more explicit declaration of Confederate Christian sainthood, mapping these leaders' identities onto biblical characters and the war onto biblical narratives. St. Paul's Episcopal Church in Richmond, known as "the Cathedral of the Confederacy," contains four

magnificent, floor-to-ceiling stained glass windows: two dedicated to
Davis and two to Lee, both of whom were church members during the
Civil War. Congregants sitting in the main level of the nave, the central
part of the sanctuary, are flanked by a Lee window on the left and a
Davis window on the right. Those sitting in the upper-level balcony
are similarly situated between the upstairs windows.

The two windows dedicated to Robert E. Lee were installed in
1892 by Henry Holiday, a well-known British painter and stained
glass designer. According to a history published by the church entitled *Windows of Grace: A Tribute of Love—The Memorial Windows
of St. Paul's Episcopal Church, Richmond, Virginia*, the window on
the main floor depicts Lee as a young Moses "in the attire of a prince
turning away from the house of Pharaoh and dropping his wand of
office."[34] The balcony window features the general as an older Moses
who is depicted kneeling, with a halo around his head and a gray
beard similar to Lee's at the end of the war.

Though thick with mind-bending irony, the analogy is clear: just
as Moses refused service to Pharaoh in order to lead his people out of
slavery and into freedom in the promised land, so Lee refused service
to the Union army in order to lead his people in the South to uphold
their freedom to hold slaves and preserve their way of life. And, like
Moses, Lee didn't live to see the promised land; but the ultimate end
of the story is that God's chosen people—the children of Israel and the
whites of the South—would.

The two Davis windows, installed by Tiffany Studios in 1898,
are more complex. The lower sanctuary window picks up a New
Testament story of Saint Paul, who was imprisoned for two years
by Roman authorities for preaching the gospel. Davis is portrayed
as Saint Paul, standing in chains but dignified, defending Christian
doctrines before the Roman authorities. A clear likeness, the image
evokes Davis's two-year arrest and imprisonment by US federal authorities, which southerners considered an unnecessarily humiliating
and unjust treatment of their former leader. The balcony window of

Davis is more abstract. According to the St. Paul's walking-tour brochure, it depicts two large "Angels of Goodness and Mercy," who "by their downcast eyes, are implying that Jefferson Davis merits their attributes." The windows present Davis not as a traitor but as a martyr who is faithful to Christian principles even when wrongfully imprisoned. Even the angels testify deferentially to his virtues and the righteousness of the Lost Cause against the US government, which is depicted as Rome.

Perhaps the most prominent and successful UDC effort involved the placement of four large four-by-six-foot stained glass windows honoring Lee and Stonewall Jackson in the nave of the National Cathedral in Washington, DC. The second-largest religious building in the country, the National Cathedral holds pride of place because of its symbolic importance as both a religious and civic space. The cathedral has served as the site of state funerals or memorial services for presidents, from Woodrow Wilson in 1924 to George H. W. Bush in 2018; as the setting for other semiofficial state events such as presidential inaugural prayer services; and as the gathering place for national mourning in the wake of horrific events such as the terrorist attacks on September 11, 2001.

The "Lee-Jackson windows," as they came to be called, were installed in 1953 and represented the culmination of a long effort by the United Daughters of the Confederacy to mark this symbolic sacred space. Two windows each are dedicated to Lee and Jackson, with each divided into an upper and lower pane featuring images from different times in the generals' lives. All four windows contain either the Confederate battle flag or the less familiar Stars and Bars, the first official flag of the Confederacy, and each ties them specifically to Christian iconography.

The second Lee window is particularly striking, featuring a Christlike image of him. Dressed in long robes and subtly haloed, he is standing with outstretched arms and open palms, surrounded by the words "Lord now lettest thou thy servant depart in peace," an allusion to a New Testament passage where a righteous man declares that his life has been fulfilled because he has lived to see the Messiah.[35]

The first Jackson window depicts a uniformed Jackson kneeling with an open Bible in his hands in a war camp setting. Above his head flies the Confederate battle flag, and to his left are the words "Reading the Bible." The second Jackson window portrays the general as a Christian knight in white armor, stretching his arms wide as he steps across a river. In front of him are heaven's bright, golden, open gates and large trumpets. His figure is surrounded by the words "And he passed over and all the trumpets sounded for him," a line alluding to the dignified death of Mr. Valiant-for-Truth, a courageous character in John Bunyan's *The Pilgrim's Progress from This World, to That Which Is to Come*, and also echoing Jackson's final words before his death.

Symbols: The Confederate Battle Flag

Like the debates around Confederate monuments, debates about the Confederate flag are often based on the erroneous assumptions that the flag's current prevalence and cultural placements are tied directly to a continuous and consistent use from the time of the Civil War forward. But like the monuments, the flag's postwar deployment is rooted less in Civil War history itself and more in assertions of white supremacy and opposition to black equality and civil rights.

Today's most familiar Confederate symbol is technically the Confederate battle flag, which was designed for use by the army and was not typically flown in civilian spaces. The chief feature of the design, called the Saint Andrew's cross, has northern European and Christian origins. The X-shaped cross recalls the martyrdom of Andrew, a first-century Christian who was sentenced to be crucified but who told his executioners he was unworthy to be crucified on an upright cross as Jesus had been. Andrew's remains were later moved to Scotland, where he became the nation's patron saint. Scotland incorporated the Saint Andrew's cross into its national flag, and it was also incorporated into the British Union Jack in the early 1600s.[36]

The final design of the Confederate battle flag was square rather than rectangular and featured a blue Saint Andrew's cross emblazoned on a field of red, with thirteen white stars representing the Confederate states arranged symmetrically on the cross. It was first adopted in late 1861 by the Confederate army for use in battle, and by 1863 was officially acknowledged by the Confederate Congress as "the battle flag." It was also the symbol that aroused the most popular sentiment both on the battlefield and at home. Notably, the first Confederate battle flags commissioned by the army were completed as a patriotic church and state cooperative project: the Confederate government purchased large quantities of silk, and then seventy-five volunteer women, working predominantly in four prominent Richmond churches, went to work, completing 120 flags by October 1861.[37]

The deployment of the new battle flag was pushed especially by leading generals Joseph Johnston and Pierre Gustav Toutant Beauregard, and it was initially presented to troops in the field with a solemn ceremony. On November 28, 1861, General Beauregard assembled his men in formation and issued a general order that reads in part: "A new banner is intrusted [sic] to-day, as a battle-flag, to the safe keeping of the Army of the Potomac. Soldiers: Your mothers, your wives, and your sisters have made it. . . . Under its untarnished folds beat back the invader, and find nationality, everlasting immunity from an atrocious despotism, and honor and renown for yourselves—or death."[38] Two years later, an 1863 issue of Richmond's *Southern Illustrated News* demonstrated how deeply this symbol resonated with the general populace: "The baptism of blood and fire has made the battleflag [sic] of General Johnston our national emblem. It is associated with our severest trials and our proudest achievements."[39]

While the roots of the Confederate battle flag as the dominant cultural expression of support for slavery and white supremacy are beyond serious dispute, this fact of history doesn't settle the question of what the flag means today. Answering that bigger question requires tracing the broad contours of its deployment after the Civil War. A basic pattern emerges that roughly follows the timeline of monument placement—that public uses of the Confederate battle flag increased as black demands for justice advanced and white supremacy was threatened.

The question of what the Confederate battle flag stands for and the timing of its twentieth-century resurrection in American culture has never been that mysterious among African Americans. Acknowledging the midcentury uptick in the display of Confederate symbols, a 1951 issue of the black newspaper the *Chicago Defender* explained that "in a large measure, the rebel craze is an ugly reaction to the remarkable progress of our group."[40] And its use by government officials in state capitols is also fairly plain for those with eyes to see. As Yale University law professor James Foreman Jr. flatly concluded after a 1991 study of the Confederate battle flag's presence at state capitols, "The flag has been adopted knowingly and consciously by government officials seeking to assert their commitment to black subordination."[41]

In the first few decades following the Civil War, the Confederate battle flag was largely confined to events such as decorating graves on Confederate Memorial Day or parades of Civil War veterans' groups, where it was carried by men who'd actually fought under the flag in battle. In this period, the flag was, to be sure, connected to the southern vindication project of the Lost Cause, but it was also still organically connected to the Civil War generation and their children.

Beginning in the late nineteenth century, however, the Confederate battle flag took on more political and ideological meaning, as southern whites clawed their way back to power after Reconstruction and began to systematically disenfranchise African Americans with Jim Crow laws. Most notably, it was flown regularly in the 1920s and 1930s, alongside the American flag, by the second incarnation of the KKK at parades and rallies.[42] It could also be seen regularly at

University of Mississippi football games beginning in the late 1930s. These broader cultural adoptions were not directly connected to the Civil War but rather to a more generic assertion of white power and ownership of civic space.

In 1948, the Confederate battle flag was adopted by the short-lived Dixiecrat political party, an offshoot of the southern-dominated Democratic Party. After the Democratic Party adopted a platform supporting civil rights and nominated Harry Truman, the Dixiecrat Party nominated segregationist South Carolina governor Strom Thurmond and affirmed the following central plank in its platform:

> We stand for the segregation of the races and the racial integrity of each race; the constitutional right to choose one's associates; to accept private employment without governmental interference, and to earn one's living in any lawful way. We oppose the elimination of segregation, the repeal of miscegenation statutes, the control of private employment by Federal bureaucrats called for by the misnamed civil rights program. We favor home-rule, local self-government and a minimum interference with individual rights.[43]

While the Dixiecrat Party ceased to exist officially after the 1948 election, the connections it created, not only among southern Democratic politicians, but between these politicians and religious leaders, continued to bear fruit. In 1956, W. A. Criswell, the powerful pastor from the prominent First Baptist Church in Dallas, Texas, gave a defiant speech defending segregation at a South Carolina evangelism conference. The next day, he was invited by Strom Thurmond to address the General Assembly of the South Carolina State Legislature, where he spelled out the Christian foundations of segregation. In his fiery remarks, he called integration "unChristian" and "a denial of all that we believe in." He concluded his remarks this way: "Don't force me by law, by statute, by Supreme Court decision . . . to cross over in those intimate things where I don't want to go.... Let me have my church. Let me have my school. Let me have my friends. Let me have my home. Let me have my family."[44]

Throughout the 1950s and 1960s, as support for the civil rights movement grew, the Confederate battle flag was adopted by civic groups such as the White Citizens' Councils and displayed regularly by groups of whites gathering to protest school desegregation and civil rights for blacks. In the 1970s and 1980s, the decades in which I grew up, it invaded pop culture and was generally associated with white "redneck" culture.[45] The popular TV show *The Dukes of Hazzard*, which had a five-year run from 1979 to 1984, featured the flag emblazoned on the roof of a Dodge Charger nicknamed "the General Lee," whose horn played the first twelve notes of "Dixie." The 1970s rock band Lynyrd Skynyrd, from Jacksonville, Florida, put the flag on its album cover, and you could generally buy Confederate battle flag T-shirts, bathing suits, and other clothing in most malls in the South. By the 1990s, the flag had gone global: it showed up in Baltic state celebrations of liberation from Soviet rule, and it has served as a substitute rallying symbol for some neo-Nazis in Germany, where displaying the swastika or a Nazi flag is illegal and punishable by up to three years in prison.[46]

Paying attention to when the Confederate battle flag has been the subject of official state action also corroborates its use as a political tool of white supremacy. There are five southern states that continue to include Confederate symbols in their flags. Notably, four of the five (Alabama, Arkansas, Mississippi, and Georgia) are also among the top ten states containing the highest percentages of white evangelical Protestants in the country. The state of Alabama straightforwardly retains a red Saint Andrew's cross on a white field, which it adopted three decades after the close of the Civil War, in 1895. Arkansas adopted its first state flag in 1913, which has a diamond outlined by a blue stripe filled with white stars, reminiscent of the Confederate battle flag, on a red field. Inside the diamond, on a white background, is the word *Arkansas*, with three large blue stars representing the nations the state has been a part of: Spain, France, and the United States. In 1924 the legislature added a fourth star above the state name, symbolizing its affiliation with the Confederate States of America. From 1868 to 1900, the state of Florida's flag was white, with the state seal in the middle. But in 1901 voters approved a new flag that added a red Saint Andrew's cross, similar to the Alabama flag, behind the seal.

The state of Georgia has had a complex flag history. From 1879 to 1956, its flag closely mimicked the first Confederate flag, the Stars and Bars, although over time minor changes incorporated different versions of the state seal on the left blue canton. But in 1956, two years after the *Brown v. Topeka Board of Education* ruling that ordered public schools must be desegregated, the legislature replaced the more subtle red and white horizontal bars with a full version of the Confederate battle flag to the right of the blue canton. This flag flew until 2001, when Governor Roy Barnes led a move to replace it with a new flag containing a large state seal in the center on a field of blue, with a small homage to the previous state flags, flanked by two American flags, embedded in a narrow ribbon below the seal. This shift away from Confederate symbols was short-lived, however. In a 2004 referendum, voters approved by a margin of three to one a new design that even more closely resembles the Stars and Bars than the original pre-1956 flag, featuring, for example, a circle of thirteen stars that represent the states of the Confederacy.[47]

Mississippi, my home state, is currently the only state that continues to include the Confederate battle flag in its flag. Notably, the first state flag of Mississippi, adopted after secession in 1861, was the "Magnolia flag," which had a Magnolia tree centered on a field of white, with a blue canton containing a single white star and a red vertical bar on the far right of the flag. That flag was replaced in 1894 with the current flag, which vividly incorporates the battle flag as the canton, and contains three broad horizontal stripes that are also reminiscent of the Stars and Bars. In a 2001 referendum, Mississippi voters chose by a margin of two to one to retain the current flag over an alternative design that removed the Confederate battle flag.[48]

Beyond their presence on state flags, Confederate flags have been used in other official ways on capitol grounds. In 1963, when US Attorney General Robert Kennedy came to Montgomery, Alabama, to discuss desegregation with Governor George Wallace, Wallace ordered the Confederate battle flag—a symbol he used frequently during his segregationist political campaign—raised above the Alabama State Capitol.[49] In Florida, the Confederate Stainless Banner flag flew over the west entrance of the capitol from 1978 to 2001 as part of a display of four national flags that had flown in Florida (the other three were those of Spain, France, and England), until Governor Jeb Bush quietly ordered that it not be replaced when it came down for a scheduled cleaning.[50]

In South Carolina—a site of recent controversy—the Confederate battle flag rose above the state capitol building on April 11, 1961, as part of the opening celebrations marking the centennial of the firing on Fort Sumter. At the opening celebration event, with Confederate battle flags surrounding him as a backdrop, segregationist senator Strom Thurmond reminded the mostly white crowd of the meaning of the war and the flag. He reassured them that nowhere in the US Constitution "does it hint a purpose to insure equality of man or things" and warned that without white diligence, "advocacy by Communists of social equality among diverse races" could lead to the destruction of the country.[51]

The Sumter Centennial ended, but the flag stayed up. The following year, the legislature passed a resolution authorizing the flag to fly over the capitol another year, but the resolution did not dictate a time for the flag to come down. It stayed in place for another thirty-eight years. The flag was finally lowered from the capitol in 2000, after an NAACP boycott of South Carolina's tourism industry finally secured a compromise from the legislature to relocate the flag to a Confederate monument, also on the capitol grounds. That tenuous compromise held until 2015, when the killing of African Americans at Emanuel AME Church shifted the ground in what has been dubbed the "heritage versus hate" debate.

A Turning Point? The Massacre at Emanuel AME Church in Charleston

There is evidence that for many whites, who have been guilty of a willful blindness to the social function of these symbols, the 2015 massacre of nine worshippers in an African American church in Charleston, South Carolina, may have been a turning point. This horrific event has spurred not just new conversations about the contemporary meaning of Confederate symbols but also actions.

On the evening of Wednesday, June 17, 2015, Dylann Roof calmly walked into the historic Emanuel AME Church as a small Bible study group was beginning. According to witness accounts, he sat next to the pastor while the discussion went on for about an hour. He then voiced some disagreements with participants, which escalated into a negative rant about African Americans. When he brandished a gun, one of the members pleaded with him not to hurt anyone, saying, "You don't have to do this." The twenty-one-year-old replied coolly, "Yes. You are raping our women and taking over the country." Roof then opened fire, killing nine church members, including the pastor, Reverend Clementa C. Pinckney. A few members survived by playing dead, but Roof deliberately spared one woman, telling her that he was going to let her live so she could tell the story of what happened. After being captured the next day, he confessed to the murders, explaining that his goal had been "to start a race war."[52]

When police began investigating, they found a digital footprint rife with Confederate and neo-Nazi symbols and references. On his website, Roof had posted a photo of himself posing with a Glock .45-caliber handgun, the weapon in his possession at his arrest, in one hand,

and a Confederate battle flag in the other. The website contained more than photographs, many featuring Roof posing at sites and museums associated with the Confederacy or slavery. Most prominently, the website contained a 2,500-word manifesto. As he explained his motivations in that document, his radicalization began when he googled information about Trayvon Martin, an unarmed black teenager who was fatally shot by a neighborhood vigilante in Sanford, Florida, while walking home from a convenience store in 2012. Roof noted that "the first website I came to was the Council of Conservative Citizens"—a modern reincarnation of the old segregationist White Citizens' Councils and a group that was active in resisting the removal of the Confederate battle flag from the South Carolina Capitol. He praised the website for raising his awareness of what he dubbed "black on White [*sic*] crime," declaring, "I have never been the same since that day."[53]

He concluded the manifesto with these foreboding words: "I have no choice.... I chose Charleston because it is [the] most historic city in my state, and at one time had the highest ratio of blacks to Whites [*sic*] in the country. We have no skinheads, no real KKK, no one doing anything but talking on the internet. Well someone has to have the bravery to take it to the real world, and I guess that has to be me."[54]

Roof was not successful in starting a race war and has now been convicted and sentenced to death. But his murderous acts did begin to open the eyes of many white religious and civic leaders across the country, rekindling tabled conversations and pushing them out of a sleepy status quo and into action. Across the country, a familiar pattern has emerged. The 2015 Emanuel AME Church shooting sparked long-overdue conversations, and the disturbing and deadly August 2017 "Unite the Right" white supremacist rally in Charlottesville around a Robert E. Lee monument has created an urgency for action.

The Evangelical Lutheran Church in America

Although it received little press and was rarely incorporated into explanations of his motivations, Dylann Roof's identity as a white Christian was central to his worldview. As he became more radicalized by contact with white supremacist websites, reading materials, and organizations, the evidence suggests that his Christian identity easily accommodated this shift. At the time he committed the murders, Roof was a baptized member in good standing at St. Paul's Lutheran Church in Columbia, a church associated with the Evangelical Lutheran Church in America (ELCA), a white mainline Protestant denomination. According to his stepmother, Roof regularly went to church growing up, including catechism classes.[55]

After his arrest, Roof articulated his motivations in a journal that was found in his jail cell, which ultimately became government "exhibit 500" in his trial.[56] Six of the first seven pages contain prominent Christian imagery. In the forty-two pages of the journal, Roof includes no less than eighteen sketches of different types of crosses. The most prominent depiction of a cross takes up an entire page. It has the word *Jesus* over the top of a large three-dimensional cross, with "In God we trust" above the horizontal bar. The background contains clouds and what seem to be large raindrops falling behind the cross.

But the most arresting image in Roof's journal is on page 5: a full-page, detailed pencil drawing of a bearded, white Jesus emerging from the tomb after his resurrection. Roof's drawing (see figure 4.2, page 141) is not the work of a neophyte; it reflects a detailed knowledge of traditional Christian iconography. Jesus is depicted with a halo around his head, indicating his divine nature. At the top of the halo, Roof put the word *Jesus*; to the left and right of the head, within the halo, are the abbreviations *IC* and *XC*—a traditional abbreviation of the Greek words for *Jesus Christ* that is a popular depiction in Eastern Orthodox Christianity. Jesus is depicted as stepping toward the viewer through the open tomb door, with a white foot extending forward under his long robes.[57]

Roof also seemingly spent hours designing his own personal logo, which appears multiple times throughout his journal. The most notable feature of his design is that the anchoring image in the center of the logo is a cross. Specifically, it is a variant of the cross developed and used most by the Russian Orthodox Church, which contains two additional small horizontal bars representing the inscription above the head of Jesus and the footrest to which his feet were nailed at his crucifixion. In the four quadrants created by the main bars of the cross, Roof placed four white supremacist symbols (from top left, going clockwise): (1) "14": a reference to the "14 words," a popular white supremacist slogan: "We must secure the existence of our people and a future for white children"; (2) "88": a coded reference to "Heil Hitler" (Roof predicts in the journal that Hitler will one day be declared a Christian saint); (3) a swastika; and (4) a "life rune" image, an icon appropriated by the Nazis to refer to an ideal Aryan/Norse heritage. Below all this are his initials in bold block letters: "*D S R*."

Finally, there's this—Roof's take on his own Christianity:

"I see some people who seem to use Christianity as an excuse for not doing anything. They tell themselves they are being pious, but they are really being cowardly. Their piety is their excuse. But Christianity doesn't have to be this weak cowardly religion. There is plenty of evidence to indicate that Christianity can be a warrior's religion."[58]

Clearly, Roof's worldview was anchored in his self-understanding as a white Christian in relationship to a white Jesus. And although neither the press nor law enforcement described him this way, the most accurate term for him is a "white Christian terrorist." Certainly law enforcement officials, politicians, and the public would have easily labeled him a "radical Islamic terrorist" if the notebook had been filled with crescent images, a portrait of Muhammad, and reflections on Islam as a "warrior's religion."

It's vital, if we are to properly understand the problem, that we not

FIGURE 4.2 Dylann Roof's Depiction of a White Jesus

Source: Journal of Dylann Roof, Government Exhibit 500,
Contents of Cell Search, August 15, 2015.

flinch from the clear evidence that Roof's Christianity wasn't incidental to his motivations and his racist views. It was integral to his identity and helped fuel this horrific violence. He understood himself as a
white Christian warrior who consciously launched this attack on sacred ground, targeting a historic black church in the hopes of encouraging his fellow white Christians to rise up and "become completely
ruthless to the blacks." Roof summarized his actions in the journal as
follows: "I did what I thought would make the biggest wave. And now
the fate of our race sits with my white brothers who continue to live
freely."[59]

While the Christian underpinnings of Roof's racist violence were
mostly ignored by the public, it was not lost on his home denomination, the Evangelical Lutheran Church in America. In addition to
its connection to Roof, the ELCA also had connections to two of the
victims: Reverend Pinckney, the senior pastor, and Reverend Daniel
Lee Simmons Sr., a retired pastor who regularly attended Bible study
at the church. Both were graduates of Lutheran Theological Southern Seminary, an ELCA seminary. The day after the shooting, Reverend Elizabeth A. Eaton, the presiding bishop of the ELCA, issued a
statement acknowledging the denomination's intimate connection to
both the perpetrator and the victims: "The suspected shooter (Dylann
Roof) is a member of an ELCA congregation. All of a sudden and for
all of us, this is an intensely personal tragedy. One of our own is alleged to have shot and killed two who adopted us as their own."[60]

While stopping short of locating racism in the church itself, Reverend Eaton's public statement did note the widespread structural racism in American culture:

"We might say that this was an isolated act by a deeply disturbed
man. But we know that is not the whole truth. It is not an isolated
event. And even if the shooter was unstable, the framework upon
which he built his vision of race is not. Racism is a fact in American
culture."[61]

The statement called for Lutherans to mourn, but it also urged them to "get to work" and "to be honest about the reality of racism within us and around us."[62]

Significant work has commenced in the denomination. These events led ELCA pastor Lenny Duncan to write *Dear Church: A Love Letter from a Black Preacher to the Whitest Denomination in the U.S.*, a hard-hitting book to his fellow Lutherans.[63] Reverend Duncan pulls few punches in calling his denomination to go beyond easy condemnations of personal racism. While the churches have called racism a sin, Duncan argues that focusing on the personal misunderstands the nature and magnitude of the problem: "White supremacy doesn't need active racists to function. It is a demonic system with a life of its own. It is radical evil."[64] And Duncan also notes that dismantling this system is going to take some very difficult introspection and uncomfortable reparative actions on the part of white Christians: "As Lutherans, we have been trained to search for reconciliation. Like the person clearing their throat when I pause during the confession and forgiveness [portion of the liturgy], we don't like waiting in between repentance and reconciliation. That silent pause is a moment for us to see ourselves for who we really are, and it's scary as fuck."[65]

Since 2015, Reverend Eaton has led the denominational leadership into this uncomfortable space. The 2019 ELCA Churchwide Assembly took a number of actions aimed at recognizing and dismantling "the overt and covert ways that a culture of white supremacy denies full humanity to all people."[66] In recognition of the quadricentennial remembrance of American slavery, the denomination passed a resolution condemning white supremacy and issued a public apology to all people of African descent. That resolution specifically committed white Lutherans to seek a "deeper understanding of slavery and its legacy, of institutional and structural racism, of white privilege, and of attitudes and foundations of white supremacy."[67] Second, the assembly voted to establish June 17 as "Emanuel 9 Day of Repentance," commemorating the martyrdom of the nine African American members who were murdered by Roof, whom they explicitly identify as "a violent white supremacist . . . who grew up in the ELCA."[68] Perhaps most significantly, they have committed themselves to an ongoing relationship of fellowship and accountability with the African Methodist Episcopal Church, the home denomination of Mother Emanuel Church, "to develop new models that move us from dialogue to *diapraxis*, or dialogue in action, for the sake of our witness to our unity in Christ in these divisive and deadly times."[70]

The South Carolina Capitol Grounds

The murders at Emanuel AME Church also led to a fairly dramatic series of events at the South Carolina Capitol. The day after the shooting, Republican governor Nikki Haley ordered the American and South Carolina flags over the capitol to be lowered to half-mast as a sign of mourning. But the Confederate battle flag remained at full mast, because when the flag was moved from the capitol dome to the Confederate monument on the capitol grounds, the Republican-controlled legislature passed a law specifying the height at which it was required to be flown and made no provisions for exceptions in the law. Only a new act of the legislature could lower the flag.

Outraged activists took the matter into their own hands. On June 27, ten days after the murders, Bree Newsome, who is African American and the daughter of the dean of Howard University Divinity School, Clarence Newsome, climbed the flagpole and removed the flag with the assistance of a white male fellow activist. As she descended with the flag, she declared, "The Lord is my light and my salvation, whom shall I fear?" Both Newsome and her fellow activist were arrested. The flag was back at full mast within an hour.[70]

Faced with mounting pressure, Governor Haley called for the state legislature to act. A bill passed the senate quickly on July 7 and came to the floor of the house on July 8. After a tense and heated thirteen-hour debate that continued until one in the morning on July 10—in which some white Republican lawmakers continued to argue that the flag merely represents southern "heritage"—a bill to remove the Confederate battle flag completely from the capitol grounds finally passed 94 to 20.[71] Governor Haley immediately signed the bill that morning, using nine ceremonial pens, which would be sent to the families of each of the nine victims of the Emanuel AME Church shooting. The flag was removed later that morning.

At 10:00 a.m. on July 10, a three-man State Trooper honor guard, in their dress uniforms and white gloves, arrived to remove the flag. Standing at attention, two white Troopers lowered the flag and folded it into a long rectangle with military precision. They then turned in unison, handing it to an African American trooper, who crisply turned on his heels and walked away from the monument— ending the Confederate battle flag's fifty-four-year presence at the state capitol.

Speaking after the bill-signing ceremony, Haley called for the state to look to a new future:

"In South Carolina, we honor tradition, we honor history, we honor heritage, but there's a place for that flag, and that flag needs to be in a museum, where we will continue to make sure people will honor it appropriately. But the statehouse, that's an area that belongs to everyone. And no one should drive by the statehouse and feel pain. No one should drive by the statehouse and feel like they don't belong."[72]

Churches Affiliated with the Episcopal Church in America

The 2015 massacre at Emanuel AME Church resonated far beyond South Carolina, sparking significant actions among a number of churches affiliated with the Episcopal Church in America. Although the Confederate cause is more likely to be associated with white evangelicals in the South, it was the Episcopal Church, not the Baptists or the Methodists, that was the church of the Confederate elite. Both Jefferson Davis and Robert E. Lee, for example, were active members of the Episcopal Church, as were leading military leaders such as General Leonidas Polk, who served simultaneously as an Episcopal bishop and a Confederate officer.

The Charleston murders launched a conversation about the Lee-Jackson windows at the National Cathedral. The cathedral's initial response in 2016 was to remove only the two small panes containing the Confederate battle flag (leaving the larger windows intact, including two panes containing the Stars and Bars). But after the white supremacist rally around a statue of Robert E. Lee in Charlottesville resulted in the death of one person and injury to nineteen others in August 2017, the cathedral made the decision to remove the windows immediately. In its official announcement of the decision, the cathedral stated that the continued presence of the windows was "inconsistent with our current mission to serve as a house of prayer for all people" and that they had concluded that "their association with racial oppression, human subjugation and white supremacy does not belong in the sacred fabric of this Cathedral."[73]

On September 6, 2017, the windows were removed, and the church held an official deconsecration service. The service closed with the hymn "In Christ There Is No East or West." Sung to a tune adapted by an African American composer from a Negro spiritual, it contains this second verse: "Join hands disciples of the faith, what-e'er your race may be. / Who serves my Father as his child is surely kin to me."[74]

The Emanuel AME shooting also reverberated in Richmond. In August 2015, St. Paul's Episcopal Church held two "prayerful conversations about the historic Confederate imagery and symbols in the church." These meetings led the church to establish a "History and Reconciliation Initiative" with the following mission: "In light of our Christian faith, to trace and acknowledge the racial history of St Paul's Episcopal Church in order to repair, restore and seek reconciliation with God, each other, and the broader community." As one of the initial steps in this process, the church completed a thorough inventory of the Confederate symbols and references in the church. The list was daunting. In addition to the Lee and Davis Memorial

Windows, the church recorded seventeen plaques, two other stained glass windows related to Confederate leaders, and padded kneelers at the altar with cross-stitched covers containing images of the Confederate battle flag.[75]

Some modest initial steps have been taken: the kneelers with the Confederate flag have been removed, and when visitors and members enter the narthex (essentially the foyer inside the main entrance) of the historic sanctuary, a large, prominent video screen explains the History and Reconciliation Initiative. The church website has also been updated to reflect this critical work. The first two sentences of the "About Us" section of the website read as follows: "At St. Paul's, we value truth telling. Our history humbles us. Our members enslaved our fellow Christians, and told the story of Proslavery Gospel that led us into a bloody war in the 1860's." The "Our History" section also notes that the sanctuary was built with slave labor and that "[our] parishioners helped write Virginia's Jim Crow laws." Moreover, the congregation has held forums with outside civil rights activists, historians, and others to help shape this initiative. Most significantly, the initiative is conceived to be a permanent, ongoing part of the congregation's future identity, with a long-term ministry goal of "changing the image of St. Paul's from the Church of the Confederacy to a Church of Reconciliation."[76]

Just days after the Charlottesville rally, the Very Reverend Gail Greenwell, the dean of Christ Church Cathedral, an Episcopal church in Cincinnati, called on the church to remove two tributes to Confederate generals in the sanctuary: a stained glass window depicting Robert E. Lee receiving a blessing from then Virginia bishop William Meade and a plaque honoring General Leonidas Polk, who was consecrated in 1838 in Cincinnati as a bishop. Both men represented a mix of Christianity and the Confederacy. Much has been made of Lee's Christian faith, and he was a lay leader in his local Episcopal churches; Polk was known to wear his church vestments over his military uniform when performing his duties as bishop.

In a sermon, Dean Greenwell declared, "The church itself has been complicit in enshrining systems and people who contributed to white supremacy, and they are here in the very corners of this cathedral."[77] After a yearlong structured congregational conversation, a "Christian Heroes" Committee made a recommendation that was approved by the church leadership. In August 2018 the windowpane featuring Lee and Meade was removed, and plans are under way to replace it with a new one depicting Frederick Douglass and Harriet Tubman, a former slave who became a leading abolitionist and political activist.[78]

Even Episcopalian churches that remain unrepentant about their support for the men behind the symbols have been pushed to take action, a sign of a real shift in the culture. At the height of the Lost Cause resurgence at the turn of the twentieth century, a Lexington, Virginia, church voted to change its name from Grace Episcopal Church to R. E. Lee Memorial Episcopal Church in honor of the late Confederate general, who'd moved to town after the war, joined the church, and served as senior warden until his death in 1870.

In a pattern echoing those of the congregations above, this decision remained largely unquestioned until the church leadership received a letter from a distraught parishioner after the 2015 shooting in Charleston. That discussion led to no immediate recommendations (although it did bring about the resignations of two lay leaders over the inaction); but the 2017 white supremacist rally in Charlottesville rekindled the conversation and pushed the church to act.[79] In a closely divided ballot (7 to 5), church leaders voted on September 18, 2017, to return to the original name. The church's rector, Reverend Tom Crittenden, explained the decision in terms more pragmatic than moral: "It's been a very divisive issue for two years. But Charlottesville seems to have moved us to this point. Not that we have a different view of Lee historically in our church, but we have appreciation for our need to move on."[80]

New Orleans, Louisiana

A week after the 2015 Charleston massacre, New Orleans mayor Mitch Landrieu decided he needed to address the presence of the city's prominent Confederate monuments. Landrieu called for the removal of the four most prominent monuments in public spaces. "Symbols matter and should reflect who we are as a people," the mayor declared. "These monuments do not now, nor have they ever reflected the history, the strength, the richness, the diversity, or the soul of who we are as a people and a city."[81]

In addition to being morally appalled by the shooting, Landrieu noted one other major factor in his decision: an earlier conversation he had had with an African American friend, renowned jazz musician Wynton Marsalis, whom Landrieu had known from their high school days in the city. Landrieu sketched their conversation in his book *In the Shadow of Statues: A White Southerner Confronts History*, which chronicled the harrowing resistance he encountered to taking down the monuments. The conversation begins with Marsalis responding to Landrieu's request to serve on a committee planning the New Orleans 2018 tricentennial celebration:

I'll do that. But there's something I'd like you to do.

What's that?

Take down the Robert E. Lee statue.

You lost me on that…

Let me help you see it through my eyes. Who is he? What does he represent? And in that most prominent space in the city of New Orleans, does that space reflect who we were, who we want to be, or who we are?… You ever think about what Robert E. Lee means to someone black?[82]

Landrieu was convinced he needed to act, but he faced a daunting task. The city of New Orleans rivaled Richmond in Confederate monument-building fervor in the late nineteenth century. In an article summarizing Confederate monument activity, the inaugural 1893 issue of the *Confederate Veteran* declared, "New Orleans has taken the lead." The article then enumerated with pride the monuments already erected to Confederate soldiers in Greenwood Cemetery (1867): to the Washington artillery (1880); to the army of West Virginia (1881)— which at the time contained the remains of Jefferson Davis; to Robert E. Lee (1884); and to the army of Tennessee, which featured General Albert Sidney Johnston on his horse Fire-eater (1877). These monuments, the article boasted, represented a remarkable investment of $140,000—nearly $4 million in today's currency.[83]

As in Richmond, New Orleans's white residents continued building monuments to the Lost Cause well into the twentieth century, and these monuments were increasingly, and intentionally, built not in Confederate cemeteries but in prominent civic spaces. Of the early monuments, only Lee's was in a prominent civic space, located on St. Charles Avenue. In 1894, the year after the *Confederate Veteran* story ran, a monument was erected to honor the White League, the white supremacist militia group that attempted to overthrow the results of the 1872 Reconstruction-era election in both Colfax and New Orleans, in which Republicans and some African Americans took office. It was placed in a prominent traffic circle on Canal Street. In 1911 the city erected a monument to Jefferson Davis, also on Canal Street and at a cross street that became known as Jeff Davis Parkway. And in 1915 a monument to General P. G. T. Beauregard went up at the main entrance to City Park, the massive 1,300-acre central green space in the city.

With the Charleston massacre and Marsalis's words weighing on his mind, Landrieu pushed the city council to take up a measure to remove these monuments to the Confederacy in public spaces. On December 17, 2015, three months after his request, city leaders voted

six to one to remove the four most prominent monuments: the obelisk dedicated to the White League, as well as statues of Beauregard,
Davis, and Lee. The ordinance itself dubbed the monuments "public
nuisances" that "honor, praise, or foster ideologies which are in conflict with the requirements of equal protection for citizens as provided
by the constitution and laws of the United States, the state, or the laws
of the city and suggests the supremacy of one ethnic, religious, or racial group over another."[84]

In a sign of the pivotal times in which we live, what should have
been a straightforward job of removing four statues turned into a
two-year ordeal. Legal challenges took more than a year and a half
to resolve, winding through no fewer than five different courts and
thirteen judges, before the US Fifth Circuit Court of Appeals finally
affirmed the city council's authority to remove statues on its own public property. As the legal fog lifted and the project was cleared to move
forward, Landrieu received a wave of hate mail and death threats,
both at the mayor's office and at home. Landrieu described one encounter in particular that illustrates the ways in which a defense of
the Lost Cause and Christianity, this time white Catholicism, were
intertwined among the opposition:

> We felt the cold shoulders, the averted eye contact and gazes
> elsewhere by some neighbors and certain people we thought
> were friends. I had one of the most startling experiences while
> riding my bike in the park early each morning. I would be yelled
> at consistently by the same woman. One particular Sunday, it
> was more vicious and nasty than normal. You can imagine my
> surprise when a few hours later, Cheryl and I were at Mass and
> I saw her giving out Communion—she was a eucharistic min-
> ister. It was surreal.[85]

Landrieu and his staff pressed on. But the mayor encountered another
unanticipated problem: despite hundreds of millions in construction

dollars being spent in the wake of Hurricane Katrina, he couldn't find a single company that would take the city contract to remove the monuments, for fear of retaliation. In the end, a single African American contractor agreed to remove the larger monuments—provided that the city provide extra police protection—and another contractor agreed to remove the smaller White League obelisk. Even then, a contractor's car was torched, sand was put in the gas tank of one of the cranes, and drones were flown into the construction site to thwart the work.[86] The necessary security precautions rivaled a war zone and, indeed, ultimately required the city to hire an outside security firm with experience doing military and civil construction in conflict areas around the world. Landrieu described the extraordinary scene at the removal of the first monument:

"The operation began at two in the morning on April 24, 2017. The police SWAT team had sharpshooters in strategic perches with K-9 units circulating to insure the workers' safety. Men driving trucks, operating equipment, and other workers wore bulletproof vests, helmets, and face masks to guard their anonymity. Cardboard covered the company name on the vehicles and the license plates."[87]

In the end, all four monuments were removed by May 17, 2017, without any major riots or violence. But the threats and protests in the white community had brought the city's security bill alone to more than $1 million, five times what the removal project should have cost under normal circumstances.

After the removal of the final monument, to Robert E. Lee, Landrieu gave a public speech to mark the significance of the event, which went viral online. The mayor minced no words about the cultural function of the Confederate monuments, straightforwardly addressing his white audience, telling them that he wanted to "try to gently peel from your hands the grip on a false narrative of our history that I think weakens us":

"These monuments purposefully celebrate a fictional, sanitized Confederacy; ignoring the death, ignoring the enslavement, and the terror that it actually stood for. After the Civil War, these statues were a part of that terrorism as much as a burning cross on someone's lawn; they were erected purposefully to send a strong message to all who walked in their shadows about who was still in charge in this city."[88]

But the most powerful part of the speech was a vision of history and the future addressed to everyone. Tapping New Orleans's recent 2018 tricentennial celebration, Landrieu challenged them to widen the lens from "a four-year brief historical aberration that was called the Confederacy" in order to "celebrate all three hundred years of our rich, diverse history as a place named New Orleans and set the tone for the next three hundred years."[89]

According to polls toward the end of his second term in office, Landrieu lost half of his white support in the city over the monument removals. Reflecting on the tumultuous time, he noted that his own Christian faith, particularly the Jesuit values instilled in him by his Catholic high school of being "men for others," had been central to his convictions and perseverance on this issue—although it had taken horrific violence in the name of white supremacy and a conversation with a trusted African American friend to awaken and connect his Christian senses to these issues.

The changes described above are only a small window into the ripple effects. Clearly, something of significance has shifted in the culture, even among white Christian churches, since the 2015 Charleston attack. The Southern Poverty Law Center has documented 114 Confederate symbols that have been removed from public spaces since then, but 1,747 are still standing.[90] A handful of churches and denominations have embarked on soul-searching missions, but most are maintaining their centuries-long silence. While the horrific events in Charleston, along with the aftershocks from Charlotte, have clearly been felt, the country, and white Christians in particular, are taking only the first steps of a long journey.

Conclusion

The historical witness is clear: as Confederate symbols migrated from cemeteries and veterans' parades, they became less about honoring the past and more about upholding white supremacy in the present. In fact, the relationship is inversely proportional. The further the distance from the cemetery and the past, the more nakedly obvious their role in asserting white supremacy becomes. As Landrieu concluded in his assessment of Confederate monuments in the civic spaces of New Orleans, these symbols were premeditatively designed and deployed as "political weapons" in the service of preserving white supremacy.[91] A corollary conclusion also extends to the realm of religion. As Confederate symbols were intentionally installed in prominent sacred spaces, where they were enmeshed with Christian symbols and justified by white Christian theology, they became religious weapons in the service of baptizing white supremacy.

The murders at Emanuel AME Church in Charleston surely haven't changed everything; but they do seem to have changed something. This awful violence—committed in the name of white supremacy within the walls of a black church—has begun to wake at least some well-intentioned whites from their moral slumber, depriving them of a familiar, comfortable complacency. For a critical mass of whites, the once-unassailable naïveté of appeals to "heritage" are finally losing their power. Like the aging granite pedestals, the edifice of southern vindication and innocence has finally begun to crack under the weight of its own duplicity.

But the examples in this chapter are best understood as initial tremors, which are only beginning to disturb the stubborn footings of 150 years of post–Civil War white supremacy. Ultimately, the construction of a new foundation will require white Americans to do something we have never been willing to do: reanimate our own histories and confront a violent and unflattering past.

− 5 −

Mapping

The White Supremacy Gene in American Christianity

In previous chapters, I've discussed the prominent, historical role white Christians, churches, and other institutions such as seminaries have played in creating and sustaining white supremacy in America. But in order to assess the impact of this history on the present, we'll need some new tools that can give us a reliable understanding of the current relationship between white supremacy and Christian identity among whites. We'll also need a systematic approach that looks for any imprint that centuries of accommodation to white supremacy may have left on contemporary white Christians.[1] Specifically, I aim to answer these central questions: How prevalent are racist and white supremacist attitudes among white Christians today? To the extent that they exist, are these attitudes merely incidental to, or have they come to be, over time, actually constitutive of white Christian identity? And is this relationship limited to white evangelicals or white Christians in the South, or do these attitudes also persist among white mainline and white Catholic Christians outside that region? These are sensitive, difficult questions to sort out, and this chapter proceeds one step at a time.

The Living Legacy of Slaveholding
Among White Americans

When people think about the contemporary effects of slavery, they typically consider external effects such as the continued economic and social inequalities between black and white Americans, which are indeed stark. But in the book *Deep Roots: How Slavery Still Shapes Southern Politics*, political scientists Avidit Acharya, Matthew Blackwell, and Maya Sen demonstrate something less acknowledged: the remarkably enduring impact of slavery on how contemporary white people think, feel, and act today.

In a rigorous statistical analysis linking county-level slave ownership from the 1860 US Census and public opinion data collected between 2006 and 2011 by the Cooperative Congressional Election Study (CCES), a large-scale national survey of the American electorate conducted by nearly forty universities, they find that whites residing in areas that had the highest levels of slavery in 1860 demonstrate significantly different attitudes *today* from whites who reside in areas that had lower historical levels of slavery: (1) they are more politically conservative and Republican leaning; (2) they are more opposed to affirmative action; and (3) they score higher on questions measuring racial resentment.[2] After accounting for a range of other explanations and possible intervening variables, Acharya and his colleagues conclude that "present-day regional differences, then, are the direct, downstream consequences of the slaveholding history of these areas."[3]

One remarkable feature of this research is that the results are sensitive at the county level, not just within the South but also within individual states. While on average 36.7 percent of the population in southern counties was enslaved in 1860, there was a wide variation even within the same state, as two examples from Arkansas demonstrate. In the northwestern county of Benton, which was less

suited to cotton farming, only 4.1 percent of the population was enslaved. But in the southeastern county of Chicot—where my parents
lived while I was in graduate school, with a backyard emptying into
Lake Chicot and a front yard emptying into cotton fields as far as you
could see—81.4 percent of the population was enslaved.[4]

Even smaller variations in slave-owning percentages produce
measurable attitudinal differences today. For example, moving from
Alabama's Clay County to Barbour County (associated with about a 25
percent increase in slave owning in 1860) is associated *today* with a
5.6 percent decrease in the share of whites who identify as Democrats,
a 7.8 percent decrease among whites in support for affirmative action,
and a 4.8 percent increase in attitudes reflecting racial resentment.[5]

This research demonstrates that the deep racial prejudice that
was created by a slaveholding society is still measurably present in
the contemporary South, and that this relationship is not just corre-
lational but *causal*. Even when comparing neighboring counties that
differ in slaveholding percentages and adjusting for state-by-state
variation and cotton-farming suitability, the relationship between
the level of slaveholding in 1860 in a county and its current political
and racial conservatism remains robust. As Acharya and his coauthors summarize the findings, "It's not simply that more conservative
people live in these areas—these are more conservative areas *because*
of their past."[6]

These findings are provocative. But for our purposes, they have
two limitations. First, the authors give scant attention to religion in
their analysis. Second, by design, the study is limited to measuring the
effects of southern slaveholding. To answer the broader questions I
am raising about white Christian identity, I'll draw on recent national
public opinion surveys by PRRI in order to bring religion into the
analysis more deliberately and widen the field of vision beyond the
South.

The Distinctive Racial Attitudes
of White Christians Today

One of the most remarkable, consistent findings in contemporary public opinion data is the chasm between two groups who otherwise share both geographic proximity and a common evangelical religious orientation: black Protestants and white evangelical Protestants. On a range of religious measures—belief in God, belief in a literal heaven and hell, belief in a literal interpretation of the Bible, frequency of church attendance and prayer—black and white evangelical Protestants are largely aligned. But as these religious beliefs and behaviors are refracted through the lens of race, they produce starkly divergent opinions and behaviors in political space.[7]

More recently, as the ranks of religiously unaffiliated Americans have grown—from single digits in the 1990s to a quarter of Americans today—the gap between white Christians of all kinds and white religiously unaffiliated Americans has become another defining feature of the religious landscape. As we proceed through the analysis below, we'll keep all of these groups in view: white evangelical Protestants, white mainline Protestants, white Catholics, and religiously unaffiliated whites. For comparison, we'll also examine the views of these white groups alongside the views of African American Protestants.

Attitudes about African Americans and racism can be challenging to assess through public opinion surveys. The biggest hurdle is that a researcher obviously cannot get accurate results from asking respondents outright whether they are white supremacists or racists. Even with online surveys, where participants complete surveys privately on their own devices and with assurances of anonymity, many may be reluctant to reveal their true views. Or they may privately hold white supremacist or racist views that they themselves would not identify with those labels.

The slipperiness of individual questions on the sensitive topic of race can be seen in the following example from PRRI's "2018 American Values Survey."[8] White Christians were asked to say how warmly they feel toward African Americans as a group on what social scientists call "a feeling thermometer": a scale ranging from 1 to 100, where 1 is cold, and 100 is warm. White mainline Protestants (mean = 65) and white Catholics (mean = 66) on average report views close to the general population (mean = 67), while white evangelical Protestants report even warmer feelings (mean = 71).[9] But when white Christian attitudes are illuminated by more specific questions about the symbols of white supremacy, about economic and social inequality between African Americans and whites, or about unequal treatment of African Americans in the criminal justice system, white Christian attitudes appear considerably less warm, and the differences between white Christians and other Americans are revealed in stark relief.

The Confederate Flag and Confederate Monuments

Not surprisingly, attitudes about what the Confederacy symbolizes today are one of the most powerful differentiators among these groups. PRRI's 2019 "American Values Survey" found that 86 percent of white evangelical Protestants, along with 70 percent of white mainline Protestants and 70 percent of white Catholics, believe that the Confederate flag is more a symbol of southern pride than of racism. By contrast, only 41 percent of white religiously unaffiliated Americans and 16 percent of African American Protestants agree; approximately six in ten religiously unaffiliated whites and three-quarters of African American Protestants report that they see the Confederate flag mostly as a symbol of racism.[10]

On a similar question, a 2018 PRRI survey found that more than eight in ten white Christians overall—including 85 percent of white evangelical Protestants, 85 percent of white mainline Protestants, and 80 percent of white Catholics—say that Confederate monuments

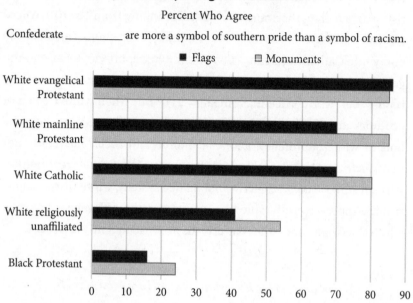

FIGURE 5.1 Perception of Confederate Symbols, by Religious Affiliation

Percent Who Agree

Confederate _____ are more a symbol of southern pride than a symbol of racism.

Source: PRRI, American Values Surveys, 2019 (Flags), 2018 (Monuments).

are more a symbol of southern pride than of racism. These views are shared by only 54 percent of religiously unaffiliated whites and a mere 24 percent of their fellow African American Protestants.[11]

The Killing of African American Men by Police

Current events related to racial injustice also produce differing opinions among white Christians than among religiously unaffiliated whites. Nearly two-thirds (64 percent) of white Christians overall believe the killings of African American men by police are isolated incidents rather than part of a broader pattern of how police treat African Americans. There is some daylight here between white evangelicals (71 percent), white Catholics (63 percent), and white mainline Protestants (59 percent), but each group has solid majorities agreeing with this statement. And there is a 26-percentage-point gap between white Christians overall and religiously unaffiliated whites (38 percent agree they are isolated incidents) and a nearly 50-percentage-point gap between white Christians and African American Protestants (15 percent agree).

There is an even larger attitude gulf related to protests about this issue, such as NFL players kneeling during the national anthem. More than seven in ten (72 percent) white Christians overall believe that professional athletes should be required to stand during the national anthem at sporting events, a view held by only 34 percent of religiously unaffiliated whites and only 21 percent of African American Protestants. Again, all white Christian subgroups have majorities agreeing with this statement: 81 percent of white evangelicals, 71 percent of white Catholics, and 65 percent of white mainline Protestants.[12]

Notably, white Christian objections are not due to a misunderstanding of the nature of these protests by African American players. PRRI's January 2018 sports poll found that more than seven in ten white Americans correctly identified these athletes' actions as protesting police violence against African Americans.[13]

Perceptions of Structural Injustice

White Christians also stand out as a group on questions related to structural injustice and perceived barriers to black social mobility. More than three-quarters of white Christians overall—including 83 percent of white evangelicals, 75 percent of white Catholics, and 71 percent of white mainline Protestants—believe that racial minorities use racism as an excuse for economic inequalities more than they should. While these views are also shared by 52 percent of religiously unaffiliated whites, the gap between them and the closest white Christian subgroup is nearly 20 percentage points. Only 30 percent of black Protestants agree. Similarly, two-thirds of white Christians overall, including similar numbers of all white Christian subgroups, agree that black Americans should be able to overcome prejudice and "work their way up without any special favors." Only about half of religiously unaffiliated whites and roughly three in ten African American Protestants agree.[14]

Perhaps most fundamentally (see figure 5.2), more than six in ten white Christians overall *disagree* with this basic statement: "Generations of slavery and discrimination have created conditions that make it difficult for blacks to work their way out of the lower class." Sixty-seven percent of white evangelical Protestants, 62 percent of white mainline Protestants, and 57 percent of white Catholics disagree with this sentiment, compared with only 40 percent of religiously unaffiliated whites. Only 31 percent of black Protestants disagree with this statement, while more than two-thirds agree.[15]

Across a range of questions, the overall pattern that emerges is abundantly clear. On the one hand, white Christians explicitly pro-

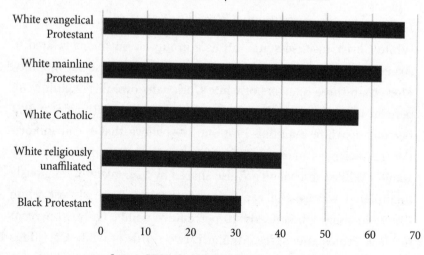

FIGURE 5.2 Impact of Structural Injustice on Black Economic Mobility

Percent Who Disagree

Generations of slavery and discrimination have created conditions that make it difficult for blacks to work their way out of the lower class.

Source: PRRI, American Values Survey, 2018.

fess warm attitudes toward African Americans. At the same time, however, they strongly support the continued existence of Confederate monuments to white supremacy and consistently deny the existence not only of historical structural barriers to black achievement but also of existing structural injustices in the way African Americans are treated by police, the courts, workplaces, and other institutions in the country. And, notably, Christian affiliation remains a powerful differentiator among whites, with differences between white Christians and religiously unaffiliated whites running from 20 to nearly 40 percentage points across these questions. In every case, it is religiously unaffiliated whites who stand closer than white Christians do to their African American Christian brothers and sisters.

Foreign Protectionism: White Christians and Negative Attitudes About Immigrants

We find similar attitudinal patterns across questions related to resisting demographic changes in the country and to protecting a perceived "American way of life" from changes by foreign influences. The largest gulf between white Christians and religiously unaffiliated whites appears on a general question about cultural protectionism. Approximately two-thirds of white Christians overall—including 71 percent of white evangelical Protestants, and 62 percent of both white Catholics and white mainline Protestants—believe that the American way of life needs protecting from foreign influence. This attitude puts them strongly at odds with religiously unaffiliated whites and with African American Protestants, among whom less than half perceive such a cultural threat (38 percent and 48 percent, respectively).

There is also notable support among white Christians for President Donald Trump's signature immigration policies. While most of the policy debates have focused on illegal immigration, one of the strongest areas of agreement among white Christians is actually in the area of limiting *legal* immigration. Nearly two-thirds (65 percent) of white Christians overall, including nearly identical numbers of white Christian subgroups, favor stricter limits on the number of *legal* immigrants coming to the United States. That level of support is 20 to 30 percentage points higher than support among religiously unaffiliated whites (37 percent) or African American Protestants (45 percent).

Similarly, white Christians are also strongly behind Trump's Muslim travel ban policy. Nearly two-thirds of white Christians favor temporarily preventing people from some majority Muslim countries from entering the United States. White evangelical Protestants are particularly supportive of this policy (72 percent), but 63 percent of mainline Protestants and 60 percent of white Catholics also back it. By contrast, only 35 percent of religiously unaffiliated whites and 34 percent of African American Protestants support this policy.

Finally, majorities of all white Christian subgroups support Trump's signature project, building a wall on the southern border. White evangelicals stand out for their particular enthusiasm: two-thirds of white evangelical Protestants favor building a wall along the US border with Mexico, including nearly four in ten who *strongly* favor this policy. Fifty-six percent of white Catholics and 52 percent of white mainline Protestants also support this policy. Only 28 percent of religiously unaffiliated whites and African American Protestants agree, reflecting a 30-percentage-point difference compared with white Christians overall (58 percent).

Compared with the questions about African Americans, there is more variation here among white Christian subgroups, with white evangelicals generally staking out more anti-immigrant positions than either white mainline Protestants or white Catholics. But even with this variation, the differences between white Christians overall and religiously unaffiliated whites are on average a robust 30 percentage points, and it remains true that religiously unaffiliated whites are closer than white Christians to the attitudes of Christians of color.

Religiously unaffiliated whites are far less likely than their Christian counterparts to perceive demographic and cultural changes as negative or to support policies designed to protect the country from such perceived external threats.

What Role Do Racial Attitudes Play in Structuring White Christian Identity?

The correlations in the descriptive statistics above are consistent and clear. But in order to assess what role racist attitudes *independently* play in structuring white Christian identity, we have to employ some additional statistical tools. This more rigorous analysis proceeds in two steps. First, we want to ensure that the particular questions we analyzed above are not peculiar in their results, and that they have not been chosen in a way that produces a skewed set of findings. To address this concern, I have integrated these questions into a broader Racism Index composed of a total of fifteen separate questions related to this history of white supremacy and perceptions of African Americans. By combining these questions into a single scale, we can ensure that we are measuring a more general underlying sentiment rather than what might be an outlier response to the specifics of a single question.

Second, I test this Racism Index for the possibility that the correlations between racial attitudes and white Christian identity are explained by some other intervening variable. For example, perhaps white evangelicals hold negative attitudes about African Americans not because they are evangelical Christians but because they overwhelmingly identify with and support the Republican Party, which has consistently opposed civil rights legislation since the 1960s, or because they reside overwhelmingly in the former states of the Confederacy, or because of some other demographic attribute. If that is the case, the correlation between holding racist attitudes and white

Christian identity may be coincidental or even spurious. But if this relationship holds up in statistical models that account for these other possible explanatory variables, we gain confidence that this relationship is real—in other words, that holding racist attitudes is directly and independently linked to white Christian identity.

I realize that, for nontechnical readers, references to "statistical models" may prompt a search for the beginning of the next chapter. But we need these tools if we want to know whether racist attitudes are important drivers of white Christian identity, or the reverse—whether white Christian identity is an important driver of racist attitudes—not just in the past but also in the present. Generally speaking, these models are the way social scientists determine the strength of relationships between attitudes, behaviors, and concepts. Humans are complex animals, and it is impossible to determine every element that explains our political and social attitudes. However, statistical analyses allow us to explain, in this case, white Christian identity, and to isolate the impact of holding racist attitudes relative to other factors such as partisanship, socioeconomic status, or where one lives. While we'll need a working knowledge of these concepts for the discussion that follows, I've sequestered most of the technical discussion and the math to the endnotes and appendices. For nontechnical readers who may still struggle with the statistical analysis, I have included a summary of the findings, sans data, at the conclusion of the chapter.[16]

A more general way of thinking about this exercise is to imagine it as an attempt to sociologically map the genome of white Christianity to see whether white supremacist attitudes have become integrated into its DNA as part of what it *means* to be a white Christian in America. If the initial correlations we see between white supremacist attitudes and white Christianity cannot be explained away by other factors, white Christians have some serious soul-searching to do.

The Racism Index

The table below lists the fifteen questions included in the Racism Index.[17] These questions cover a lot of ground: attitudes about Confederate symbols; racial inequality and African American economic mobility; racial inequality and the treatment of African Americans in the criminal justice system; and general perceptions of race, racism, and racial discrimination. For the analysis below, I have combined these fifteen questions into a single composite index that is calibrated from 0 to 1, with 0 representing the least amount of racist attitudes across all questions and 1 representing the highest amount of racist attitudes across all questions. The breadth of this scale, along with the fact that these questions produce an internally consistent scale, give us a high degree of confidence that we are measuring a broader underlying sentiment.[18]

The Racism Index • Individual Question Wording

Confederate Symbols

Do you see monuments to Confederate soldiers more as symbols of southern pride or more as symbols of racism?

Just your opinion: What should be done with Confederate monuments that are currently standing on public property such as statehouses, county courthouses, public universities or city parks? Should they be:
a) removed and destroyed;
b) removed but allowed to be reinstalled in a museum or on private property;
c) left in place but have a plaque added that explains their historical context; or
d) left in place just as they are.*

Racial Inequality and African American Economic Mobility

Generations of slavery and discrimination have created conditions that make it difficult for blacks to work their way out of the lower class.*

It's really a matter of some people not trying hard enough; if blacks would only try harder, they could be just as well off as whites.

Irish, Italians, Jews, and many other minorities overcame prejudice and worked their way up. Blacks should do the same without any special favors.

Over the past few years, blacks have gotten less than they deserve.*

Racial minorities use racism as an excuse more than they should.

White people in the U.S. have certain advantages because of the color of their skin.*

Racial Inequality and the Treatment of African Americans in the Criminal Justice System

Do you think recent killings of African American men by police are isolated incidents, or are they part of a broader pattern of how police treat African Americans?

Professional athletes should be required to stand during the national anthem at sporting events.

A black person is more likely than a white person to receive the death penalty for the same crime.*

Perceptions of Race, Racism, and Racial Discrimination

I am fearful of people of other races.

Racial problems in the U.S. are rare, isolated situations.

I am angry that racism exists.*

Today discrimination against whites has become as big a problem as discrimination against blacks and other minorities.

* Note: Response options for these questions were reverse-coded so that they run the same ideological direction as other questions in the scale.

SOURCE: PRRI, AMERICAN VALUES SURVEY, 2018.

FIGURE 5.3 Distribution of Racism Index Scores among White Religious Subgroups

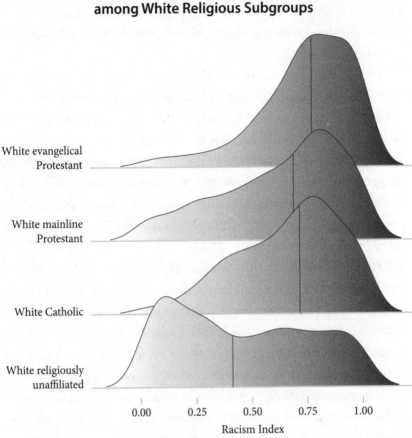

White evangelical
Protestant

White mainline
Protestant

White Catholic

White religiously
unaffiliated

0.00   0.25   0.50   0.75   1.00

Racism Index

Note: Median lines shown.
Source: PRRI, American Values Survey, 2018.

Analysis of the composite Racism Index confirms the general pattern from the individual question analysis above: white Christians overall are more likely than white religiously unaffiliated Americans to register higher scores on the Racism Index, and the differences between white Christian subgroups (white evangelical Protestants, white mainline Protestants, and white Catholics) are largely differences of degree rather than kind. Figure 5.3 shows the median scores with vertical lines—the score at which there are equal numbers of group members falling above and below—and the distribution of attitudes on the Racism Index among each white Christian subgroup, along with the comparison group of whites who are religiously unaffiliated.

Even a brief glance at the median scores for each group shows the similarity of attitudes among each white Christian group. Not surprisingly, white evangelical Protestants have the highest median score (0.78) on the Racism Index. But the median scores of white Catholics (0.72) and white mainline Protestants (0.69) are not far behind. To put these scores into perspective, the median score for each white Christian subgroup is significantly above the median scores of the general population (0.57), white religiously unaffiliated Americans (0.42), and black Protestants (0.24).

The shapes of the distributions are also informative. Among white evangelicals, attitudes are distributed nearly perfectly on either side of a high peak near the median score, indicating a great degree of homogeneity in opinion around this mark. The distribution of white Catholics looks similar to that of white evangelical Protestants, but with the median score just to the left of the curve peak—reflecting slightly more respondents with lower scores on the Racism Index. White mainline Protestants have the most variation in attitudes. Like white evangelicals, this group also shows a (lower) peak around 0.8, but the median score is well to the left of that peak, reflecting the presence of significantly more white mainline Protestant respondents toward the lower end of the Racism Index scale compared with the other two white Christian subgroups. By contrast, the distribution of religiously unaffiliated whites is significantly heavier toward the low end of the index, with a peak around 0.1.

We can now compare the scores from the Racism Index to the previously mentioned findings from the "feeling thermometer" question. Although all white Christian groups record similarly warm feeling thermometer scores to Americans overall in the analysis above, each group's score on the Racism Index is significantly *higher* than the general population's. White evangelical Protestants, for example, report the warmest attitudes toward African Americans (an average score of 71 on a scale of 1 to 100), while simultaneously registering the highest score on the Racism Index (0.78 on a scale of 0 to 1). While this stunning contradiction is most pronounced for white evangelical Protestants, the pattern also exists among white mainline Protestants and white Catholics. In other words, by asking multiple questions about concrete policies and specific attitudes rather than relying on more general sentiments, the Racism Index helps us see a paradox that is critical for understanding racial attitudes among white Christians. White Christians think of themselves as people who hold warm feelings toward African Americans while simultaneously embracing a host of racist and racially resentful attitudes that are inconsistent with that assertion. If we want to understand the legacy of white supremacy in American Christianity, we'll need to move beyond self-reported general sentiment toward African Americans, and the Racism Index gives us a lens to help us see its concrete effects.

This first step in the analysis confirms that the Racism Index is a stable, broad measure of underlying racial attitudes about African Americans, and that attitudes on this index are strongly related to the three largest white Christian subgroups: white evangelical Protestants, white mainline Protestants, and white Catholics. This tells us that there is a robust relationship between holding racist attitudes and identifying as a white Christian. But it's still possible that this correlation is the result of some other intervening variable.

In order to eliminate that possibility, we need to tap some more sophisticated statistical tools that allow us to control for the influence of a range of other variables. That analysis will allow us to measure how much holding racist attitudes *predicts independently* the probability of identifying as a white Christian. As another way to understand the relationship between these two concepts, we'll also flip the direction of the analysis, measuring how much identifying as a white Christian *predicts independently* the likelihood of holding racist attitudes. In short, we'd like to know whether holding racist attitudes makes one more likely to identify as a white Christian and, conversely, whether identifying as a white Christian in itself makes one more likely to hold racist attitudes.

Does Holding More Racist Attitudes Increase the Likelihood of Identifying as a White Christian?

To sort this out, we turn to what social scientists call "multivariate regression models," a fancy term for a statistical technique that can unravel the simultaneous influence of multiple concepts in predicting how another attitude or behavior changes. In our case, we need to measure how strongly holding racist attitudes predicts four different white Christian identities: (1) white Christian overall, (2) white evangelical Protestant, (3) white mainline Protestant, and (4) white Catholic. For comparison, we also need a fifth model to predict being white and religiously unaffiliated.[19]

To ensure that the relationship between the Racism Index and white Christian identity is a direct and independent one, we also need a robust set of independent control variables representing other factors that could theoretically influence the relationship between racial attitudes and white Christian identity. Unless otherwise noted, the control variables in the analysis below are political party affiliation, education level, region, gender, age, household income, home ownership, frequency of church attendance, and living in a metropolitan area. Additionally, I included an Immigration Index variable, a composite variable based on nineteen separate questions measuring attitudes about immigrants and immigration policy.[20] The Immigration Index was included to ensure that the attitudes in the Racism Index were, in fact, measuring negative attitudes about African Americans specifically and not negative attitudes about nonwhite racial groups or general threats to cultural change.

One way of understanding the function of a regression model is to think about it as a science project constructed to understand electrical circuitry. We can imagine the science project as a box with multiple electrical switches attached to its left end and a single lightbulb inserted into a socket on the right end. The box itself contains complex circuits connecting all the switches to the light in a way that accounts for how the currents running between these switches and the light might interact with one another to produce a final current to the light. When the bulb is first inserted into the socket, the default state of the experiment—with all switches set in neutral positions—produces a light with a glow set by the average level of electrical current specific to that bulb. The goal of the science project would be to understand the effect that manipulating a single switch might have on the light.[21]

Turning back to our regression models, we can envision the independent variables (the items whose influence we are interested in testing, such as the Racism Index) as the set of switches attached to one side of our box. We can imagine the dependent variable (the item we are curious to see impacted, such as a specific white Christian identity) as the lightbulb inserted into the socket on the opposite side of the box. And we can think of the regression model as the box itself.

Using this thought experiment, a number of things could theoretically happen when a switch is flipped. If there is no significant, independent relationship between a switch and a particular bulb, we could flip the switch on and off in vain, seeing no effect at all on the light. For example, with other controls in place, education level had no independent impact on white Christian identity, so flipping that switch would have no effect on the light. If there were a weak relationship between an independent variable and white Christian identity, flipping the switch would produce only a modest change in the light: slightly brighter for a positive relationship and slightly dimmer for a negative relationship. For example, with other controls in place, higher household income was positively predictive of white Christian identity (in other words, more income = more likely to identify as white Christian), but the magnitude of this effect is very modest, so flipping that switch would only slightly brighten the light in our thought experiment. Only if there were a strong relationship between an independent variable and a particular white Christian identity would flipping the switch produce a very bright light. Because of the work of the box circuitry, we would know this effect was not caused by any other variable.

The results below spell out what happens when we flip the Racism Index switch on the box and look to the light on the other side representing some variety of white Christian identity. Figure 5.4 summarizes the independent impact of the Racism Index on the likelihood of white Christian identity overall, among the three largest white Christian subgroups, and among whites who are religiously unaffiliated. In other words, if we insert the lightbulb representing each of these target groups one at a time and flip the Racism Index switch, here's what happens.

These results are striking. Even with all the statistical controls in place, the Racism Index remains an independent predictor of white Christian identity overall for each of the three white Christian subgroups individually, and—in the opposite direction—for religiously unaffiliated whites. In the model, when the RI shifts from least racist to most racist (a move from 0 to 1 on the RI), that shift *independently* makes an average respondent 18 percentage points more likely to identify as white mainline Protestant, 19 percentage points more likely to identify as white evangelical Protestant, and 20 percentage points more likely to identify as white Catholic. For white Christian identity overall, which accounts for the combined effect of all three identities, maximizing the Racism Index score makes a respondent 57 percentage points more likely to identify as a white Christian.[22] By contrast, the corresponding shift in the RI has only a very weak effect on white religiously unaffiliated identity.[23]

Translating these results to our thought experiment, we can imagine having a lightbulb—one for each of these white Christian identities (white evangelical Protestant, white mainline Protestant, and

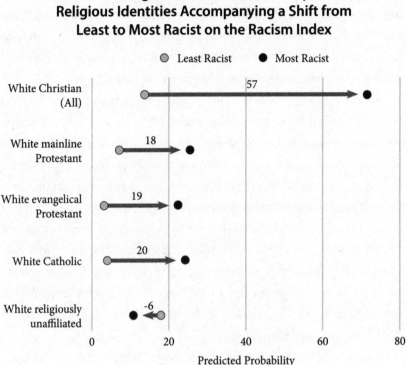

FIGURE 5.4 Change in Predicted Probability of White Religious Identities Accompanying a Shift from Least to Most Racist on the Racism Index

○ Least Racist ● Most Racist

White Christian (All) — 57

White mainline Protestant — 18

White evangelical Protestant — 19

White Catholic — 20

White religiously unaffiliated — -6

Predicted Probability

Source: PRRI, American Values Survey, 2018.

white Catholic) plus white religiously unaffiliated identity—whose brightness ranges from 0 to 100. We attach these bulbs to our science fair box one at a time and flip on the switch representing the RI to its maximum value. In each case, flipping the RI switch produces a light that is approximately 20 percentage points brighter than that bulb's default state. And when the bulb representing all white Christians is attached, it produces a truly incandescent light, nearly 60 percentage points brighter. By contrast, when the RI switch is flipped with the white religiously unaffiliated bulb plugged in, the light dims slightly.

The models reveal that, in the United States today, the more racist attitudes a person holds, the more likely he or she is to identify as a white Christian. And when we control for a range of other attributes, this relationship exists not just among white evangelical Protestants but also equally strongly among white mainline Protestants and white Catholics.[24] And there is also a telling corollary: this relationship with racist attitudes has little hold among white religiously unaffiliated Americans; if anything, the relationship is negative.

A look at the role of church attendance levels casts further light on the relationship between holding racist attitudes and white Christianity. Some have argued, in defense of white Christian churches and institutions, that this link is driven primarily by those who claim a Christian identity but who have little connection to Christian churches. There's even an acronym for this condition: CINO (Christians in name only). Those loosely connected white Christians, the theory goes, are more likely to hold racist views, while those who attend religious services more often—with more exposure to sermons, Sunday school, Bible study, and other forms of Christian discipleship offered within congregations—are more likely to be in solidarity with their African American brothers and sisters.[25]

But there is no evidence that higher church exposure has any mitigating effect on racist attitudes; if anything, the opposite is true. For all white Christian subgroups, there is a positive relationship between holding racist attitudes and white Christian identity among *both* frequent (weekly or more) and infrequent (seldom or never) church attenders. For white Catholics, there are no attendance differences: a move from least racist to most racist on the Racism Index makes both frequent and infrequent church attenders more likely to identify as white Catholic (21 percentage points and 19 percentage points, respectively). For white mainline Protestants, infrequent church attenders see a bigger boost in probability of identification related to holding more racist views (22 percentage points), but the identification boost due to racist views among frequent church attenders is also positive and significant (12 percentage points).

For white evangelical Protestants, there is, strikingly, a stronger boost in likelihood of affiliation due to racist attitudes among *frequent* church attenders than among *infrequent* church attenders. A move from least racist to most racist on the Racism Index makes frequent church attenders 34 percentage points more likely to identify as white evangelical Protestants, compared with an increase of only 9 percentage points among infrequent church attenders. In other words, holding racist views is nearly four times as predictive of white evangelical Protestant identity among frequent church attenders as among infrequent church attenders.

Moreover, if we ask the question of where church attendance has the largest influence on white evangelical Protestant identity, we get a startling answer, which can be seen in the gap between the two lines in figure 5.5. The largest gap between the frequent and infrequent church

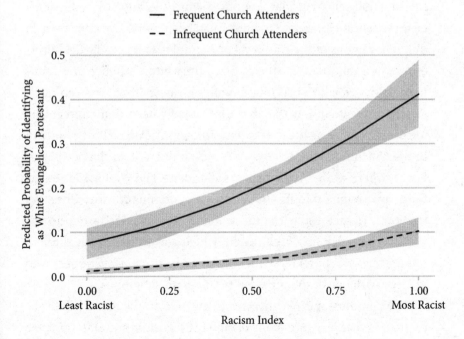

FIGURE 5.5 Predicted Probability of White Evangelical Protestant Identity, by Racism Index Score and Church Attendance Frequency

—— Frequent Church Attenders

– – Infrequent Church Attenders

Source: PRRI, American Values Survey, 2018.

attenders is among those with the highest (most racist) scores on the Racism Index. It's the opposite pattern that anyone thinking of the church as a moderating force on race relations would expect. Among Americans holding the most racist views (Racism Index = 1), frequent church attenders are 31 percentage points more likely than infrequent church attenders to identify as white evangelical Protestant. By contrast, among Americans with the least racist views (Racism Index = 0), the likelihood of white evangelical Protestant identification between frequent and infrequent church attenders is nearly indistinguishable.

Racist Attitudes and White Christian Identity at the Regional Level

As explosive as these findings are, the national numbers tell only part of the story. An examination of the regional variations within each of these models provides important, unanticipated insights into how the relationship between racial attitudes and white Christian identity functions closer to the ground. Historically, and still today, each of these white Christian traditions has been culturally dominant in different regions of the country. For example, white evangelical Protestants are dominant in the South, and white Catholics are dominant in the Northeast. White mainline Protestants have been more evenly distributed, but they have historically been dominant in the Midwest, notable as the prevailing expression of white Protestantism in the Northeast, and, to a lesser extent, influential in the peripheral South, where white Methodists are abundant. The West stands out as the census region that has not had a clear, dominant white Christian tradition. In fact, today the most dominant "religious" group in the West is the religiously unaffiliated, which constitutes about three in ten westerners, compared with only about one in ten westerners who identify with one of the three white Christian subgroups.

If we understand negative racial attitudes to be about white supremacy—that is, expressions of support for white social dominance and control—we might expect the relationship between racist attitudes and white Christian identity to be stronger for each white Christian subgroup within the region in which they are culturally dominant. This is exactly what we see at the regional level, as the chart on the next page indicates. In figure 5.6, the black dots represent the *increase* in probability of each type of white Christian identity, within each region, that accompanies a shift from least to most racist (from 0 to 1) on the Racism Index. The lines on each side of the dots are "error bars," indicating how precise an estimate is, based on the sample sizes and distribution of each subgroup. The shorter the error bar, the more precise the estimate. [26]

For white evangelical Protestants, the largest boost in the predicted probability of affiliation due to increased racist attitudes is in the South. Whereas the predicted probability of identifying as a white evangelical Protestant due to racist attitudes is 19 percent nationally, it jumps to 29 percent in the South. Similarly, whereas the predicted probability of identifying as a white Catholic due to racist attitudes is 20 percent nationally, it soars to 54 percent in the Northeast. For white mainline Protestants, who are geographically more distributed, the regional differences are weaker; but the predicted probability of identifying as a white mainline Protestant due to racist attitudes moves from 18 percent nationally to 23 percent in the Northeast, the region with the highest effect. Notably, for white mainline Protestants, the predicted probabilities in the Midwest (19 percent) and the South (21 percent) are also substantial.

These regional contingencies suggest that within specific geographic regions, especially where a particular white Christian group holds a dominant cultural position, the connections between racist attitudes and white Christian identity are notably stronger. In the South, white evangelicalism receives a significant affiliation boost due to racist attitudes. While white evangelicalism benefits little from increasing racist attitudes in the Northeast, white Catholicism and, to a lesser extent, white mainline Protestantism become the beneficiaries

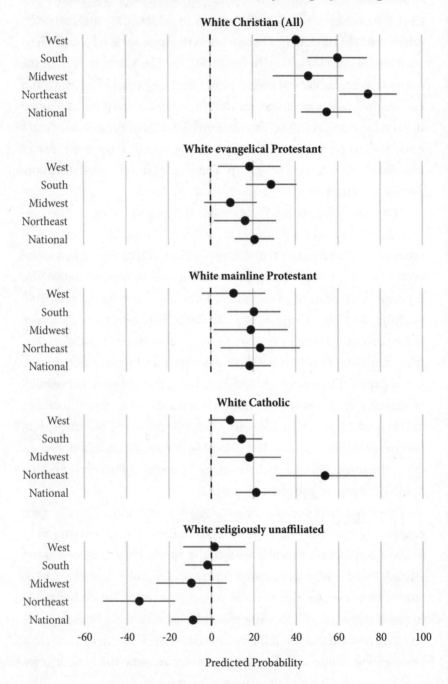

FIGURE 5.6 Change in Predicted Probability of White Religious Identities Accompanying a Shift from Least to Most Racist on the Racism Index, by Geographic Region

Source: PRRI, American Values Survey, 2018.

in that region. White mainline Protestants receive a more evenly distributed boost in the probability of affiliation due to racist attitudes across the Northeast, Midwest, and South. Each form of white Christian identity receives a boost in the probability of affiliation as a result of racist attitudes, and for white evangelicals and white Catholics in particular, this boost is turbocharged in the regions where they are culturally dominant.

The combined white Christian model also reveals some surprising insights. Most notably, the region in which white Christianity receives the highest boost in affiliation due to racist attitudes is not the South but the Northeast. This unexpected finding is due to the fact that unlike the South, where white evangelicals are the single dominant group, the Northeast has two culturally dominant white Christian groups: one Protestant (mainline) and one Catholic. Like product diversification in the marketplace, the presence of two groups that are compatible with white supremacist affinities effectively gives whites with strong racist attitudes two possible Christian identities with which to affiliate. The South clocks in as the region with the second-highest boost in affiliation due to racist attitudes, based principally on the strong effects among white evangelical Protestants, with a smaller boost from white mainline Protestants. The Midwest ranks third, primarily because of the presence of white mainline Protestants and, to a lesser extent, white evangelical Protestants. With no culturally dominant white Christian group, the West ranks last, with the smallest boost in white Christian identity due to racist attitudes.

Compared with white Christian identities, the differences in the patterns predicting white religiously unaffiliated identity are telling. Increased racist attitudes have virtually no impact on the probability of white religiously unaffiliated identification in the West or the South. In the Midwest, while these effects are modest, they flow in a *negative* direction: higher scores on the Racism Index make one slightly *less likely* to be white and religiously unaffiliated. And in the Northeast—the region where both white Catholicism and white mainline Protestantism are strong beneficiaries of racist attitudes—holding more racist attitudes results in a 34 percent *reduction* in the likelihood of identifying as white and religiously unaffiliated. In other words, particularly in the Northeast, holding racist attitudes has become a strong differentiator between white Christians and white religiously unaffiliated residents; those holding the strongest racist attitudes are more likely to feel at home with either white mainline or Catholic Christians, as compared with religiously unaffiliated whites.

The data suggest that white Christian churches, both Protestant and Catholic, have served as institutional spaces for the preservation and transmission of white supremacist attitudes. Rather than deconstructing this racist ideology, most white Christian churches have protected white supremacy by dressing it in theological garb, giving it a home in a respected institution, and calibrating it to local cultural sensibilities. And this analysis shows just how much this legacy has become embedded in the DNA of white Christianity today.

Flipping the Analysis: How Much Does White Christian Identity Predict Higher Racist Attitudes?

Reversing the direction of the analysis above also helps us confirm the strong relationship between racist attitudes and white Christian identity. If we shift the Racism Index to be the dependent variable (make it the bulb instead of a switch in our imaginary science experiment), and move white Christian identities to be independent variables (make them switches), we can see how much each white Christian identity predicts independently an increase in racist attitudes as measured by the RI. This analysis largely confirms the previous findings. (See appendix C for full model output.[27])

Using the same control variables in the models above, being affiliated with each white Christian identity is independently associated with a nearly 10 percent increase in racist attitudes, compared with those who do not identify as a white Christian: 9 percent for white evangelical Protestant identity, 8 percent for white mainline Protestant identity, and 9 percent for white Catholic identity.[28] By contrast, there is no significant relationship between white unaffiliated identity and holding racist attitudes.

Notably, looking at the analysis in this direction, church attendance has no significant impact on the relationship between white Christian identities and holding racist views, confirming the findings of the analysis above. In other words, there is no evidence that going to church every week, at least at the churches white Christians are currently attending, makes a white Christian any less likely to be racist. Whatever Christian formation and discipleship is happening is not impacting the white supremacist attitudes that are deeply embedded in white Christian institutions of all types. White evangelical Protestants, white mainline Protestants, and white Catholics who go to church frequently are as likely as their less-frequently-attending counterparts to hold racist attitudes.

The relationship, then, between the Racism Index and white Christian identity is a broad two-way street: an increase in racist attitudes independently predicts an increase in the likelihood of identifying as a white Christian, and identifying as a white Christian is independently associated with an increased probability of holding racist attitudes.

A Summary of the Statistical Findings

We've covered a lot of statistical ground in this chapter. Below is a summary of the main findings:

- White Christians think of themselves as people who hold warm feelings toward African Americans while simultaneously embracing a host of racist and racially resentful attitudes inconsistent with those warm feelings. The Racism Index provides a more accurate reading of white Christians' views toward African Americans.

- Harboring more racist views is a positive independent predictor of white Christian identity overall and for each of the three white Christian subgroups individually: white evangelical Protestant, white mainline Protestant, and white Catholic. By contrast, holding more racist views has only a very weak effect on white religiously unaffiliated identity, and that effect is in the negative direction.
- Attending church more frequently does not make white Christians less racist. On the contrary, there is a positive relationship between holding racist attitudes and white Christian identity among *both* frequent (weekly or more) and infrequent (seldom or never) church attenders. And for white evangelical Protestants, holding racist views has nearly four times the power to predict the likelihood of identification among frequent church attenders than among infrequent church attenders.
- The relationship between racist attitudes and white Christian identity is even stronger for each white Christian subgroup within the region in which they are culturally dominant: white evangelical Protestants primarily in the South and white Catholics in the Northeast; for the more geographically diffuse white mainline Protestants, the strongest relationship is in the Northeast, but the relationship is also significant in the South and Midwest.
- When we reverse the analysis to predict racist attitudes, being affiliated with each white Christian identity is independently associated with an approximately 10 percent increase in racist attitudes. By contrast, there is no significant relationship between white religiously unaffiliated identity and holding racist attitudes.
- Looking at the analysis in this reverse direction, church attendance has no significant impact on the relationship between white Christian identities and holding racist views. Frequently attending white evangelical Protestants, white mainline Protestants, and white Catholics are as likely as their counterparts who attend less frequently to hold racist attitudes.

This analysis leaves us with some remarkable conclusions. If you want to predict whether an average person is likely to identify as a white Christian, and you could know only one attribute about that person, you would be better off knowing how racist he or she is than how often he or she attends church. Or, to put it even more bluntly, if you were recruiting for a white supremacist cause on a Sunday morning, you'd likely have more success hanging out in the parking lot of an average white Christian church—evangelical Protestant, mainline Protestant, or Catholic—than approaching whites sitting out services at the local coffee shop.

Conclusion

While the persistence of racist attitudes among white Christians today may seem astonishing at first blush, the three authors of *Deep Roots*, Acharya, Blackwell, and Sen, note just how close the Civil War and the institution of slavery are to us. The last known person to have been born into slavery, Sylvester Magee, died in Hattiesburg, Mississippi, in 1971,[29] and Ruth Odom Bonner, a child of former slaves, lived long enough to stand alongside President Barack Obama to ring the bell opening the National Museum of African American History and Culture in 2016, at the age of ninety-nine.[30]

Avidit Acharya and his coauthors also demonstrate how cultural beliefs and behaviors can persist over time. They argue that beliefs and behaviors can become socially self-reinforcing; once a fork in the cultural road has been chosen, especially among a social group, it becomes harder to deviate from that path because of the social pressure that accumulates over time from parents and grandparents, settled communal norms, and institutions that codify and preserve these beliefs and bridge generations. They sum up this dynamic as follows: "Similar to religion and language, attitudes—including political and racial attitudes—are passed down from generation to generation, fostered and encouraged by families and social structures, such as schools and churches."[31]

While Acharya and his colleagues explicitly mention religion and churches early in their book as general examples of the kind of institutional, connective tissue they theorize is at work in passing down attitudes about race across generations, this mechanism largely drops out of their statistical analysis and findings. At the conclusion of the book, they are perplexed that the successes of the civil rights movement and the fall of Jim Crow laws have not done more to mitigate the continued effects of slaveholding on the contemporary attitudes of whites in the South. They note that these sweeping social and legal changes have been less effective than one might expect at attenuating "differences in behavioral outcomes—including political attitudes, opinions on race, and support or opposition for race-related policies."[32] They conclude simply, "The fact that we can still detect this kind of divergence between whites living in these areas and whites living in other parts of the South is a testament to slavery's lasting political and cultural legacy."[33]

This much is true. But the authors miss the opportunity to identify a key conduit of the ongoing cultural transmission of white supremacy: white Christian churches.[34] Even as Jim Crow laws have been struck from the books in the political realm, most white Christian churches have reformed very little of their nineteenth-century theology and practice, which was designed, by necessity, to coexist comfortably with slavery and segregation. As a result, most white Christian churches continue to serve, consciously or not, as the mechanisms for transmitting and reinforcing white supremacist attitudes among new generations.

This chapter demonstrates—with rigorous quantitative evidence— a disturbing fact: that Frederick Douglass's nearly two-hundred-year-old observations about the positive correlation between white supremacy and Christianity continue to be supported by the contemporary evidence. Not only in the South but nationwide, higher levels of racism are associated with higher probabilities of identifying as a white Christian; and, conversely, adding Christianity to the average white person's identity moves him or her toward more, not less, affinity for white supremacy. White supremacy lives on today not just in explicitly and consciously held attitudes among white Christians; it has become deeply integrated into the DNA of white Christianity itself.

That last statement, standing alone, sounds shocking. But an honest look at the historical arc of white Christianity in America suggests that we should instead be astonished if it were otherwise. For centuries, through colonial America and into the latter part of the twentieth century, white Christians literally built—architecturally, culturally, and theologically—white supremacy into an American Christianity that held an *a priori* commitment to slavery and segregation. At key potential turning point moments such as the Civil War and the civil rights movement, white Christians, for the most part, did not just fail to evict this sinister presence; history confirms that they continued to aid and abet it. The weight of this legacy is indeed overwhelming. But as the next chapter shows, there are signs that at least some white Christians are facing the reality of this history and have taken a few steps along a new path toward repentance and repair.

– 6 –

Telling

Stories of Change

The extent to which white supremacy is entrenched among white Christians, not just evangelicals in the South but also white mainline Protestants and white Catholics in other parts of the United States, is indeed daunting. But as I traveled the country doing research for this book, it also became clear that Americans, at both the national and local levels, are attempting to tell a more truthful story about our racist past, to understand how this past is manifesting itself in our fraught present, and to begin to shape a better future. These stories are emerging in both private moments and public monuments, particularly—but not exclusively—in the American South. Through these recent stories of transformation, we can see how white Christian Americans might begin to face our own personal and family stories and wrestle with the ways in which white supremacy has distorted our sense of reality and ourselves.

Jackson, Mississippi:
The Mississippi Civil Rights Museum

In my hometown of Jackson, Mississippi, I visited the Mississippi Civil Rights Museum just a few weeks after it opened in December 2017. Given my own experiences and the state's track record on civil rights, I was not expecting this museum to be a sign of hope; I was highly skeptical that I would encounter anything near an honest accounting of the state's civil rights history. The museum has the distinction of being the first, and currently the only, civil rights museum built with public funds. While such an investment might indicate a deep commitment to the topic in many other states, my assumption was that official state funding would whitewash the narrative.

I was also suspicious of the "two museums" marketing, which tied the Civil Rights Museum opening to the reopening of the Museum of Mississippi History after the original was closed due to damage from Hurricane Katrina in 2005. Such couplings by the white power structure are familiar tactics in the South, potentially signaling to whites that there was one museum for them (covering fifteen thousand years, from the Stone Age to the present, including the state's two hundred years of existence) and one for blacks (focused on the thirty years between World War II and the mid-1970s).

Moreover, the official opening ceremony had been marred by Governor Phil Bryant's having invited "my friend" President Donald Trump, who just a few months before had refused to condemn white supremacists who marched in Charlottesville, Virginia, rallying around a statue of Confederate general Robert E. Lee while chanting, "White lives matter!" "Jews will not replace us!" and the Nazi slogan "Blood and Soil!" Trump's invitation caused Representative John Lewis, the Georgia congressman who marched with Martin Luther King Jr., and who was arrested in Mississippi during Freedom Sum-

mer in 1964, to threaten a boycott if Trump spoke at the opening. Ignoring the backlash, the president accepted the invitation and pushed
forward with his plans to speak. The museum scrambled and struck a
compromise that allowed Trump to address an invitation-only crowd
inside the museum before being whisked away ahead of the official
public ceremony outside.[1]

Despite my misgivings, I discovered that the museum had succeeded in doing the near impossible in Mississippi: telling the whole
truth about our state's shameful record on slavery, Jim Crow, massive
resistance to civil rights, and our uneven progress today. It is an impressive and courageous achievement.

It was all there: murders of civil rights workers in Neshoba
County, the assassination of Medgar Evers and the failure of all-
white juries to convict his self-acknowledged killer, Governor Ross
Barnett's resistance to James Meredith being enrolled as the first
black student at Ole Miss, the stark white robes of the KKK. In one
of the first galleries, an 1858 poster advertised boldly, "One Hundred
Negroes for Sale." In addition to the slaves immediately available for
purchase, the fine print assures potential customers that "additional
lots" would be regularly available "during the season"—a reference
to the slave trade practice of timing the arrivals of slaves to coincide
with harvest, in order to ensure higher prices at peak demand times.

One panel, depicting publications of the White Citizens' Councils
and the KKK in the Jim Crow era, featured an eye-catching bright red
cover to the introductory issue of *White Patriot* magazine, with this
subtitle in bold white lettering: "Americans for the preservation of the
white race / If it is not preserved—it will be destroyed." This single
magazine cover powerfully captures the seamless integration of white
supremacy, nationalism, and Christianity. At the top center of the
cover, with crossed staffs, are the American flag and the Confederate
battle flag. Each has an inscription under the image: "Forever shall
she wave for that which she was originally raised" for the former and
simply "The flag of inspiration" for the latter. At the bottom center

are two sketched facial profiles of a white girl and a freckled white boy beside an icon representing a school, labeled "Our Most Precious Possession." And flanking these left and right are monthly calendars featuring the most important dates of the year. January features "New Year's" and "Robt. E. Lee," while December declares "Christ was born."

To my surprise, the museum doesn't avoid highlighting the role of white churches as sites of strong resistance to black claims to equality. One prominent exhibit features a replica of a plain, white, wood-clad church building. Inside that structure, there is an immersive "Organizing Mississippi" exhibit that allows you to sit on worn wooden pews and hear what an organizing meeting for civil rights might have sounded like inside a black Mississippi church. Outside, an exterior church wall tells a different story of organized resistance to integration by white Christian churches. It features news stories and photos of police arresting racially mixed groups of worshippers who had been blocked by church deacons on the steps of white churches during the Jackson Church Visit Campaign of 1963. While the major emphasis is rightly on the nearly unanimous white Christian resistance to desegregation, the exhibit also features smaller "Points of Light" portraits of the few Jackson ministers who spoke out—at significant personal risk and cost—for civil rights, such as Rabbi Perry Nussbaum, Reverend Edwin King, and Dr. W. B. Selah.

The most haunting parts of the museum are the black floor-to-ceiling columns throughout that inscribe in crisp white lettering the names of more than six hundred lynching victims in the state, the dates they were murdered, and their alleged crimes. There is an entire alcove devoted to fourteen-year-old Emmett Till, who was tortured and murdered in 1955 after being accused of whistling at a white storekeeper's wife during a short visit to a candy store. The display includes Till's coffin and the *Jet* magazine photo featuring his battered body lying in the casket that his mother insisted be open to expose the brutality of his murder. And in the center of another room is a replica prison cell from Parchman Penitentiary, where many Freedom Riders were jailed; and on the wall are large mugshots of Freedom Riders who were arrested in 1961, including John Lewis.

It's a difficult museum to visit, especially if you are a white Protestant Mississippian. But it is encouraging that my family weren't the only whites attending that day. While the two Mississippi history museums share a common admissions desk, one could easily imagine whites taking their tickets to the left to the state history museum and African Americans taking theirs to the right to the civil rights museum. But the civil rights museum was crowded, and my fellow visitors that day were a racially diverse crowd, approximately 60 percent black and 40 percent white. And many family groups—including mine that day—included three generations exploring the exhibits together, sparking a range of conversations about how things have and haven't changed.

The mere existence of the Mississippi Civil Rights Museum, with its unflinching portrayal of the terror and violence whites unleashed to protect their dominance and thwart black equality, is itself a testament of hope. It is a sign that the country is beginning—but only just beginning—to face how centrally white supremacy has shaped our communities, our culture, and our faith. When the Mississippi Civil Rights Museum was first conceived in 2001, for example, there were only two modest memorials related to the civil rights movement in the state: an eternal flame in Meridian on the grave of James Cheney, one of three American civil rights workers who were murdered in 1964, and a statue in Jackson of Medgar Evers—compared with fifty-two public monuments to the Confederacy.[2] And although it took sixteen years of lobbying and legislative efforts to win state approval and financial support, the museum was finally built in the capital city—just down from the Old State Capitol, which was the seat of the Confederate state's congress and where some of the nation's most oppressive Jim Crow laws were passed.

Montgomery, Alabama: The National Memorial for Peace and Justice

I also visited Montgomery, Alabama, where the state's articles of secession were drawn, and which served as the first seat of the Confederate government. The state capitol building is situated prominently on a hill overlooking downtown and the river. To approach the capitol from downtown, you proceed up Commerce Street to the city fountain and bear left onto Dexter Avenue, a broad, majestic cobblestone street that rises toward the capitol building, which is set off as a silhouette against the horizon. Dexter Avenue was originally named Market Street, for the bustling slave markets along the route. The cotton-slavery connection would have been vividly evident on this street and on the aptly named Commerce Street to which it connects. At the lower terminus of Commerce Street, Montgomery merchants constructed a giant "cotton slide" to allow heavy bales of cotton to slide down from city street level to awaiting boats on the river. And slaves were marched off boats, chained together, in the other direction: up Commerce Street to awaiting slave pens and warehouses until they could be auctioned off at the intersection of Commerce and Market, near the courthouse fountain and within sight of the capitol.

The old signs of the Confederacy are still there, to be sure. Walking up toward the capitol on Dexter Avenue today, as you pass the last cross street, there is a heavy, six-foot-high triangular piece of granite on the right corner, placed by the United Daughters of the Confederacy, with this inscription: "Along this street moved the inaugural parade of Jefferson Davis. He took the oath of office as President of the Confederate States of America, February 18, 1861. DIXIE played as a band arrangement for the first time on this occasion. Placed by Sophie Bibb Chapter, U.D.C., April 26, 1942." As you ascend the capitol stairs, you pass a twenty-foot-high bronze statue of Davis just to the left, which was erected by the UDC in 1940. When you arrive on the top step, there is a bronze star with this inscription: "Placed by the Sophie Bibb Chapter, Daughters of the Confederacy, on the spot where JEFFERSON DAVIS stood when inaugurated president of C.S.A., Feb. 18, 1861." And if you walk around to the left side of the capitol building, there is an enormous eighty-eight-foot-high monument to the Confederacy, the cornerstone of which was laid by Jefferson Davis himself before a crowd of five thousand in 1886.

But the Lost Cause message of the UDC is not the only witness to history in contemporary Montgomery. Also on Dexter Avenue, in the shadow of the capitol just before that last cross street, sits Dexter Avenue King Memorial Baptist Church. The church was founded in 1877 as the Second Colored Baptist Church and met originally in a former slave trader's pen before purchasing the land on its current location in 1879. The church was Reverend Dr. Martin Luther King Jr.'s first pastoral appointment at the age of twenty-five and where he was serving when helping to organize, from the church basement, the 1955–56 Montgomery bus boycott, a yearlong campaign that ultimately ended segregation in the city's public transportation system.

While standing in that basement near a worn pulpit King used for outside speaking events, my tour guide, Wanda, a member of the church, clasped her hands together and described Montgomery this way: "We've got the Civil War and civil rights all together here in one place. All on top of one another." My visit occurred days after a mass shooting in August 2019, in which a white man killed twenty people in an El Paso Walmart, citing as his motivation "the Hispanic invasion of Texas."[3] Clearly thinking of this event and the general rise of white supremacist violence, Wanda paused. With tears in her eyes, she added, "And they're both still with us, ya'll."

One of the most poignant examples of this dueling, intertwined history is the memorial standoff created by the addition of a second marker on Dexter Avenue, placed directly across the street, on the opposite corner from the long-standing 1940 UDC marker. The newer granite marker is clearly designed to mirror the UDC marker in size, shape, and placement. It reads: "THE SELMA TO MONTGOMERY VOTING RIGHTS MARCH led by Martin Luther King, Jr. ended at the foot of the capitol steps on March 25, 1965. Here Dr. King addressed 25,000 people. 'I believe this march will go down as one of the greatest struggles for freedom and dignity in the nation's history.' Martin Luther King, Jr." Today, if you stand in the middle of Dexter Avenue, these symmetrical sentries, protecting two visions of history, frame your view of the steps rising up to the state capitol.

The city also contains signs—placed mostly in the last decade—marking the sites of slave warehouses and markets, along with significant people and events related to its rich civil rights history. A brass plaque marks the spot where Rosa Parks stepped onto the bus before refusing to give up her seat to a white man. To get the fuller story, one can visit the nearby Rosa Parks Museum. And there are public tributes to lesser-known but important heroes of the movement such as Fred David Gray, the civil rights activist and lawyer who represented Parks and also won a class-action lawsuit against the federal government for the infamous Tuskegee syphilis experiment in which the US Public Health Service conducted a study of untreated syphilis among African American men without their informed consent.

If historical marker campaigns sometimes feel like an "and also" version of history, especially amid the crowds of Confederate monuments to the Lost Cause in states such as Alabama, there is one memorial in Montgomery that has powerfully changed the balance of the narrative, not just in Montgomery but also nationwide: the National Memorial for Peace and Justice. Opened in 2018, the National Memorial is a $15 million investment in truth telling about America's violent, white supremacist past. It's difficult to overstate the impact of this memorial, which is an achievement in archival research, interactive data visualization, and architectural invocation of sacred space.

The Equal Justice Initiative, the organizational force behind not only the memorial but also a related Legacy Museum downtown on Commerce Street, as well as the local civil rights markers about town,

set out to document and memorialize every known lynching that occurred in the country between 1877 (the end of Reconstruction) and
1950. Their research, which counts only lynchings that can be verified
by two independent sources, documented more than 4,400 cases of
African American men, women, and even children who were "hanged,
burned alive, shot, drowned, and beaten to death by white mobs" during this period.

While the vast majority of these lynchings happened in twelve
southern states, the National Memorial also notes that approximately
10 percent of these lynchings took place outside the South, and these
were no less brutal expressions of racial terrorism. In Springfield,
Missouri, for example, where I lived for three years when I taught at
Missouri State University, three black men were lynched in the town
square by a mob of a thousand whites in the early hours of Easter
Sunday in 1906. Arthur Hodge, a Springfield community leader who
organized a memorial for the victims in 2018, summarized the event
this way: "They hanged them. They threw kerosene on them. They
burned them to a crisp. And then they went to church."[4]

Contemporary newspaper accounts note that the white crowd
sifted through the pile of ashes for souvenir pieces of clothing, bone,
or charred flesh. Entrepreneurial businessmen took pictures of the
grisly scene, which captured smoke still rising from the men strung
up from a tower—originally constructed to support streetcar electrical lines and featuring a miniature Statue of Liberty at the top—to sell
as postcards. A few white entrepreneurs even struck medals to com-
memorate the occasion. One read, "Easter offering."[5]

While the National Memorial makes clear that white racial terrorism was not confined to a single region, its visual depiction of the
density of violence in the South is particularly arresting. The memorial occupies a six-acre elevated site with views of downtown and the
capitol. An open-air, low-slung building houses an individual monument for each of the more than eight hundred counties in the South
where a lynching occurred. Each county's monument is a six-foot

metal cuboid box, suspended from the ceiling by a single metal pole. The boxes are arranged in neat rows, each engraved on one side with the names and dates of each victim from that county, listed in a vertical column. Constructed of Corten steel, they age naturally over time, each acquiring its own unique patina, reflecting the uniqueness of each locale and victim.

The memorial is designed for visitors to proceed through the display by walking in a square that descends into the side of a hill and back out again. At the deepest end, as the monuments rise overhead evoking in abstract form the violence of lynching, are these powerful words in bronze letters on the wall:

For the hanged and beaten.

For the shot, drowned, and burned.

For the tortured, tormented, and terrorized.

For those abandoned by the rule of law.

We will remember.

With hope because hopelessness is the enemy of justice.

With courage because peace requires bravery.

With persistence because justice is a constant struggle.

With faith because we shall overcome.

In addition to moving sculptures and a meditation garden dedicated to Ida B. Wells, who risked her life to become one of the earliest voices drawing attention to lynchings, the site contains a breathtaking set of more than eight hundred duplicate steel monuments, arranged in rows and organized by state and county in an adjacent field. These duplicate monuments, lying in state next to the memorial, are part of the memorial's ongoing project to create change across the country.

As the memorial summarizes it, these monuments "are waiting to be claimed, transported, and publicly installed in the counties they represent as a public recognition of that past and step toward a different future."[6]

Although the National Memorial for Peace and Justice has not, as of this writing, fully worked out the criteria, the idea is that local community groups will commit not just to sponsor the installation of the monument but also to foster an ongoing program of racial justice in their local communities. Once placed, the memorials will function as an acknowledgment of the past as well as a commitment to a new future. And the National Memorial will serve as a central site of accountability. It will report on which counties have "confronted the truth of racial terror" and which have not, and visitors can see whether their own counties have unclaimed memorials still resting in the field.

Macon, Georgia: Two First Baptist Churches

In the early morning of October 20, 2018, a bus pulled out of Macon, Georgia, en route to the National Memorial for Peace and Justice in Montgomery, Alabama, on a trip that had been more than four years in the making. Of the twenty-one people aboard roughly half were white and half were African American, representing two different First Baptist Churches in Macon: First Baptist Church of Christ, which is historically and predominantly white, and First Baptist Church (often called First Baptist Church "on New Street" to distinguish it from the other), which is historically and predominantly black. The two churches sit just around the corner from each other, at right angles, with their rear parking lots forming vectors that, if extended just a hundred yards or so, would intersect in a nearby park. If you stand at the corner of High Place and High Street near the park, you can see both steeples: FBC New Street to the right, and FBC of Christ up the hill straight ahead.

My family's personal connection to FBC of Christ, the white congregation, is indirect. As residents of blue-collar East Macon, my parents and relatives didn't attend FBC of Christ, but they were the beneficiaries of its work. FBC of Christ was one of the earliest churches to sponsor a mission church in East Macon. Established in 1881 as the Warren Chapel, after the name of the FBC of Christ pastor who spearheaded the effort, the church served the residents of the rows of modest, wood-clad houses in the textile "mill village" and a small surrounding neighborhood that had grown up across the Ocmulgee River from downtown after the Civil War.[7] Nestled between the city and the Ocmulgee Indian burial mounds, lingering witnesses to the displaced original inhabitants, this narrow strip of land was home to both of my parents.

The church grew and eventually became independently established as East Side Baptist Church.[8] Growing up, my parents walked a grid of rough blacktop and red clay streets to services, and when my mom was nineteen and my dad was twenty, they were married there. A familiar image from my childhood is a black-and-white wedding photo that hung near the piano in our living room and shows them standing arm in arm on the church steps. Although many in my generation have scattered to other parts of the country, "our people" are still there, and Macon is still a modest enough place to allow for small-town serendipity: when I drove down to visit the location of the two First Baptist Churches, I realized that my cousin's law offices are directly across the street from FBC of Christ.

The unlikely and somewhat confusing configuration of the two First Baptist Churches is not the result of some out-of-control church marketing competition but of an intimate, shared history: they began as one church. In 1826 Macon was a town of only a few thousand people, and First Baptist Church was incorporated and built by Bibb County's merchant, banker, and planter class, many of whom built large houses for their families in town, with its conveniences and services, commuting out to their plantation homes periodically. Each of the white charter members of FBC Macon were slave owners, owning between eight and twenty slaves each. For the first two decades of its existence, as was common in the South, whites and blacks worshipped together, with white slave owners sitting toward the front and enslaved people sitting separately in the back.

But by the 1840s, tensions were heating up over secession and the issue of slavery. With black members then significantly outnumbering white members, church records show that the white congregation thought it time for a new arrangement. In 1845—the same year Baptists in the South met in nearby Augusta and broke ties with their northern brethren over the issue of slavery—they issued a deed for land and a building to the black congregation to be used "for religious services and moral cultivation forever."[9] Despite the independent location, the black congregation remained under the authority and supervision of the white board of deacons, and FBC Macon continued to count them as members of the white church in official reports to the regional Baptist association; FBC New Street also had a white pastor appointed by the white church until after the Civil War.[10] Never far away from each other, both churches changed locations several times, settling into their current adjacent configuration by 1887.[11]

These two congregations sat virtually back to back for 128 years, during the reassertion of white supremacy through Jim Crow laws following the overturn of the Reconstruction government, seven documented lynchings in Bibb County, the federally mandated desegregation of Macon's public schools and the establishment of private white Christian academies, the tumultuous years of the civil rights movement, white flight from Macon's city core, and the tense silences in the decades following these changes. There was a tacit acknowledgment of their shared history but no meaningful contact between the two congregations.

That began to change only in 2014, when some mutual acquaintances encouraged the two current pastors to meet. At the time, Reverend Scott Dickison had been pastor of FBC of Christ for just two

years, while Reverend James Goolsby was a decade into his tenure at
FBC on New Street. As it turned out, this differential experience may
have been calibrated just right. In hindsight, Dickison sees that some
naiveté may have been beneficial on the white side of the relationship.
"I must admit, I had no clue about what I was getting myself into," he
told me in an interview. And Goolsby noted that his longer experience
was critical for leading his congregation, some of whom were initially
wary of the white congregation's motives: "There was a trust that I'm
not a novice, and there's a trust that I'm not easily fooled, and so they
trusted my decision."[12]

Their initial conversations led Dickison and Goolsby to connect
with the New Baptist Covenant, a group started in 2006 by former
president Jimmy Carter to help black and white Baptists begin to heal
divisions and work together for social justice. To bring the congregations together and break the ice formed from more than a century of
silence, they began with simple social events such as a joint Easter egg
roll for the kids in the adjoining park and potluck dinners. Most of
these events went smoothly, but they soon found that even seemingly
low-risk joint ventures could be more fraught than anticipated.

In 2014 FBC of Christ invited the youth from FBC on New Street
to join them on an annual youth group retreat, that year to Universal
Studios in Florida. Having had good attendance at other joint church
events, Dickison was surprised to see no African American teens
signed up for the trip as the deadline approached. Puzzled, he asked
Reverend Goolsby if he knew what was going on. Reverend Goolsby
explained that for him and many in his congregation who were parents
of teenage boys, Florida had become synonymous with the 2012 killing of Trayvon Martin, an unarmed teenager, and the state's so-called
Stand Your Ground law. In 2013 this law had permitted the acquittal
of Trayvon's killer, who said he had feared for his life when he saw
Trayvon walking home from a convenience store in a hoodie. Goolsby
straightforwardly told Dickison: "You put a hoodie on my son, and it's
just Trayvon, and there's no way in the world I [am] going to let my

son go to Florida without me."[13] These concerns about the racial climate in Florida, combined with the lack of confidence that the white chaperones understood these risks, had prevented the black parents from allowing their kids to participate.

But even at this early stage in the churches' partnership, enough trust had been established to foster an honest conversation. When Dickison brought these concerns back to the white adults signed up as chaperones, David Cooke Jr., a longtime member of FBC of Christ and also the local district attorney for Bibb County, was deeply moved by this story, which intersected with his professional work around race and the law. Cooke told Goolsby and the other black parents that he understood their concerns and promised that he personally would commit himself to carefully looking after the African American teenage boys on the trip. To his own surprise, Goolsby noted, "I felt comfortable with that, amazingly. That never would have happened had we not begun to develop that relationship." For his part, Dickison noted that the event had broken through the racial naiveté, while opening up a new path of empathy among many white parents: "Hearing that, the fear from a black father about his son and sharing that with him, I think really gave [the white parents] kind of a personal opening to some of these larger questions that, unfortunately, white America is only now confronting." Goolsby signed up his son for the trip, and others from FBC on New Street followed suit.

The most immediate result of these difficult conversations was that the youths went on their first ever racially integrated trip. But beyond that, it was a sign that the churches' initial interactions were paying dividends. Dickison noted that their modest efforts were bridging divides in contemporary Macon: "Our covenant opened up that interaction, not just between a black father and a white father, but between a black father and the DA of the city." And Goolsby saw it as a confirming milestone that allowed him to say to himself, "Okay, we're moving in the right direction."[14]

Five months after the youth trip, the two churches formalized their commitment by holding a joint service and signing a covenant to work together toward racial justice and healing. Goolsby and Dickison chose Pentecost Sunday (May 24, 2015), which celebrates the Holy Spirit coming among the fearful disciples after Jesus's death and resurrection, to empower them for a new phase of ministry. One of the most moving moments of that service was the observance of Communion, the consumption of the bread and wine representing the body and blood of Jesus. In a city where public swimming pools had been closed to prevent black children from swimming with white children after public facilities were legally desegregated, the practice of becoming united in the same spiritual fellowship, through the intimate symbols of shared bread and wine, is nothing short of radical.

While both churches are Baptist and broadly hold a shared theological understanding of Communion, each nonetheless had to adjust to cultural differences in the rituals. FBC of Christ has women deacons who assist with serving the congregation, while FBC on New Street does not. FBC on New Street approaches the ritual with a higher degree of formality, with deacons donning white gloves, while FBC of Christ does not. Even these small differences rang with broader significance in the racially charged Deep South.

For many older white deacons in an upper-middle- to upper-class church, holding a tray and serving their African American neighbors would be an image devastating to the hierarchical ethos of their childhood. And for many African American deacons, serving Communion in white gloves to well-off white folks may have evoked memories of the not-too-distant past when African Americans were confined largely to menial labor and service jobs and kept out of the white-collar economy. But Dickison and Goolsby both described the act of observing and making space for these ritual differences as powerful expressions of mutual respect and desire for community.

Just three weeks after this service launching their formal work together, white Christian supremacist Dylann Roof gunned down nine

African Americans who were attending a Bible study at Emanuel AME Church in Charleston, testing the mettle of the Macon churches' new covenant. "Charleston was so clear and blatant," Dickison said. "Like the bombing of the Sixteenth Street Baptist Church and the four little girls," a reference to a 1963 incident in Birmingham, "Charleston was a turning point. It changed our conversation."[15]

The Sunday after the Charleston massacre, Dickison and his worship team arranged the entire service to address the issue of white racism and violence. Reflecting back on that day, Dickison noted that while he would like to think that their services would have focused on that tragic event anyway, he knew that because of their covenant with FBC on New Street, the events "weighed more heavily on our congregation."[16] No one, he recalled, questioned why the service was focused on racism and racial violence, nor did they question his participation, along with Goolsby, at a rally decrying white supremacy later in the week. After Charleston, Dickison said, "A lot of white people are seeing that this doesn't have to do with 'people over there'; it has to do with us."[17]

In his mostly white congregation, Dickison has been working to build up a tolerance for the discomfort that comes from honestly confronting a past that differs from the stories told in the official church histories. This tolerance faced a serious challenge when historian Doug Thompson, director of the Spencer B. King Jr. Center for Southern Studies at Macon's Mercer University and a member of the congregation, discovered historical financial transactions with horrifying implications. In a single week in 1855, the church accounts-receivable ledger detailed income from the sale of two teenage boy slaves for $950 each, equivalent to a total of about $56,000 today. That same week, the accounts-payable ledger reflected a payment toward the pastor's salary and the church building fund. The inescapable conclusion was that at least some of the funds from the sale of church members' slaves went to pay the church's bills. When Thompson brought these transactions to the attention of Dickison and the church leadership, Dickison decided to preach about it. According to Thompson, who attended the Sunday service, when Dickison disclosed the transactions, "there was an audible gasp in the congregation."[18]

As Thompson and Dickison kept digging, they found more evidence of just how complicit the church and its most respected members had been in both slavery and the defense of white supremacy. Beyond the slave sales identified above, they discovered that the congregation's flagship 1855 church building on Second Street, constructed to impress, was likely funded by the sale of approximately twenty slaves owned by one of its prominent founding families.[19] The official history of First Baptist Church of Christ proudly described the public reception of the building in detail:

"Praise for the new building was unlimited. The editor of the *Georgia Citizen* declared it 'an ornament to the city . . . the finest church edifice in Macon . . . second to none in the State, point of architectural design and beauty.' It was also described as a "handsome and tasteful Gothic edifice, the most attractive building in the city."[20]

The land and building alone cost approximately $20,500 in 1855, equivalent to more than $600,000 in today's currency—a considerable commitment for a church with an enrollment of just 287 whites and 400 enslaved black members. On the morning of March 18, 1855, Pastor Sylvanus Landrum preached the dedication sermon based on the text "The Lord is in his holy temple; let all the earth keep silence before him."[21]

In a 2017 sermon entitled "Learning How to Remember," Dickison drove home the painful revelation of their research to the congregation: "Given what we know about our congregation at the time, that it included both slave owners and their slaves, [this means] that the church building may have been financed through the sale of some of its own members."[22] Pausing over this transaction reveals just how brutal an act this would have been. The sale of slaves at this scale would have almost certainly meant large-scale family separations:

husbands from wives, parents from children, siblings from one another, not to mention extended family connections. It's not hard to
imagine the soul-crushing experience of an African American slave
member whose family members were sold to purchase the land and
materials for the church; who was forced to work on its construction
and then later required to attend worship services, listening to paternalistic admonishments from a white preacher while sitting in one of
the rear pews his own hands had built.

In addition to selling slaves to finance church business, church
leaders were strongly committed to the cause of the Confederacy. On
January 25, 1861, the Sunday following Georgia's act of secession,
Pastor E. W. Warren—the same minister who launched what eventually became my parents' home church—delivered a sermon, printed
in full in the *Macon Daily Telegraph*, that was described as "a thor-
oughgoing defense of slaveholding supported entirely by the pastor's
interpretation of references to the Scriptures, including both Testa-
ments."[23] This sermon proved so popular that Warren expanded on
these ideas in serial publications in the *Christian Index*, and later
published them in a widely read book, *Nellie Norton: Or, Southern
Slavery and the Bible, A Scriptural Refutation.*[24]

When the Confederate Congress adopted the Stars and Bars as the
first official flag of the Confederacy and telegraphed the design speci-
fications out to the states in March 1861, the church minutes recorded
with pride the fervent activity of Mrs. Thomas Hardeman Jr., the wife
of the US congressman who had recently resigned his post to serve in
the Confederate army. The minutes note that Mrs. Hardeman, "with
her accustomed patriotism and energy devoted her labor the whole
of that night to the making of the first flag of the Confederacy which
waved upon Georgia soil."[25] In April 1862 the congregation voted to
offer its massive nine-hundred-pound bronze bell to be melted down
to create Confederate cannons.[26] Finally, because of its grandeur, the
church building also had the distinction of being the site of the last
address Confederate president Jefferson Davis gave to the people of

Macon just before the end of the Civil War. There is no record that any of this activity raised a white Christian eyebrow.

Since 2015, Goolsby and Dickison, and key leaders in their churches, have continued to slowly build trust between the congregations. Dickison's white congregation has seen a few families leave, and some who have stayed still argue defensively that these uncomfortable conversations are pointless, since no whites currently attending the church were responsible for enslaving anyone. But for the most part, the congregation remains behind the efforts, which have focused less on joint worship and more on holiday potlucks, shared programs for children and youth, and service projects. As Dickison put it, "If there's any secret to what we've done, it's that we've shared far more potato salad than pulpit swaps. It's tastier and, in the end, probably better for you."[27] And Goolsby's congregation continues mostly to trust his wisdom even if some still have concerns about the motives of the whites up on the hill.

Notably, Goolsby and Dickison recounted similar reactions to the initial stages of their covenant work, both from older members of their congregations. After a Thanksgiving potluck gathering, an older white female congregant pulled Dickison aside and said, "I didn't know how much we needed this." And after the Pentecost service, an older black male congregant told Goolsby matter-of-factly, "We've been waiting for this to happen."[28]

After four years of community building, the two churches concluded that they were ready to take a new step, to more directly confront the history of racial violence in the country through a visit to the National Memorial for Peace and Justice in Montgomery. The night before the trip, the twenty-one members from both churches, ranging in age from their twenties to their seventies, held a meeting to discuss their hopes and worries about the trip. While there were some shared anxieties about the emotional impact of the experience, especially within a racially mixed group, there were also some that were distinctive to white and black experiences.

More than one African American member said that anticipating the trip had recalled old stories, which they had somewhat suppressed, about family members disappearing. One recalled cautionary lessons he had received as a child about "how you carry yourself in public and around white people" to avoid potentially life-threatening confrontations. Another worried, "Am I gonna see names I recognize? What will I feel when I see these things, and do I want to go there?" A white member from a prominent family with a "proud Confederate history," who said only half-jokingly that his wife had signed him up for the trip, shared emotionally that he was just at this pretrip meeting realizing that his hopes and fears were the same: "That I'll feel responsible."[29]

During the visit, one particularly moving moment happened between Tim, an African American man, and Cathy, a white woman. As Cathy descended to the building's deepest point, where the rectangular steel county memorial columns to lynching victims become suspended overhead, she felt emotionally overwhelmed and sat down on a bench to collect her thoughts. Tim, who had just encountered the list of names inscribed on the column representing the county in which he grew up, caught her eye. He sat down next to Cathy without a word, and the tears came for both of them.

At a reflection service after the trip, Cathy summed up this simple but powerful moment: "We sat and shed tears together, neither of us completely knowing or understanding the source of those tears, but we were there for each other."[30] The racial complexity of this moment, however, was thick for Tim. He later confessed to Cathy that he couldn't help but think about what the evidence all around them demonstrated: that the simple physical proximity of a white woman and a black man was precisely the catalyst for the torture and murder of many a black man remembered on the columns suspended above them.

"We had some pretty holy moments come out of that trip," noted Dickison. Importantly, the two churches have done enough hard work together to realize that the goal "wasn't about making it okay; it was just about the power of mourning together these things."[31] And especially for the white church members, this kind of mourning together challenges the racial naiveté that whites have cultivated over centuries. Neither a trip to Florida nor two people grieving side by side is a simple thing when not all parties are white. And the massacre of African American worshippers by a Lutheran white supremacist is not an isolated incident perpetrated randomly by a madman; it is, rather, the harvest from the seeds of racism that white Christians allowed to flourish within a culture that saw itself as God's ideal civilization, even while condoning and theologically underwriting white Christian terrorism.

Looking ahead, the two First Baptist Churches are exploring some concrete next steps in their journey together. In addition to continuing their ongoing work with the New Baptist Covenant, they have engaged in a conversation with the Equal Justice Initiative to become sponsoring organizations that would "claim" the Bibb County steel column at the National Memorial. While talks are still under way and criteria still being worked out with EJI at the time of this writing, this work would entail bringing the memorial back to Macon, placing it somewhere prominent in the city, and committing to an ongoing slate of joint programming and racial justice work. Asked how far along in the journey he thought the churches are, Dickison replied, "I think everybody feels like we are still scratching the surface.... I think we're just getting started. I think people in both churches feel that way."[32]

Duluth, Minnesota: A Memorial to Lynching Victims Outside the South

The cultural distance between Macon and Minnesota is immense, but the specter of lynching found its way even here. Slavery was prohibited in Minnesota from the time it was admitted to the Union as a state in 1858. Settled initially by Scandinavian, German, and Irish immigrants after Native Americans were pushed westward, the state continues to be dominated by this cultural and religious heritage. Religiously speaking, white mainline Protestants and white Catholics account for four in ten residents. On the Protestant side, Minnesota is home to the greatest number of Lutherans of any state; in 2016, adherents to Lutheranism alone comprised 23 percent of Minnesotans.[33] The state is also one of the whitest states in the country. At the turn of the century, Minnesota's two million residents were 99 percent white; even today, about eight in ten Minnesotans are non-Hispanic whites.[34]

The city of Duluth is nestled on the tip of Lake Superior, less than two hundred miles from the Canadian border. It is also the site of one of the most widely attended and documented lynchings in the country. The three black victims—Elmer Jackson, Elias Clayton, and Isaac McGhie—were not residents of Duluth but were working as roustabouts for a traveling circus that was in town for a single day in June 1920. A young white couple accused them, without witnesses or evidence, of attacking the man and raping the woman. Although there was no evidence and no trial, the men were arrested and placed in the local jail.

That night, a white mob of more than ten thousand people—representing about 10 percent of the town's population of ninety-nine thousand—swarmed the jail, marched the men to the town square, and hung them one at a time from a lamppost. After the hangings, the crowd parted to allow a car to come through so they could use the headlights to illuminate the scene. After adjusting the rope length of one of the victims to better fit in the frame, photographs were taken, which were later sold as postcards.[35] The white police officers on duty did little to interfere.

In 2003, residents of Duluth unveiled a large memorial for the three men who were lynched. What started as a campaign to add a plaque to the site of the violence ended with the creation of a large,

fifty-three-by-seventy-foot sculpture paid for by $267,000 in dona-
tions that poured in from the community. One anonymous $10,000
donation came from a female relative of a man who had been working at the jail that fateful night, charged with ensuring the inmates'
safety; she said the events of that night had haunted him the rest of
his life.

The idea for creating the Clayton Jackson McGhie Memorial came
from Heidi Bakk-Hansen, a white Duluth resident. After reading *The
Lynchings in Duluth*—a book by a local relative of the former mayor
that was originally published under the title *They Was Just Niggers*—
Bakk-Hansen couldn't stop thinking about these crimes when she
drove past the intersection on her way to work downtown.[36] In 2000,
just ahead of the eightieth anniversary of the event, she wrote an article about it in the local alternative weekly publication the *Ripsaw
News*, entitled "Duluth's Lingering Shame."[37] The article sparked
broader interest in the anniversary vigil and in ongoing conversations
about what might be done to help the community come to terms with
this part of its history.

Bakk-Hansen soon gathered a small group of people who shared
her concerns, including fellow Duluth residents Henry L. Banks, who
is black, and Catherine Ostos, who is Latina. Together the three of
them spearheaded a campaign to create a public memorial that would
tell the truth about this terrible event in the city's history that whites
had largely repressed and tried to forget, and that the tiny minority of
black residents talked about only among themselves.

Three years later, in October 2003, that vision came to fruition.
More than three thousand people turned out for the memorial's unveiling. A processional, featuring New Orleans–style jazz music, followed the route the men had been forced to walk from the jail to the
intersection and featured the mayor, local clergy, and schoolchildren.
Most of the attendees and speakers at the event were local, but there
were also others who flew in from across the country, such as Warren Read, a fourth-grade teacher from Kingston, Washington. While

doing genealogical research on his family, Read was horrified to discover that his great-grandfather, Louis Dondino, had been convicted and sentenced to five years in prison for being one of the ringleaders of the lynching mob, although he only served about one year in prison. When he received the news about the monument unveiling, Read asked if he could come to symbolically apologize to Elmer, Elias, and Isaac, and to their families and descendants.

In his remarks at the unveiling, Read noted how the postcard image of that night had frozen that awful racial violence in time, and he expressed his hopes that the day's event would provide an alternative image of accountability and reconciliation: "I stand here today as a representative of [my great-grandfather's] legacy, and I willingly place that responsibility on my shoulders."[38] Read continued, "As a family, we have used the discovery of this as a tool for continued discovery of ourselves. This means our past, present, and future selves, and a lesson that true shame is not in the discovery of a terrible event such as this, but in the refusal to acknowledge and learn from that event."[39]

To be sure, the placing of a public monument hasn't solved all of Duluth's racial problems or prevented ongoing expressions of white supremacy. But the commitment to tell this truth has given the community a moral anchor point that has demanded a different kind of accountability and response in the face of continued challenges. For example, on Election Day in 2012, an effigy of President Barack Obama was found hanging from a billboard in Duluth. In response, the mayor's office, along with the board of trustees from the Clayton Jackson McGhie Memorial, declared that as stewards of that memorial, they were required to speak out. Their response looked to the memorial as a public commitment "to build a more just and inclusive community." Based on that down payment on a different future for the city in race relations, they declared:

"As a community, we cannot tolerate bigotry and hate. We cannot ignore or remain indifferent to the heinous nature of this act. We can speak out and defy such behavior in our community. We can commit to actively eradicate racism and hatred in our midst."[40]

Years after the unveiling of the Duluth memorial, these initial efforts have continued to pay dividends. After the opening of the National Memorial for Peace and Justice in 2018, a group of thirty-five Duluth residents gathered to make the 1,223-mile trip to Montgomery. The group included many who had been present from the beginning of this journey, including Bakk-Hansen, who was checking people onto the bus with a clipboard. But it also included some new faces, such as Mike Tusken, Duluth's chief of police, who is also the grandnephew of Irene Tusken, the white woman who falsely accused the African American men of raping her. Tusken didn't know about his own family's connection to the lynchings until the unveiling of the memorial in 2003. "This has been a journey for me, being that I didn't find out for years my family's history," Tusken noted in an interview ahead of the trip. "I can't miss this. It's too big for our nation, too big for our city."[41]

Between the 2003 Duluth memorial and the 2018 National Memorial for Peace and Justice opening, Warren Read, now fifty-one, continued his genealogical research and located the family of Elmer Jackson. He connected with Virginia Huston—Jackson's cousin, who is in her seventies and still living in Jackson's hometown of Pennytown, Missouri—and told her what he had discovered about that terrible night and his own family's connection to it.

After some email exchanges, the two agreed to meet in Montgomery during the Duluth delegation's visit and to tour the National Memorial together. Standing outside the EJI Legacy Museum on Commerce Street, the companion museum to the National Memorial, Huston introduced Read to others who didn't know the connection, saying:

> Warren is my baby brother now. He brought the research to us
> to let us know what happened. We didn't know what happened

to Elmer, but with his research, we now know. We have closure. Warren's great-grandfather, he was instrumental in getting the lynch mob. But that's not Warren. He shouldn't have any guilt feelings or anything. We're going to look forward, we're not looking back. We're going to build ourselves up, and live for today and live for tomorrow. He will always be my brother, and I love him very much.[42]

Following the tour of the National Memorial for Peace and Justice, Chief Tusken was visibly moved, and noted that the experience had convinced him that feelings of grief or shame had to give way to commitments to action. "Leaving this memorial, I think everyone has to ask themselves, 'What are you personally going to do to confront racism? To make sure that people have access and equality?' And that really is the takeaway everyone should leave with: What are you going to do?"[43]

Each of these contemporary stories of hope is, against the historical backdrop of racial injustice, modest. But they are concrete and meaningful efforts at confession coupled with steps toward, or at least a strong conviction about the necessity of, repair. And they serve as examples of contemporary wakefulness in the face of centuries of white apathy and slumber. Looking ahead, the large Edmund Burke inscription on the walls behind the life-size bronze statues of the three Duluth lynching victims is a good description of where we are, at the very beginning of this journey: "An event has happened, upon which it is difficult to speak and impossible to remain silent."

Retelling Our Own Stories

In addition to telling more honest public stories, those of us who have grown up under the protective canopy of white Christian America need to tell a more truthful story about our own lives, both in the present and the past. My own experience has been that it has taken first an openness to the possible existence of a different story and only a modest amount of initial effort—a week of daily journaling, for example—before the light shifts, the forgotten or repressed stories begin to emerge, and the scenery transforms slowly. Then it takes some digging with enough conviction and curiosity to overcome the inevitable defensiveness that rears its head as the veneer of innocence encasing treasured family lore begins to chip away. But while there is anxiety, and even some shame and terror, in recovering a truer narrative about ourselves, there is also something far more valuable: the possibility of a return to health, with these painful revelations serving as the first signposts marking the path out of what can only be called a kind of self-induced insanity.

In *The Fire Next Time*, James Baldwin wrote that one of the reasons African Americans, on the whole, had felt so little hatred toward white Americans, compared with what history might suggest was due, was that they perceived white Americans to be stuck in a form of madness that prevented them from coming into full human maturity. Baldwin described this insight this way:

> The American Negro has the great advantage of having never believed that collection of myths to which white Americans cling: that their ancestors were all freedom-loving heroes, that they were born in the greatest country the world has ever seen, or that Americans are invincible in battle and wise in peace, that Americans have always dealt honorably with Mexicans and Indians and all other neighbors or inferiors.... The tendency has really been, insofar as this was possible, to dismiss white people as the slightly mad victims of their own brainwashing. One watched the lives they led. One could not be fooled about that; one watched the things they did and the excuses that they gave themselves, and if a white man was really in trouble, deep trouble, it was to the Negro's door that he came. And one felt

that if one had had that white man's worldly advantages, one would never have become as bewildered and as joyless and as thoughtlessly cruel as he.[44]

This journey toward self-realization and sanity isn't a simple one, but it begins with the act of telling a more complete, and truer, story. Here's what the beginning of mine looks like.

On a top shelf in my house is a family Bible that belonged to my fifth great-grandfather on my mother's side. Printed in 1815, it is inscribed on the front inside cover with the following words: "Presented by Nathaniel Ellis to his friend Pleasant Moon, July 17th, 1825." Pleasant Moon (1800–1843) was among the first generation of my mother's family to be born in Georgia, where five generations of my family have lived in either Twiggs County or Bibb County, the adjacent county on the north that is the home of Macon. Both of my parents grew up in East Macon, and our family was one of the few that had moved away; I have warm memories of visiting a host of aunts, uncles, and cousins on both sides during our yearly pilgrimage back "home." Pleasant's father, William H. Moon, my sixth great-grandfather, had been born in 1740 in Albemarle County, Virginia, and served in the Revolutionary army. Sometime after 1790, he moved his family to the Georgia frontier, on land that was being seized by the Georgia government from the indigenous inhabitants of the land, the Creek and Cherokee Indians, and distributed via rolling lotteries to white settlers.[45]

Although I have not been able to locate a will for my fifth great-grandfather, I have been able to locate one for his uncle (his father's brother) and namesake, Pleasant Moon Sr. (1742–1818), who also made the journey from Virginia to Georgia with the extended family at the close of the eighteenth century. The will of my sixth great-uncle is an illuminating window into the role slavery played in my family's modest fortunes, and more generally its role among what we'd think of today as white lower-middle-class families. While they had means to relocate from Virginia, my Baptist Georgia ancestors weren't in the wealthy planter class of *Gone with the Wind*. Typical land lots dispensed by the state of Georgia during this period, for example, were between 160 and 200 acres—large enough to farm beyond mere subsistence but nowhere near the size of the major cotton plantations in the area.[46]

At his death in 1818, the county recorded both his will and an "Inventory of the Goods and Chattles [*sic*] of Pleasant Moon, Deceased." The inventory was thorough, including items like "1 young bay mare @ $60. And 1 bay horse cart @ $35"; "1 cow at $15 and 7 head of sheep at $11"; "1 feather bed and furniture @ $90"; and "1 shot gun @ $11." Not counting the land, my sixth great-uncle's estate was fairly modest, totally $2,293.22, or approximately $46,000 in 2019 dollars.

Most surprising, though, were two listings near the top of the household inventory: "1 negro woman named Naomi @ $800, & 1 named Susan @ $450," totaling $1,250; and on the line below that, "1 named Eliza at $275, & 1 named Bird, a boy @ $150," totaling $425. To put this into perspective, there is no other single line in the entire page-long household inventory that registers more than $100. Taken together, these two lines of human slave property totaled $1,675, accounting for an astonishing 73 percent of the assets of the estate. In other words, even among my barely-above-subsistence-farming ancestors, their way of life and economic well-being were thoroughly dependent on owning slaves.

On September 20, 1920, Isham Andrews, my great-grandfather and the husband of Pleasant Moon's great-granddaughter, was killed. He was supervising the pulling of a post at the John Sant & Sons clay mines near Dry Branch, Georgia, when a steel cable snapped and struck him, breaking his arm and crushing his skull. This event sent shock waves through my mother's side of the family, leaving my great-grandmother Beulah with little money and four small children. It was ultimately too much for her to cope with. She essentially left the four kids to fend for themselves—leaving the two older ones who were in their early teens at the time to care for the two younger ones—while she pursued two subsequent husbands and started another family with one of them. This family disarray righted itself only two generations later with my mother, Beulah's granddaughter through her second marriage, who was adopted and raised in a stable household by Beulah's daughter from the first marriage and her husband.

I grew up vaguely knowing this story of the tragic, premature death of my great-grandfather at the age of thirty-six. But when I was in high school, my great-uncle (Isham's son) told me a more sinister side of the story that reflected the racial dynamics of the time. Although the *Atlanta Constitution* reported that my great-grandfather's death was an accident, and no evidence was ever publicly presented otherwise, according to my great-uncle, Isham's coworkers blamed his death on an African American working that day.[47] The next week, as my great-uncle told the story, the black man they singled out was "accidentally" crushed by a heavy cart of clay at the mine.[48]

I know what havoc my great-grandfather's death wreaked in my mother's family. But I have no way of knowing what demons this retributive white racial violence unleashed in that African American man's family. I certainly know that he was a black man living in Jim Crow–era Georgia in the 1920s, one of the most brutal periods of white racial terrorism in the country. And I know that my white great-grandfather was a supervisor, while the African American man was a line worker, most likely living near poverty in a highly segregated society with few resources. He probably lived with some sense of vulnerability and the fragility of life on a daily basis. Given the dangers of clay mining, I'm sure he worried that a mistake with the heavy machinery in the open-pit mines could lead to serious injury or death. And given the ferocity of white supremacy in 1920s middle Georgia, I can only assume that both he and his family wondered, as he left for work each day, whether a misstep with his white coworkers or the wrong encounter on the road might be more perilous than the mine.

When my great-uncle first told me this story, I simply accepted it. I don't remember asking any questions. But I was also puzzled about the significance of it and why he would take pains to pass it along to me. Over the years, it has stayed with me. As I reflect on it now, the word that comes to me to describe my great-uncle's disposition as he told the story is *satisfaction*. While he never spelled out its full meaning, the story seemed designed to convey a reassurance about our place in the social pecking order—that even if accidental, the death of a white man would demand retribution. When a white man was killed, in other words, the universe lurched sideways. Retaliatory racial violence promised to balance the scales, reinscribing white dominance particularly through its arbitrariness.

With the exception of the few preschool years I lived in Wichita Falls, Texas, I have never lived in a county that is free from a history of lynching. In reverse chronological order, here are the counties in which I've lived and the number of documented cases of white racial terrorism: Montgomery County, Maryland (2); Greene County, Missouri (4); DeKalb County, Georgia (4); Tarrant County, Texas (1); Hinds County, Mississippi (22); Bexar County, Texas (6). The place in which I spent most of my formative years, from the time I was seven to twenty-one, particularly stands out. At twenty-two lynchings, it is the county with the fourth-highest number of lynchings in Mississippi and is tied for fifteenth place as the county with the most lynchings nationwide. At the National Memorial for Peace and Justice, the engravers had to use a smaller font to fit all the names and dates on the six-foot steel memorial for the county. Even this awful tally understates the case. My home state, which lauds itself as "the hospitality state," contains such a density of counties with legacies of lynching that they drive up the total to 654, giving Mississippi the dishonor of having the highest number of recorded lynchings of any state.

My experience through the lens of the nicknames of my high school and college reenacted the history of white oppression in reverse order. As I noted earlier, my high school's nickname was the Rebels, the mascot was Colonel Reb, and the band played "Dixie" as a cheerleader ran down the sidelines with a large Confederate battle flag each time the football team scored a touchdown. My college experience wasn't much better. My Southern Baptist–affiliated college, Mississippi College, were the Choctaws, and the mascot was an Indian figure with a cartoonish oversized head in full headdress. Women's social clubs (Greek sororities weren't allowed on campus) were "tribes" named after Indian-sounding or Indian-derived names such as Nenamoosha, Swannanoa, and Kissimee. To rouse the crowd at sporting events, the band played stereotyped, minor-key music (think bad early westerns) while the crowds—which included me at the time—made an up-and-down tomahawk motion in unison with our right arms bent at the elbow, chanting, "Scalp 'em, Choctaws, scalp 'em!"

Conclusion

I'm thoroughly convinced that my story is unremarkable. My ancestors weren't large plantation owners, Confederate generals, or, as far as I know, active members of the KKK. My parents were the first in each of their families to go to college. My ancestors were more carried along by than shapers of the great currents of history. Somehow I had a sense that this more modest history provided some inoculation against white supremacy's potency. As I've moved through the process of writing this book, of retelling my own story, however, I've been astonished at how ubiquitous the claims of white supremacy have been on my life. I grew up knowing that my parents had made a conscious decision to shield me and my siblings from the worst of the racism that was ubiquitous in our grandparents' generation and before. But even with that protection, the ways in which white supremacy crept into my worldview, my faith, and even my body are overwhelming.

I'd wager that many—maybe even most—white people, with little effort, could uncover a very similar narrative about their own family and experience, and the ways in which white supremacy, like kudzu, has crept its way forward through the family tree. If we're going to save ourselves, and our country, from being strangled by this invasive parasite, we will first need to develop the discernment to distinguish between it and the healthy branches straining under its weight. And even then, we will need to find the resolve not just to prune the parasite back for a season but also to kill it, root to stem.

Reckoning

Toward Responsibility and Repair

Where do we go from here? One of the most common responses I hear when this question is raised is that time will take care of most of our racial problems—a euphemism for the extinction of older whites who hold racist views. I've heard variations of this argument from a wide array of sources: from young people who have tried unsuccessfully to raise these issues within their churches, to progressive political operatives doubling down on the inevitability of the "New America."

I even witnessed a visceral expression of this sentiment during my visit to Richmond to conduct research for this book. As I was leaving the headquarters of the United Daughters of the Confederacy, where I had been doing archival research, four demonstrators who looked to be in their sixties or seventies had set up five ten-foot staffs topped with large Confederate battle flags on the sidewalk near a busy intersection, accompanied by a placard that read "Save our Monuments." During the ten or fifteen minutes I observed, most passing motorists ignored them. A few honked their approval but at least three times as many yelled objections, such as "No racism in Richmond!" or "Go home and take that flag with you!" But one incensed younger white man put his gray minivan in park at the light, stormed around the front of his car to the sidewalk, and stood in front of them, yelling, "I can't wait 'til all you old human pieces of shit just die, so I can piss on your grave." With that, he returned to his car, put it into gear, and sped off.

While it's tempting, especially faced with the enormity of the problem, to believe that the oldest generation of whites will take white supremacy with them to the grave, finally removing it from our religious and political lives, such blind hopes misunderstand the nature of white supremacy, particularly its tenacious ability to endure from generation to generation. Contrary to the assertions of white Christian theology's freewill individualism, the hosts of white supremacy are not just individuals. Even after the last white American who grew up in Jim Crow America has died, the legacy of white supremacy will survive because, after hundreds of years of nurturing and reinforcement, it has become part of our culture and institutions. Sometimes it lies dormant, but until it is excised, it remains potentially active in overt and subtle ways.

If we get past denial, if we get past the magical thinking that time will settle our moral obligations for us, the next challenge for white Christians today is to deal with the paralyzing notion that the weight of this history is so enormous that meaningful action is impossible. At one early meeting between the white and black members of the two First Baptist Churches in Macon, a white member confessed that she was simply overwhelmed and didn't know what to do. After a painful pause, an African American woman responded calmly, "Of course you are."[1] This reply was a palpable moment of compassion and accountability. While giving the white woman permission to feel overwhelmed, the African American woman's response also gently affirmed that this discomfort was not an excuse for inaction.

Several common defense mechanisms protect the place of the white supremacy gene in Christianity. Once we acknowledge its presence, these tactics become more apparent. Southern Baptist Seminary president Al Mohler, for example, insists that "we must repent of our own sins, we cannot repent for the dead"—while refusing to have even a cursory conversation about financial reparations related to the seminary's slaveholding past.[2] In stark contrast, Virginia Theological Seminary, affiliated with the Episcopal Church of America, announced in 2019 the creation of a $1.7 million endowment fund, the annual proceeds of which will be allocated to the descendants of enslaved people who worked at the seminary and to African American alumni who are working at historically black churches. The Very Reverend Ian S. Markham, president of the seminary, noted in a statement, "This is a start. As we seek to mark [the] Seminary's milestone of 200 years, we do so conscious that our past is a mixture of sin as well as grace. This is the Seminary recognizing that along with repentance for past sins, there is also a need for action."[3]

Popular white evangelical author John MacArthur Jr.—in a statement that has garnered more than eleven thousand approving signatures—denies that "one's ethnicity establishes any necessary connection to any particular sin" and rejects "critical race theory" or "any teaching that encourages racial groups to view themselves as privileged oppressors or entitled victims of oppression."[4] And US Senate majority leader Mitch McConnell, having declared that America has mostly dispensed with the "sin of slavery" by electing Barack Obama as president, dismisses any serious discussion of slavery reparations because "it'd be pretty hard to figure out who to compensate."[5]

Each of these responses, from the theological to the practical, is actually evidence of the moment of reckoning that is upon us. They are the desperate seizures of white consciences, squirming to escape the convicting evidence and protect their own innocence. In a 2019 interview with Religion News Service, Eric Metaxis—white evangelical author, radio host, and strong Donald Trump supporter—illustrated the tortured self-deception such defensiveness produces. Asked about the relationship between Christianity and racism, Metaxis responded as follows:

You always hear about slave-owning Christians, or you hear about people using the Bible to justify slavery. Well, even though that's true, do you hear about the fact that it was what we would today call "Evangelical Christians" who led the battle for the abolition of the slave trade? They were in the front lines of saying that slavery is wrong—and you can look to the civil rights movement. It's very similar. The churches were the place where you found that.... I can tell you most Christians that I know, if they really see racism or injustice, they get more angry about it than any secular people I know. They would rightly get outraged by it. The idea that being a white evangelical means you are sort of comfortable with white privilege is deeply offensive to people—because not only do they disagree with it, but their whole lives are meant to represent the opposite of that.[6]

As incredulous as such assertions are against the plain witness of history and current public opinion, this sort of knee-jerk defensiveness is understandable, even predictable, as a first response. Mercer University history professor and FBC of Christ church member Doug Thompson witnessed firsthand the challenges the evidence of the church's racist past had created, especially for its most faithful and long-standing members. Thompson noted that the church's self-perception was, like most, self-congratulatory: "We were good people who did good things."

It took time, courage, and relationships with African American fellow Christians for the church to finally admit, in a spirit of honesty and repentance, that while that self-perception contained some truth, "it's not an accurate depiction."[7] FBC pastor Scott Dickison vividly described his personal experience with the process this way: "It is painful and at times humiliating, and in the end requires nothing less than the death of a vision of ourselves that we may be surprised to learn is so deeply rooted within us."[8]

Allowing this discomfort—and at times extreme anguish—to come, allowing the waves of the past to crash on the shore of the present until the rhythm is familiar enough to ring in the ears, is a critical step toward healing and wholeness. It is also perhaps the biggest challenge for us white Christians, who have been conditioned to move through our lives preoccupied with personal sin but unburdened by social injustice. The moral call now before us is not to solve an insurmountable problem but to begin a journey back to ourselves, our fellow citizens, and God.

Reckoning with White Supremacy in American Christianity

The etymology of the word *reckoning* highlights two branches of historical meaning: one more narrative and one more transactional. On the Old English side, *reckoning* means to give a full verbal account of something, but its Dutch and German roots connote notions of economic justice, a fair settling of accounts. In religious terms, these meanings could be translated to confession and repair, and sustained forms of both will be necessary to move toward health.

As they emphasized in conversations with me, Reverend Goolsby and Reverend Dickison, the pastors of the two First Baptist Churches in Macon, don't pretend to have figured it all out, nor do they have a grand master plan for the future. But they have learned a few important lessons that can help us understand what an honest reckoning looks like. The earliest work they did together, their first tentative steps along a murky path, focused strictly on building community. As they built trust, they were able to begin moving toward a fuller accounting. They were able to start asking some hard questions, trying to understand the ways in which racism and the ideology of white supremacy had shaped their relationship to each other—and, for the members of the white church, how it had distorted their own self-understanding and their faith. These conversations have led them through some initial, deliberate work of confession.

One of the most impressive things about the journey of the two

First Baptist Churches in Macon is that FBC of Christ has not suc-
cumbed to a mistake that most white Christians make when they engage in this work: reaching too directly for reconciliation. Dickison
had this to say about the challenges of the reconciliation paradigm:

> I've stopped using the word *reconciliation* . . . for what we're
> doing. I've started using *justice work* more, not saying *racial
> reconciliation*, but really talking about *racial justice*. When
> we throw around the word *reconciliation*, especially as white
> Christians, white people, we're betraying our desire to just kind
> of move through all of the hard stuff just to get to the happy
> stuff. So, when we're talking about justice work, for me we're
> getting into these much stickier questions of what has been
> lost, what is owed.[9]

And justice, rather than reconciliation, takes white Christians into difficult terrain indeed. Even with all of the work done at FBC of Christ
to come to terms with the church's history, Dickison says, "We have lamented that, we have confessed that to a degree, but what we haven't
done is repented for that." That next step, repentance, involves the
difficult question of restitution and repair.

Dickison also indicated that the inevitable destination on his
church's journey will be the question of restitution:

> When I look down the road and think what would it look like
> for us to have really done the work that I believe we're called
> to do, it has to be a measure of restitution and accounting—a
> tangible economic accounting for what was taken and what is
> owed. The gospel lesson this past Sunday is, "For where your
> treasure is, there your heart will be also," and I think what Jesus
> means there by "treasure" is a pretty broad definition of every-
> thing that is meaningful to us. But unless we really account for
> our possessions, our economic possessions, resources, if we

leave that out of it, we are leaving a huge part of our heart behind. That has to be a part for us.[10]

Such conversations are bound to be difficult. But one thing Goolsby
and Dickison have discovered is that people are capable of changing along the way. What sounds like an impossible demand now may
seem like a natural next step flowing from an expanded perspective at
a later point in the journey.

Reconsidering "the Mark of Cain"

Inside both the National Memorial for Peace and Justice visitor center and the Legacy Museum in downtown Montgomery, there is an
installation composed of rows and rows of glass jars on wooden racks,
containing soil samples from lynching sites. These samples were collected as part of EJI's Community Remembrance Project, which seeks
to place historical markers at lynching sites, while bringing back soil
to a central location as a tangible way of documenting and memori-
alizing these victims of racial violence. The jars are labeled with the
names, dates, and locations of the victims in uniform white letters,
which contrast with the different colors and textures of the soils. Some
hold the sand of coastal regions, while others contain dark-black Delta
cotton soil, the red clay of Alabama and Georgia, or the mossy loam
of the low country. While these are contemporary soil samples that do
not literally contain human remains from the lynchings, the way they
bridge space and time is affecting.

Although I didn't find any biblical references near the Community
Remembrance Project exhibits, for those familiar with the Bible, the
jars of soil powerfully evoke a story from the book of Genesis about
the first set of brothers, Cain and Abel, born to Adam and Eve. In
the ancient story, Cain becomes jealous of his younger brother, Abel,
and, in a fit of anger, murders him in a field, far from the eyes of his

parents. Afterward, God confronts a defiant and indignant Cain, who lies about the murder:

> Now Cain talked with Abel his brother; and it came to pass, when they were in the field, that Cain rose up against Abel his brother and killed him.
> Then the Lord said to Cain, "Where is Abel your brother?"
> He said, "I do not know. Am I my brother's keeper?"[11]
> The LORD said, "What have you done? Listen! Your brother's blood cries out to me from the ground. Now you are under a curse and driven from the ground, which opened its mouth to receive your brother's blood from your hand. When you work the ground, it will no longer yield its crops for you. You will be a restless wanderer on the earth."[12]

Notably, this story is "the mark of Cain" narrative that has served (in tandem with the "curse of Ham" story) as the most prominent theological justification of white supremacy.[13] When Cain complains that his punishment is too harsh and that he will be killed if he is driven from his homeland, God agrees to mark him in some way as a visible sign of God's protection, even while he remains under the curse. For generations, white Christians have interpreted this passage to describe the origins of dark-skinned humans, whom they understood as a race created not from the nobility of divine breath but from human acts of jealousy, murder, and deception.

In the reflections of these glass jars of dirt dug from lynching site grounds, however, a different understanding materializes, one that inverts the traditional white interpretation of this story. I'll be blunt: it is white Americans who have murdered our black and brown brothers and sisters. After the genocide and forced removal of Native Americans, the enslavement of millions of Africans, and the lynching of more than 4,400 of their surviving descendants, it is white Americans who have used our faith as a shield to justify our actions, deny our responsibility, and insist on our innocence. We, white Christian Americans, are Cain.

And despite our denials, equivocations, protests, and excuses, as the biblical narrative declares, the soil itself preserves and carries a testimony of truth to God. Today God's anguished questions—"Where is your brother?" and "What have you done?"—still hang in the air like morning mist on the Mississippi River. We are only just beginning to discern these questions, let alone find the words to voice honest answers.

These queries are, of course, rhetorical, even in the biblical story. God certainly knows the answers, and, if we're honest with ourselves, so do we. I've always found it puzzling that God asks these questions of Cain. When I was younger, I thought perhaps God was playing a divine game of "gotcha" with Cain, laying a trap and testing him to see if he would lie. But I think the better interpretation, and one that is relevant for us, is that God is giving Cain the opportunity for confession, for honesty, knowing that this would be the best path for Cain to begin reckoning with the traumatic experience of having killed his own brother, the pain he has unleashed for himself and others, and the consequences that will inevitably come. God's questions were a compassionate invitation to Cain, giving him an opportunity to avoid the twisting of his personality that this trauma, and the perpetual deception required to cover it up, would inevitably bring.

But just as we have, Cain doubles down. Throwing his own rhetorical question back at God—"Am I my brother's keeper?"—Cain not only indignantly denies any knowledge of his brother's fate but also rejects the very idea that he should be expected to answer God's questions. Here, it's clear that Cain's decision to lie about his hand in the murder and to deny responsibility makes his future harder, just as our denials threaten our own future. The challenge for white Americans today, and white Christians in particular, is whether and how we are going to answer these questions: "Where is your brother?" and "What have you done?"

As we contemplate our answers, there are certainly important pragmatic considerations. Continued racial inequality, injustice, and unrest harm our ability to live together in a democratic society. Racial prejudice and divisions provide weapons for our enemies who wish to weaken us. White supremacy is sand in the gears of the economy and a source of life-threatening conflict in our communities.

But another important consideration, and one that we white Americans have given very little thought to, is the ways in which our complicity in this history, and our unwillingness to face it, have warped our own identities. Just as Cain was separated from his natural family, we have allowed white supremacy to separate us not just from our black brothers and sisters but also from a true sense of who we are.

We are Cain. It is white Christian souls that have been most disfigured by the myth of white supremacy. And it is we who are most in need of repentance and restoration, not just for the sake of the descendants of those whom our ancestors kidnapped, robbed, whipped, murdered, and oppressed; not just for those who today are unjustifiably shot by police, unfairly tried, wrongfully convicted, denied jobs, and poorly educated in failing schools; but for the sake of our children and our own future. And there's hope here in the Genesis story. Even for the guilty and unrepentant Cain, God acts to preserve the possibility of a new future.

The White Problem

This brings us to the crux of the matter; what James Baldwin powerfully articulated as "the white problem." Writing just months after the assassinations of Martin Luther King Jr. and Bobby Kennedy, which precipitated violent protests in more than 120 cities in tumultuous and bloody 1968, Baldwin penned the following in a *New York Times* op-ed:

I will flatly say that the bulk of this country's white population impresses me, and has so impressed me for a very long time, as being beyond any conceivable hope of moral rehabilitation. They have been white, if I may so put it, too long; they have been married to the lie of white supremacy too long; the effect on their personalities, their lives, their grasp of reality, has been as devastating as the lava which so memorably immobilized the citizens of Pompeii. They are unable to conceive that their version of reality, which they want me to accept, is an insult to my history and a parody of theirs and an intolerable violation of myself.[14]

These are sharp words from a man who, despite his own experiences with racial bigotry and injustice and his extraordinary perceptive abilities, consistently held out hope for change in his writings, refusing to dip his pen in the well of racial hatred. When he was young, and a black minister told him that he should, under no circumstances, give his seat to a white woman on public transportation, Baldwin reported that his response was this: "But what was the point, the purpose, of *my* salvation if it did not permit me to behave with love toward others, no matter how they behaved toward me?" When he was gaining recognition as a writer, he was recruited by the founder and leader of the Nation of Islam, Elijah Muhammad. But Baldwin wrote that he knew an insurmountable barrier stood between him and that movement: that, whatever white people's sins, which were many, he could not sign on to the idea that whites were literally "devils."[15]

But even with his stubborn orientation toward love, Baldwin saw that any progress could come only if whites, and white Christians, specifically, could wrestle with the difficult truths of the intertwined histories of blacks and whites in America. "If we are going to build a multiracial society, which is our only hope," Baldwin said in his 1968 testimony before a US House Select Subcommittee that was considering a bill to establish a National Commission on Negro History and

Culture, "then one has got to accept that I have learned a lot from you, and a lot of it is bitter, but you have a lot to learn from me, and a lot of that will be bitter. That bitterness is our only hope. That is the only way we get past it."[16]

For Baldwin, this bitterness, of coming into fuller acknowledgment of the harm we have done, is the beginning of the path to freedom. Far from believing in the inevitability of oppression, he declared, "I think that people can be better than that, and I know that people can be better than they are."[17] In the end, Baldwin appeals to his fellow white citizens, arguing that love is the thing that can ultimately resolve the racial dilemma we currently face. "Love," Baldwin writes, "takes off the masks that we fear we cannot live without and know we cannot live within." Love requires us to see who we really are and to respond to the voices still crying out to us from the ground.

Conclusion: Seeing What's at Stake

Four hundred years after the first African slave landed on our shores, and more than 150 years after the abolition of slavery, a combination of social forces and demographic changes has brought the country to a crossroads. We white Christians must find the courage to face the fact that the version of Christianity that our ancestors built—"the faith of our fathers," as the hymn celebrates it—was a cultural force that, by design, protected and propagated white supremacy. We have inherited this tradition with scant critique, and we have a moral and religious obligation to face the burden of that history and its demand on our present. And we have to accept, given the way in which white supremacy has burrowed into our Christian identity, that refusing to address this sinister disorder in our faith will continue to generate serious negative consequences not just for our fellow Americans but also for ourselves and our children. Inaction is a tacit acceptance of white supremacy inhabiting our Christianity. Doing nothing will ensure that, even despite our best conscious intentions, we will continue to turn deaf ears to calls for racial justice.

The disruptive experience of current trends—particularly demographic change and the exodus of younger white adults from Christian churches over the last few decades—may provide motivation for change. But at this late point in our history, real reforms may arise only from the ashes of the current institutional forms of white Christianity.[18] One thing is clear: any lasting changes will necessarily involve extreme measures to detect and eradicate the distortions that centuries of accommodations to white supremacy have created.

Perhaps the most important first step toward health is to recover from our white-supremacy-induced amnesia. It is indeed difficult—and at times overwhelming—to confront historical atrocities. But if we want to root out an insidious white supremacy from our institutions, our religion, and our psyches, we will have to move beyond the forgetfulness and silence that have allowed it to flourish for so long. Importantly, as white Americans find the courage to embark on this journey of transformation, we will discover that the beneficiaries are not only our country and our fellow nonwhite and non-Christian Americans, but also ourselves, as we slowly recover from the disorienting madness of white supremacy.

This last point is only beginning to dawn on us white Christian Americans, who still believe too easily that racial reconciliation is the goal and that it may be achieved through a straightforward transaction: white confession in exchange for black forgiveness. But mostly this transactional concept is a strategy for making peace with the status quo—which is a very good deal indeed if you are white. I am not trying to be cynical here, but merely honest about how little even well-meaning whites have believed they have at stake in racial reconciliation efforts. Whites, and especially white Christians, have seen this project as an altruistic one rather than a desperate life-and-death struggle for their own future.

What few whites perceive, and this is a truth that has come late to me, is that we have far *more* at stake than our black fellow citizens in setting things right. As Baldwin provocatively put it, the civil rights movement began when an oppressed and despised people began to wake up collectively to what had happened to them.[19] The question today is whether we white Christians will also awaken to see what has happened to us, and to grasp once and for all how white supremacy has robbed us of our own heritage and of our ability to be in right relationships with our fellow citizens, with ourselves, and even with God. Reckoning with white supremacy, for us, is now an unavoidable moral choice.

Acknowledgments

I've dedicated this book to my spouse, Jodi Kanter, a writer, artist, and professor of theatre at George Washington University. Through four books and thirteen years of marriage, she has been my partner in every sense of the word. As I've accompanied her on her own academic journeys—especially the one leading to her most recent book, *Presidential Libraries as Performance: Curating American Character from Herbert Hoover to George W. Bush*—she's taught me how to see the world through a performance-studies lens. This perspective has deepened my understanding of the ways public memorials preserve and transmit social memory and communal values over time. It has fundamentally changed the way I see monuments, museums, flags, and other markers in public space. I am also grateful to Jodi for believing in this project, which was often challenging because of its personal nature, and helping protect time for writing amid our family's busy schedules. Jodi read every page and every revision, often on the same day it was drafted; I'm grateful to her for always being my earliest sounding board and my first and best editor.

I've also dedicated this book to the people of the two First Baptist Churches in Macon, Georgia: one predominantly black and one predominantly white. Together with their leaders—Reverend James W. Goolsby Jr., pastor of First Baptist Church (on New Street), and Reverend Scott Dickison, pastor of First Baptist Church of Christ—these congregations have begun to heal 170 years of racial injustice and division by courageously reckoning with the history of slavery, the Civil War, Reconstruction, segregation, and continued resistance among whites to full equal rights for African Americans. Beyond their example, I am grateful to both pastors for talking to me honestly about this challenging journey and to Reverend Dickison for hosting me in Macon for an additional set of conversations about the changes this deepening relationship was creating among his white congregation. These congregations are signs of hope in our fractured time and witnesses to the truth that racial healing and reconciliation, while possible, can only be realized as the mature fruits of repentance and reparative justice.

Books are always team projects, and I have been blessed to be a part of a vibrant intellectual community at Public Religion Research Institute (PRRI) for a decade now. The PRRI senior leadership team—Director of Research Natalie Jackson, Senior Director of Communications and External Affairs Jioni Palmer, and Chief of Staff Sean Sands—each read portions of the manuscript and gave me invaluable feedback. Melissa Deckman, PRRI board chair and the Louis L. Goldstein Professor of Public Affairs at Washington College, talked with me about the central ideas long before they coalesced into a book and helped me think through how to present the technical results of statistical models to a general audience.

I am deeply grateful to two other political scientists in the PRRI orbit for their assistance with the statistical modeling and analysis in chapter 5: Juhem Navarro-Rivera, a former PRRI research associate and the current political research director and managing partner at Socioanalitica Research, and Paul Djupe, associate professor of political science at Denison University. Juhem helped develop and test an early round of statistical models, and Paul independently helped develop and test the final set of models and graphics. While I am deeply indebted to Paul and Juhem, any shortcomings or errors in the analysis are of course my responsibility. Finally, Tim Duffy, PRRI's graphics design consultant, expertly produced production-ready versions of all the tables and charts in the book; and Drew Keavaney, a former PRRI intern, provided rigorous and efficient copyediting for the manuscript.

I have had the good fortune of working with Bob Bender, vice president and executive editor at Simon & Schuster, for both *The End of White Christian America* and *White Too Long*. Over these two projects, Bob has helped me adapt technical writing for a general audience, and he has an exceptionally steady hand as an editor. I'm also grateful for the efficiency and attentiveness of associate editor Johanna Li, who has kept the project moving on a tight timeline. My book agent, Roger Freet, has also gone above and beyond the call of duty, serving as a sounding board, strategist, and even occasional cheerleader when I've needed it. In-depth, early conversations with Roger helped shape the project, and I'm grateful to him for encouraging me to allow my personal stake in the research to show up on the page.

Funding for the PRRI surveys that informed the book was generously provided by the Carnegie Corporation of New York, the Nathan Cummings Foundation, the New World Foundation, and the Unitarian Universalist Veatch Program at Shelter Rock. Additionally, the principal survey for the analysis in chapter 5, PRRI's 2018 American Values Survey, was part of a decade-long partnership between PRRI and the Brookings Institution. Brookings senior fellows E. J. Dionne Jr. and Bill Galston have been amazing partners on this annual survey and were instrumental in creating, analyzing, and releasing the initial report at a public event at the Brookings Institution in October 2018.

Intellectual debts are always difficult to discern fully. I am especially indebted to a number of African American scholars, religious leaders, reporters, and writers who have shaped my thinking and my work, particularly on the question of how the Christian church has been complicit in abetting white supremacy: Adelle Banks, Charles M. Blow, James H. Cone, Jonathan Capehart, Kelly Brown Douglas, Lenny Duncan, Michael Eric Dyson, Eddie Glaude Jr., Obery M. Hendricks Jr., Willie James Jennings, Jacqui Lewis, Bryan N. Massingale, Toni Morrison, Joy Reid, Howard Thurman, Jemar Tisby, and Cornel West. And there are also the rarer white voices who have helped me deepen my insights into the problem that whiteness presents for Christians: Will Campbell, Gary Dorrien, Carolyn Renée Dupont, Michael O. Emerson, Jennifer Harvey, Paul Harvey, Richard Hughes, Bill Moyers, Walter Shurden, Christian Smith, Ted A. Smith, Jim Wallis, and James Wilson-Hartgrove.

I owe a particular debt to James Baldwin, from whose writing the title of this book is taken. I came to his work only in the last few years, but I was immediately captivated by how clearly he perceived the roots of racial strife and violence in America, flipping the script from the common parlance of "the Negro problem" to "the white problem." While it's perhaps surprising that the writing of a black, gay author hailing from Harlem a generation before my time would resonate with me—a white, straight southerner—I was moved that his unflinching perceptiveness, coupled with his own life experiences, did not fill him with hate and despair. I also found familiar his own deep wrestling with a Christianity that both attracted and disappointed him. Throughout the writing process, I was haunted by his call to whites in America, and particularly to white Christians, to wake up from their self-induced white supremacist nightmare. White Christians were plainly unprepared to heed this call to repentance a generation ago, and we still may be incapable today. But one way of reading this book is as an attempt to begin a white Christian response to Baldwin's invitation.

Finally, I am deeply grateful for my parents, Pat and Cherry Jones. My parents were both raised in Jim Crow–era Macon, Georgia. And the church in which they grew up and in which they were married was founded as a mission of the white First Baptist Church of Christ. While they inherited the Christian and southern culture of their time, handed down from four previous generations of our Baptist family who lived in Bibb and Twiggs Counties, Georgia, they made intentional decisions to shield me and my siblings from the overt prejudices that accompanied that legacy. While our family and our home church were comfortably apolitical in ways that only white families can be, my parents taught us everyone was equal, and—what is most important for children—they lived in a way that convinced us they believed it. This book is my attempt to understand and reckon with the power white supremacy continues to hold within white Christianity, even when there are good-faith efforts to resist it. While that work remains in process, without those consistent parenting decisions, both big and small, I would not have found the light to assess it critically.

My hope is that this book sheds more light on that path for my own children. The truth is—and this makes me more optimistic about the future—that I'm often catching up to them. While I was working on this book, my daughter was wrapping up her senior year at a public high school named after a member of President Abraham Lincoln's cabinet, and one of her favorite classes was an African American literature class. My fourth-grade son, Jasper, already knows the names of civil rights leaders, gleaned from school lessons that were not just conducted during Black History Month; and when we visited Harpers Ferry, he wrestled with the moral questions raised by John Brown's raid, sympathizing particularly with the story of Dangerfield Newby, one of Brown's men who was killed while trying to free his enslaved family. Their diverse friendship circles and their worldviews indicate that they are carrying far less baggage from our white supremacist past; but they also know enough of our history to realize that an ongoing diligence is needed, since people whose families have thought of themselves as white and Christian can still be blind to these dynamics. Thankfully, they are demonstrating that the same light that reveals the painful ugliness of the past also points the way to a more healthy future for white Christians and a more just future for us all.

— Appendix A —

Multivariate Regression Model Outputs Predicting Religious Identity

The table on page 245 contains the output tables for five different multivariate regression models conducted using PRRI's "2018 American Values Survey." Each column in the table represents a different model: model one predicts white Christian identity, model two predicts white evangelical Protestant identity, model three predicts white mainline Protestant identity, model four predicts white Catholic identity, and model five predicts white religiously unaffiliated identity.

The variables in the rows are the independent variables—the variables whose influence we are testing. The numbers in rows next to the dependent variable names represent their estimated effects in the analysis, showing how much a one-unit shift in the independent variable changes the dependent variable. A positive number means the probability of being in the dependent variable group (for instance, white evangelical Protestant) goes up as the independent variable increases; a negative number indicates the opposite—that the likelihood of being in the dependent variable group goes down. The numbers in parentheses below each estimate are "robust standard errors" and refer to the uncertainty in the estimate. A quick way to read this table is to look for an asterisk (*** p < 0.01, ** p < 0.05, * p < 0.1), which tells us that the effect is statistically significant; that is, that the effect is distinguishable from 0 (no effect). As a general rule, and unless otherwise specified, I have used the 95 percent confidence level (p < 0.05) as the threshold for significance in the discussion of the findings.

- The Racism Index refers to the composite variable described in chapter 5, with a higher score on the index representing more racist views. A score of 0 (least racist views) is the reference category. The values in the table represent the effect of a score of 1 (most racist views).

- "Party affiliation" was measured in a 5-point scale, with identifying as a Democrat as the reference category.

- "Education" was measured in a 4-point scale, with having no high school diploma as the reference category.

- "Region" was measured across four categories, with living in the Northeast as the reference category.

- "Women" was measured in two categories, with the reference category as men.

- "Age" was measured as a continuous variable running from 18 to 91.

- "Household income" was measured with eighteen categories, from those earning less than $5,000 to those making more than $200,000.

- "Own home" was measured in two categories: owning versus being rented or occupied without payment of cash rent. The latter is the reference category.

- "Church attendance" was measured in six categories, running from those who never attend on the low end to those who attend more than once a week on the high end.

- "Metropolitan area" was measured in two categories: living in a metropolitan area versus living in a nonmetropolitan area. The latter is the reference category.

- The Immigration Index refers to the composite variable described in appendix B, with a higher score on the index representing more anti-immigrant views. A score of 0 (least anti-immigrant views) is the reference category. The values in the table represent the effect of a score of 1 (most anti-immigrant views).

Multivariate Regression Model Outputs Predicting White Christian Identities

DEPENDENT VARIABLE

	Model 1 White Christian	Model 2 White Evangelical	Model 3 White Mainline	Model 4 White Catholic	Model 5 White Unaffiliated

INDEPENDENT VARIABLES

Racism Index (low to high)	3.25***	2.40***	1.51***	2.13***	-0.72
	(0.38)	(0.55)	(0.42)	(0.49)	(0.53)

Party Affiliation

Reference: Democrat

Leaning Democrat	0.14	0.90***	-0.04	-0.19	0.43**
	(0.19)	(0.30)	(0.22)	(0.28)	(0.22)
Independent	-0.59**	0.16	-0.44	-0.45	0.84**
	(0.29)	(0.47)	(0.42)	(0.42)	(0.38)
Leaning Republican	0.18	1.11***	-0.16	-0.25	0.67**
	(0.22)	(0.34)	(0.25)	(0.33)	(0.34)
Republican	0.79***	1.49***	0.00	0.03	-0.90**
	(0.22)	(0.32)	(0.25)	(0.28)	(0.36)

	Model 1 White Christian	Model 2 White Evangelical	Model 3 White Mainline	Model 4 White Catholic	Model 5 White Unaffiliated
Education Level					
Reference: No high school diploma					
High school graduate	0.11	0.21	0.86*	-0.66	0.60
	(0.30)	(0.42)	(0.46)	(0.42)	(0.49)
Some college	0.25	0.56	0.78*	-0.68*	0.84*
	(0.28)	(0.38)	(0.46)	(0.40)	(0.47)
BA degree or higher	0.26	0.22	0.93*	-0.55	1.07**
	(0.30)	(0.40)	(0.49)	(0.42)	(0.48)
Region					
Reference: Northeast					
Midwest	0.04	0.20	0.83***	-0.93***	0.38
	(0.20)	(0.29)	(0.24)	(0.23)	(0.28)
South	-0.77***	0.62**	0.26	-1.63***	-0.23
	(0.20)	(0.28)	(0.25)	(0.24)	(0.27)
West	-1.02***	0.40	-0.02	-2.12***	0.15
	(0.21)	(0.31)	(0.27)	(0.27)	(0.28)
Reference: Men					
Women	0.43***	0.19	0.39***	0.07	-0.52***
	(0.13)	(0.18)	(0.15)	(0.18)	(0.18)
Age (in years)	0.02***	0.00	0.02***	0.02***	-0.01*
	(0.00)	(0.01)	(0.00)	(0.01)	(0.01)
Household income (low to high)	0.04**	-0.03	0.02	0.07***	0.03
	(0.02)	(0.02)	(0.02)	(0.02)	(0.02)

	Model 1 White Christian	Model 2 White Evangelical	Model 3 White Mainline	Model 4 White Catholic	Model 5 White Unaffiliated
Reference: Not homeowner					
Own home	0.47***	0.06	0.43**	0.40*	0.48**
	(0.16)	(0.20)	(0.18)	(0.23)	(0.22)
Church attendance (low to high)	1.10***	2.79***	-1.11***	0.17	-6.93***
	(0.21)	(0.31)	(0.24)	(0.23)	(0.54)
Reference: Nonmetropolitan area					
Metropolitan area	-0.55***	-0.74***	-0.28	0.16	-0.39
	(0.20)	(0.24)	(0.21)	(0.27)	(0.27)
Immigration Index (low to high)	-0.44	-0.66	0.20	-0.50	-0.05
	(0.56)	(0.83)	(0.63)	(0.77)	(0.78)
Constant	-4.08***	-5.78***	-4.91***	-3.48***	0.05
	(0.54)	(0.76)	(0.66)	(0.66)	(0.72)
Observations	2,337	2,337	2,337	2,337	2,337

SOURCE: PRRI, AMERICAN VALUES SURVEY, 2018.

– Appendix B –

The Immigration Index

Just your impression: In the United States today, is there a lot of discrimination against any of the following groups, or not?

a. Blacks

b. Asians

c. Hispanics

Do you strongly agree, agree, disagree, or strongly disagree with the following statements?

a. It bothers me when I come into contact with immigrants who speak little or no English.

b. The American way of life needs to be protected from foreign influence.

Would you say that, in general, the growing number of newcomers from other countries threatens traditional American customs and values, or strengthens American society?

Which of the following statements comes closer to your own views:

Immigrants today strengthen our country because of their hard work and talents, or immigrants today are a burden on our country because they take our jobs, housing, and health care.

As you may know, US Census projections show that by 2045, African Americans, Latinos, Asians, and other mixed racial and ethnic groups will together be a majority of the population. Do you think the likely impact of this coming demographic change will be mostly positive or mostly negative?

In general, how well do you think each of the following describes immigrants coming to the US today?
a. They are hardworking.
b. They make an effort to learn English.
c. They mostly keep to themselves.
d. They have strong family values.
e. They burden local communities by using more than their share of social services.

We would like to get your views on some issues that are being discussed in the country today. Do you strongly favor, favor, oppose, or strongly oppose the following?
a. Passing a law that places stricter limits on the number of *legal* immigrants coming to the US.
b. Building a wall along the US border with Mexico.
c. Passing a law to prevent refugees from entering the US.
d. Temporarily preventing people from some majority Muslim countries from entering the US.
e. An immigration border policy that separates children from their parents and charges parents as criminals when they enter the country without permission.
f. Allowing immigrants brought illegally to the US as children to gain legal resident status.

Note: Cronbach's alpha, a measure of internal consistency that is scaled from 0 to 1, is high (0.92), indicating these questions are closely related as a group.

SOURCE: PRRI, AMERICAN VALUES SURVEY, 2018.

— Appendix C —

Multivariate Regression Model Outputs Predicting Racist Attitudes

The table on the following page contains the output table for a multivariate regression model predicting the level of racist attitudes, measured by a composite score on the Racism Index (the dependent variable). The variables in the rows are the independent variables, the variables whose influence we are testing. For more details on how to read this table and about the independent variables, see appendix A.

Multivariate Regression Model Outputs Predicting Racism Index Score

DEPENDENT VARIABLE   *Racism Index*

INDEPENDENT VARIABLES

White Religious Groups

White Catholic	0.09***
	(0.01)
White Mainline	0.08***
	(0.01)
White Evangelical	0.09***
	(0.01)
White Unaffiliated	0.01
	(0.01)

Party Affiliation

Reference: Democrat

Leaning Democrat	0.04***
	(0.01)
Independent	0.09***
	(0.03)
Leaning Republican	0.12***
	(0.01)
Republican	0.10***
	(0.01)

Education Level

Reference: No high school diploma

High school graduate   0.01
                            (0.02)

Some college   -0.01
                            (0.02)

BA degree or higher   -0.03
                            (0.02)

Region

Reference: Northeast

Midwest   -0.01
                            (0.01)

South   -0.01
                            (0.01)

West   0.02*
                            (0.01)

Reference: Men

Women   -0.03***
                            (0.01)

Age (in years)   0.00
                            (0.00)

Household Income   -0.00
(low to high)   (0.00)

Reference: Not homeowner

Own home	0.01
	(0.01)
Church attendance (low to high)	0.00
	(0.02)

Reference: Nonmetropolitan area

Metropolitan area	-0.00
	(0.02)
Immigration Index (low to high)	0.93***
	(0.03)
Constant	0.03
	(0.04)

Observations	2,337
R-squared	0.69

SOURCE: PRRI, AMERICAN VALUES SURVEY, 2018.

Notes

Chapter 1. Seeing: Our Current Moment

1. Walter Shurden, *Not an Easy Journey: Some Transitions in Baptist Life* (Macon, GA: Mercer University Press, 2005), 137–39.
2. Leon McBeth, *The Baptist Heritage: Four Centuries of Baptist Witness* (Nashville: Broadman Press, 1987), 382.
3. United Methodist Communications.
4. Cyprian Davis, *The History of Black Catholics in the United States* (New York: Crossroad, 1990), 28.
5. Ibid., 35.
6. Lawrence E. Lucas, *Black Priest, White Church: Catholics and Racism* (New York: Random House, 1970; Trenton, NJ: First Africa World Press, 1992), 15–16.
7. See Morrison, 1948. As I noted in *The End of White Christian America*, "Charles Clayton Morrison presided over a series of editorials addressing America's religious future: an eight-part series by field editor Harold Fey in 1944–1945 titled, 'Can Catholicism Win America?,' and a sixteen-part series he penned himself in 1946 titled, 'Can Protestantism Win America?' The articles formed what was essentially a single long-running argument that Catholicism threatened not only Protestantism but also democratic governance." See Robert P. Jones, *The End of White Christian America* (New York: Simon & Schuster, 2016), 63.
8. Slavoj Žižek, "A Permanent Economic Emergency," *New Left Review*, no. 64 (July/August 2010, https://newleftreview.org/issues/II64/articles/slavoj-zizek-a-permanent-economic-emergency.
9. Jones, *The End of White Christian America*.
10. See PRRI 2018b. Here and throughout the book, when I'm writing about demographic data, the term "white" refers to "white, non-Hispanic" respondents. Most scientific public opinion surveys, including those conducted by PRRI, ask respondents separate questions about race (for example, white,

black, and so on) and ethnicity (for instance, Hispanic origin). Therefore, respondents can identify for example as white *and* Hispanic, or black *and* Hispanic. For analytical purposes, I follow the general social science practice of allowing ethnicity to trump race. In other words, if a respondent identifies as both "white" and "Hispanic," they are counted as "Hispanic" in the analysis.

11. Merle Black and Earl Black, *The Rise of Southern Republicans* (Cambridge, MA: Belknap Press, 2003).

12. National Exit Polls, 2000–2016.

13. Chris Moody and Kristen Holmes, "Donald Trump's History of Suggesting Obama Is a Muslim," CNN online, last modified September 18, 2015, https://www.cnn.com/2015/09/18/politics/trump-obama-muslim-birther/index.html.

14. John Eligon, "Hate Crimes Increase for the Third Consecutive Year, F.B.I. Reports," *New York Times*, November 13, 2018, https://www.nytimes.com/2018/11/13/us/hate-crimes-fbi-2017.html.

15. SPLC 2019a. Southern Poverty Law Center (SPLC) online, "Hate Groups Reach Record High," accessed February 19, 2019, https://www.splcenter.org/news/2019/02/19/hate-groups-reach-record-high.

16. ADL 2019b. Anti-Defamation League (ADL) online, "Hate on Display Hate Symbols Database," accessed September 28, 2019, https://www.adl.org/hate-symbols?cat_id%5B146%5D=146.

17. PRRI 2018a. See Pew Research Center online, "An Examination of the 2016 Electorate, Based on Validated Voters," last modified August 9, 2018, https://www.people-press.org/2018/08/09/an-examination-of-the-2016-electorate-based-on-validated-voters.

18. See Pew Research Center. I should flag one caveat for these election findings. The Pew Research Center report found white evangelical support for Trump to be 77 percent, slightly lower than the exit polls, largely due to variances in third-party-candidate voters. Pew also found that white religiously unaffiliated voters supported Clinton over Trump by a margin of 62 percent to 26 percent. This reflects a more than 30-percentage-point difference between white religiously unaffiliated voters and the nearest subgroup of white Christian voters.

19. Jones, 2018.

20. Eddie S. Glaude Jr., *Democracy in Black: How Race Still Enslaves the American Soul* (New York: Crown, 2016).

21. Richard J. Herrnstein and Charles Murray, *The Bell Curve: Intelligence and Class Structure in American Public Life* (New York: Free Press, 1994).

22. James Baldwin, "On Language, Race, and the Black Writer" (1979), in *The Cross of Redemption: Uncollected Writings*, ed. Randall Kenan (New York: Vintage Books, 2010), 140–44.

23. James Baldwin, "The White Problem" (1964), in *The Cross of Redemption*, 93.

24. Toni Morrison, *Playing in the Dark: Whiteness and the Literary Imagination* (New York: Vintage Books, 1993), 4–5.

25. Ibid., 5–6.

26. Lucas, *Black Priest, White Church*, 15–16.

Chapter 2. Remembering: Christianity as the Conductor of White Supremacy

1. Glenn M. Linden, *Voices from the Reconstruction Years, 1865–1877* (New York: Harcourt Brace/Cenage, 1998), 205.

2. Ibram X. Kendi, *Stamped from the Beginning: The Definitive History of Racist Ideas in America* (New York: Nation Books, 2016), 252.

3. Richard Rubin, "The Colfax Riot," *The Atlantic*, July/August 2003.

4. Ibid.

5. W. E. B. DuBois, *Black Reconstruction in America, 1860–1880* (New York: Free Press, 1935), 30.

6. Ida B. Wells-Barnett, *Lynch Law in Georgia: A Six-Weeks' Record in the Center of Southern Civilization, as Faithfully Chronicled by the "Atlanta Journal" and the "Atlanta Constitution"* (Chicago: Chicago Colored Citizens, 1899), https://www.loc.gov/resource/lcrbmrp.t1612/?sp=1.

7. Philip Dray, *At the Hands of Persons Unknown: The Lynching of Black America* (New York: Random House, 2002), 5.

8. Ibid., 13.

9. Donald G. Matthews, *At the Altar of Lynching: Burning Sam Hose in the American South* (Cambridge: Cambridge University Press, 2018), 158.

10. Ibid., 160.

11. Edwin T. Arnold, *What Virtue There Is in Fire: Cultural Memory and the Lynching of Sam Hose* (Athens: University of Georgia Press, 2019), 102.

12. Matthews, *At the Altar of Lynching*, 1.

13. *Atlanta Constitution*, April 23, 1899.

14. DuBois, 1961.

15. Dray, *At the Hands of Persons Unknown*.

16. Samuel S. Hill Jr., *Southern Churches in Crisis* (Boston: Beacon Press, 1966).

17. John Lee Eighmy, *Churches in Cultural Captivity: A History of the Social Attitudes of Southern Baptists* (Knoxville: University of Tennessee Press, 1972).

18. Carolyn Renée Dupont, *Mississippi Praying: Southern White Evangelicals and the Civil Rights Movement, 1945-1975* (New York: New York University Press, 2013), 7.

19. A. James Fuller, *Chaplain to the Confederacy: Basil Manly and Baptist Life in the Old South* (Baton Rouge: Louisiana State University Press, 2000).

20. See ibid., 277. Throughout this section, I am indebted to the work of A. James

Fuller, professor of history at Indianapolis University, who has written the only scholarly biography of Basil Manly Sr.

21. Ibid.

22. Ibid.

23. Ibid., 291.

24. Ibid.

25. Benjamin F. Riley, *History of the Baptists of Alabama* (Birmingham: Roberts and Son, 1895), 278–80.

26. Fuller, *Chaplain to the Confederacy*, 292.

27. Ibid.

28. Ibid., 293.

29. Ibid.

30. Ibid., 294.

31. Ibid., 295.

32. Ibid.

33. Ibid., 1.

34. Ibid.

35. Bill Prochnau, "The Tale of a Pulitzer, a Paper, a Family," *Washington Post*, April 25, 1983, https://www.washingtonpost.com/archive/politics/1983/04/25/the-tale-of-a-pulitzer-a-paper-a-family/2440bfeb-b772-4612-8a10-d044 32844673c/?noredirect=on&utm_term=.87bcd4d68461.

36. Dupont, *Mississippi Praying*, 114.

37. David R. Davies, "The Civil Rights Movement and the Closed Society, 1960–1964" (presented to the *American Journalism Historians Situation, Roanoke, Virginia, October 6–8, 1994*).

38. Kathy Lally, "A Journey from Racism to Reason," *Baltimore Sun*, January 5, 1997.

39. Carter Dalton Lyon, *Sanctuaries of Segregation: The Story of the Jackson Church Visit Campaign* (Jackson: University Press of Mississippi, 2017), 179.

40. *Jackson (MS) Daily Journal*, "Greeting for Negro," September 12, 1962.

41. "Mississippi Mix? Ross Says 'Never!'," editorial, *Jackson (MS) Daily News*, September 14, 1962.

42. Lally, "A Journey from Racism to Reason."

43. Richard Pearson, "Segregationist Governor Ross Barnett Dies at 89," *Washington Post*, November 8, 1987.

44. Dupont, *Mississippi Praying*, 115.

45. John Dittmer, *Local People: The Struggle for Civil Rights in Mississippi* (Champaign: University of Illinois Press, 1995), 139.

46. Editorial Board, "Mississippi Mix? Ross Says 'Never'!" *Jackson Daily News*, September 14, 1962.

47. Lyon, *Sanctuaries of Segregation*, 14.

48. Ibid., 14–15.

49. Ibid., 15.

50. Ibid., 254.

51. Charles Marsh, *God's Long Summer: Stories of Faith and Civil Rights* (Princeton, NJ: Princeton University Press, 1997).

52. Dupont, *Mississippi Praying*, 116.

53. Lyon, *Sanctuaries of Segregation*, 28.

54. Ibid., 13.

55. Ibid., 61.

56. Ibid., 63.

57. Ibid., 64.

58. Michael Dorman, "Who Killed Medgar Evers?," *New York Times*, May 17, 1992, https://www.nytimes.com/1992/05/17/magazine/who-killed-medgar -evers.html.

59. Ibid.

60. Curtis Wilkie, *Dixie: A Personal Odyssey Through Events That Shaped the Modern South* (New York: Touchstone Books, 2002), 104–5.

61. Charles W. Eagles, *The Price of Defiance: James Meredith and the Integration of Ole Miss* (Chapel Hill: University of North Carolina Press, 2009), 333.

62. There have been four failed attempts to remove "Go Mississippi" as the official state song: Senate Bill 2960 (2000): "An Act To Designate New Official State Song 'Mississippi;' And To Repeal Chapter 654, General Laws, 1962, Which Designated The Song 'Go, Mississippi,' As The Official State Song," sponsored by State Senator William Gardner Hewes; Senate Bill 2217 (2003): "An Act To Adopt New Official State Song; 'My Home Mississippi,'" sponsored by State Senator Delma Furniss; Senate Bill 2177 (2015): "An Act To Authorize Two Official State Songs, Keeping The Existing Song, 'Go, Mississippi,' And Adding 'My Home Mississippi,'" sponsored by State Senator Robert L. Jackson; and Senate Bill 2178 (2015): "An Act to adopt 'My Home Mississippi' As The Official State Song," sponsored by State Senator Robert L. Jackson.

63. Arielle Dreher, "How Integration Failed in Jackson's Public Schools from 1969 to 2017," *Jackson Free Press*, November 15, 2017, https://www.jackson freepress.com/news/2017/nov/15/how-integration-failed-jacksons-public -schools-196/, accessed November 25, 2019.

64. I have supplemented my memory from 1985 with samples of Gooch's testimony available on YouTube (https://vimeo.com/100670017) and in his autobiography, *I'm Free*.

65. Southern Baptist Convention, "Resolution on Racial Reconciliation on the 150th Anniversary of the Southern Baptist Convention" (Atlanta, 1995), www.sbc.net/resolutions/899/resolution-on-racial-reconciliation-on-the -150th-anniversary-of-the-southern-baptist-convention.

66. Gustav Niebuhr, "Baptist Group Votes to Repent Stand on Slaves," *New York Times*, June 21, 1995, https://www.nytimes.com/1995/06/21/us/baptist -group-votes-to-repent-stand-on-slaves.html.

67. Ibid.

68. Associated Press, "Baptist Leader Criticizes Trayvon Martin Support." *Newsday* (Long Island, NY), April 14, 2012. https://www.newsday.com/news/nation/baptist-leader-criticizes-trayvon-martin-support-1.3660945

69. Michelle Boorstein, "Richard Land: A Southern Baptist Warrior Bids Goodbye to Washington," *Washington Post*, August 10, 2012, https://www.washing tonpost.com/local/richard-land-a-southern-baptist-warrior-bids-goodbye -to-washington/2012/08/10/d0f92880-e186-11e1-98e7-89d659f9c106_story .html?utm_term=.260959399a9c.

70. Albert Mohler, "The Heresy of Racial Superiority—Confronting the Past, and Confronting the Truth," Albert Mohler online, last modified June 23, 2015, https://albertmohler.com/2015/06/23/the-heresy-of-racial-superiority -confronting-the-past-and-confronting-the-truth.

71. Ibid.

72. Southern Baptist Theological Seminary, *Report on Slavery and Racism in the History of the Southern Baptist Seminary* (Louisville, KY: Southern Baptist Theological Seminary, 2018), http://www.sbts.edu/wp-content/uploads /2018/12/Racism-and-the-Legacy-of-Slavery-Report-v4.pdf.

73. Ibid.

74. Ibid., 2015.

75. Ibid.

76. Jason Fowler, "Broadus, John Albert, (1827–1895), Southern Baptist Theological Seminary Archives online, accessed May 17, 2019, https://archon.sbts .edu//?p=creators//creator&id=7.

77. Adelle M. Banks, "Southern Baptist Seminary Denies Request for Reparations," Religion News Service online, last modified June 5, 2019, https:// www.baptiststandard.com/news/baptists/southern-baptist-seminary-denies -request-for-reparations/.

78. King, 1957.

79. Wolfgang Saxon, "Obituary: Cardinal O'Boyle of Washington, Liberal Who Espoused Orthodoxy," *New York Times*, August 11, 1987, https://www.ny times.com/1987/08/11/obituaries/cardinal-o-boyle-of-washington-liberal -who-espoused-orthodoxy.html.

80. See United States Catholic Conference 1961, 205–206. While the bishop's letter laid important theological groundwork, it was ambiguous about concrete actions. For example, it called for "prudence" among Catholics, charging them to "seize the mantle of leadership from the agitator and the racist," and it warned that "changes in deep-rooted attitudes are not made overnight."

81. Richard Rothstein, *The Color of Law: The Forgotten History of How Our Government Segregated America* (New York: Liveright, 2018), 104.

82. Ibid., 103–4.

83. Ibid., 85.

84. Abigail Perkiss, "Shelley v. Kraemer: Legal Reform for America's Neighborhoods," *Constitution Daily* online, last modified May 9, 2014, https:// constitutioncenter.org/blog/shelley-v-kraemer-legal-reform-for-americas -neighborhoods.

85. Ibid., 105.

86. See Cote Brilliante Presbyterian Church online, cbpcstl.org. The Presbytery retained the property, redesignated it a mission church to African Americans, and appointed a new pastor, Reverend William Gillespie, who served the church for fifty-three years until his retirement in 2009.

87. Akilah Johnson, "The Forgotten Riot That Sparked Boston's Racial Unrest," *Boston Globe*, June 1, 2017, https://www.bostonglobe.com/metro/2017/06 /01/the-forgotten-protest-that-sparked-city-racial-unrest/0ry39I37z87Twd BfrqUnTP/story.html.

88. W. E. B. DuBois, *The Correspondence of W.E.B. DuBois*, vol. 1, ed. Herbert Aptheker (Amherst, MA: University of Massachusetts, 1997).

89. Rothstein, *The Color of Law*, 26–27.

90. Ibid., 105–6.

91. Lucas, *Black Priest, White Church*, 71.

92. Ibid., 45–46.

93. Ibid., 43–44.

94. Rothstein, *The Color of Law*, 104.

95. Ruth Rejnis, "Priests Renew Charge of Racism Against Archdiose," *New York Times*, May 14, 1972, https://www.nytimes.com/1972/05 /14/archives/priests-renew-charge-of-racism-against-archdiocese.html, accessed November 26, 2019.

96. Martin Luther King Jr., "The Christian Way of Life in Human Relations, Address Delivered at the General Assembly of the National Council of Churches of Christ in the U.S.A.," St. Louis, December 4, 1957, in *The Papers of Martin Luther King, Jr., vol. 6: Advocate of the Social Gospel, September 1948–March 1963*, ed. Clayborne Carson et al. (Berkeley: University of California Press, 2007).

97. Bryan N. Massingale, *Racial Justice and the Catholic Church* (Maryknoll, NY: Orbis Books, 2018), 55.

98. Ibid., 61.

99. Ibid., 62.

100. Ibid., 68.

101. Ibid.

102. Ibid., 69.

Chapter 3. Believing: The Theology of White Supremacy

1. Romans 8:28 (King James Version).
2. Martin Luther King Jr., "Letter from Birmingham Jail," in *Why We Can't Wait*, repr. ed. (New York: Signet Books, 1964; Boston: Beacon Press, 2011). Citations refer to the Beacon edition.
3. Glaude, *Democracy in Black*, 37.
4. The Green family are avid supporters of President Trump, and the museum opening included a controversial private gala the evening before at the Trump International Hotel.
5. Veronica Stracqualursi, "Museum of the Bible Offers Revelations, Faces Controversy as It Opens," ABC News online, last modified November 18, 2017, https://abcnews.go.com/Politics/museum-bible-faces-revelations-controversy-opens/story?id=51194500.
6. Gordon Haber, "Investigating the Hobby Lobby Family: An Interview with Candida Moss and Joel S. Baden," *Religion & Politics*, last modified November 8, 2017, https://religionandpolitics.org/2017/11/08/investigating-the-hobby-lobby-family-an-interview-with-candida-moss-and-joel-s-baden.
7. Ibid.
8. Ibid.
9. PRRI, 2015.
10. Anti-Defamation League, *Murder and Extremism in the United States in 2018* (Washington, DC: ADL online, 2018), https://www.adl.org/media/12480/download.
11. Weiyi Cai and Simone Landon, "Attacks by White Extremists Are Growing. So Are Their Connections," *New York Times*, April 3, 2019, https://www.nytimes.com/interactive/2019/04/03/world/white-extremist-terrorism-christchurch.html.
12. Fuller, *Chaplain to the Confederacy*, 213.
13. Ibid.
14. Ibid.
15. Ibid., 116.
16. Ibid., 118.
17. Ibid.
18. Ibid., 214.
19. Ibid.
20. Ibid., 215.
21. Frederick Douglass, *Narrative of the Life of Frederick Douglass, an American Slave, Written by Himself* (Boston: Anti-Slavery Office, 1845; electronic ed., Chapel Hill: University of North Carolina, 1999), https://docsouth.unc.edu/neh/douglass/douglass.html.

22. Ibid., 120–21.

23. Ibid., 51.

24. Ibid., 54.

25. Ibid.

26. Ibid., 55.

27. Ibid., 79.

28. Ibid., 77–78.

29. Ibid., 308.

30. Ibid., 310.

31. Samuel S. Hill Jr., et al., "The South's Two Cultures," in *Religion and the Solid South* (Nashville: Abingdon, 1972), 36.

32. Charles Reagan Wilson, *Baptized in Blood: The Religion of the Lost Cause, 1865-1920* (Athens: University of Georgia Press, 1980), 7.

33. Ibid., 69.

34. Ibid., 75.

35. Ibid., 11.

36. Michael O. Emerson and Christian Smith, *Divided by Faith: Evangelical Religion and the Problem of Race in America* (New York: Oxford University Press, 2000), 33.

37. George Marsden, *Religion and American Culture* (San Diego: Harcourt Brace Jovanovich, 1990).

38. Scofield did serve in the Confederate army but deserted and took the oath of loyalty to the Union so that he could pass into civilian life behind Union lines; and although he was ordained, there is no record of his completing theological training beyond attending Bible conferences. Nonetheless, he was a shrewd self-promoter who exerted enormous influence through his reference Bible, which he also leveraged into a lucrative correspondence course business. See Jean D. Rushing, "From Confederate Deserter to Decorated Veteran Bible Scholar: Exploring the Enigmatic Life of C. I. Scofield, 1861–1921" (unpublished master's thesis, East Tennessee State University, 2011).

39. C. I. Scofield, *The Old Schofield Study Bible, KJV, Classic Edition* (Oxford: Oxford University Press, 1999).

40. PRRI 2014. Public Religion Research Institute (PRRI), "Believers, Sympathizers, and Skeptics: Why Americans are Conflicted about Climate Change, Environmental Policy, and Science," November 21, 2014, accessed September 28, 2019, https://www.prri.org/research/believers-sympathizers-skeptics-americans-conflicted-climate-change-environmental-policy-science/.

41. Emerson and Smith, *Divided by Faith*, 47.

42. Romans 3:23 (King James Version).

43. Douglass, *Narrative of the Life of Frederick Douglass*.

44. King, "Letter from Birmingham Jail."

45. Ann Swidler, "Culture in Action," *American Sociological Review* 51 (1986): 273–86.

46. Emerson and Smith, *Divided by Faith*, 76.

47. Ibid.

48. Ibid., 79.

49. Ibid., 78.

50. Michael O. Emerson and James E. Shelton, *Blacks and Whites in Christian America: How Racial Discrimination Shapes Religious Convictions* (New York: New York University Press, 2012). Note that Emerson and Shelton did not break out the views of white Catholics separately in their study.

51. Ibid., 178.

52. Ibid.

53. Ibid.

54. See Amy Held, "Maryland Gets Closer to Retiring State Song That Calls Northerners 'Scum,'" NPR online, last modified March 18, 2018, https://www.npr.org/sections/thetwo-way/2018/03/16/594305719/maryland-gets-closer-to-retiring-state-song-that-calls-northerners-scum. I am leaving aside the divisive debates about "limited" versus "unlimited" atonement, whether Jesus died for all people or only for an elect subset of people. These are essentially questions of human agency. While what I have presented is more representative of the unlimited atonement conception, the focus on a personal relationship with Jesus remains, whether one actively chooses or comes to the realization that one has been chosen to be among the elect.

55. William Paul Dillingham, *Dictionary of Races or Peoples: Reports of the Immigration Commission* (Washington, DC: United States Printing Office, 1911).

56. Michael Duffy, "Jerry Falwell: Political Innovator," *Time*, May 15, 2007, http://content.time.com/time/nation/article/0,8599,1621300,00.html.

57. Randall Balmer, "The Real Origins of the Religious Right," *Politico*, May 27, 2014, https://www.politico.com/magazine/story/2014/05/religious-right-real-origins-707133.

58. Matt Stearns, "Jerry Falwell Brought Religious Conservatives into US Politics," *Mercury News* (San Jose, CA), May 16, 2007, https://www.mercurynews.com/2007/05/16/jerry-falwell-brought-religious-conservatives-into-u-s-politics.

59. Paul Harvey, *Redeeming the South: Religious Cultures and Racial Identities Among Southern Baptists, 1865–1925* (Chapel Hill: University of North Carolina Press, 1997), 22.

60. Anthony E. C. Wallace, *Religion: An Anthropological View* (New York: Random House, 1966), 30.

61. Wilson, *Baptized in Blood*, 41.

Chapter 4. Marking: Monuments to White Supremacy

1. Alice M. Tyler, *A Souvenir Book of the Jefferson Davis Memorial Association and the Unveiling of the Monument* (Richmond, VA: Whittet and Shepperson, 1907), https://archive.org/details/cu31924030945020/page/n6.
2. Ibid.; Wilson, *Baptized in Blood*, 119.
3. Wilson, *Baptized in Blood*, 133.
4. Scott Dance and Michael Dresser, "Senators Pass Bill Stripping 'Maryland, My Maryland' of 'Official' Status," *Baltimore Sun*, March 18, 2018.
5. In Lost Cause groups, Maryland was considered a kind of honorary Confederate state. The UDC Catechism for Children contains clarifying questions about Maryland's liminal status: "[24] Did Maryland take any part in the cause of the South? Yes, most valiant part, furnishing many regiments of men and other aid for carrying on the war, and those who gave this aid endured persecution and imprisonment by the Federal authorities, as well as from those at home who opposed secession. Maryland was only kept in the Union by force" (Stone, 1904). The state of Maryland itself adopted "My Maryland!" as the official state song in 1939. Eight separate legislative attempts to revoke the song's status failed. In 2018 a compromise was reached that reclassified the song as the "historical" state song rather than as its "official" one. The University of Maryland band also regularly played "My Maryland!" at football games, a practice that ended only in fall 2017, in response to the violent white nationalist riots in Charlottesville, Virginia. See Held, "Maryland Gets Closer."
6. Karen L. Cox, *Dixie's Daughters: The United Daughters of the Confederacy and the Preservation of Confederate Culture* (Gainesville: University Press of Florida, 2003), 61.
7. Ibid., 63.
8. Tyler, *A Souvenir Book of the Jefferson Davis Memorial Association*.
9. Ibid.
10. Wilson, *Baptized in Blood*, 29.
11. Mrs. W. S. Humphreys, "Children at Dedication of Monument," *Confederate Veteran* 17:6 (June 1909), 266.
12. Cox, *Dixie's Daughters*, 65.
13. Ibid., 68.
14. Ibid., 93.
15. "Chapter Report from Greenville, Virginia," *Confederate Veteran* 40, no. 5, May 1932.
16. Cox, *Dixie's Daughters*, 156.
17. Urofsky 2006, 83.

18. Ibid., 84.

19. Cox, *Dixie's Daughters*, 158.

20. Ibid., 158.

21. Debra McKinney, "Stone Mountain: A Monumental Dilemma," Southern Poverty Law Center, *Intelligence Report*, no. 164, Spring 2018, 18–22.

22. Cox, *Dixie's Daughters*, 29.

23. SPLC 2019b. Southern Poverty Law Center (SPLC) online, "Whose Heritage? Public Symbols of the Confederacy," accessed February 1, 2019, https://www.splcenter.org/20190201/whose-heritage-public-symbols-confederacy.

24. Cox, *Dixie's Daughters*, 30; SPLC 2019a.

25. SPLC 2019b, "Whose Heritage?"

26. Cox, *Dixie's Daughters*, 137.

27. Ibid., 137.

28. Ibid., 138.

29. Methodist Episcopal Church, *The Catechism of the Methodist Episcopal Church: Numbers 1, 2, and 3, in One Volume, Designed for Consecutive Study in Sunday Schools and Families* (New York: Carlton and Phillips), 1855.

30. Caroline Branch Stone, *The UDC Catechism for Children* (Galveston, TX: United Daughters of the Confederacy, 1904).

31. Ibid.

32. Wilson, *Baptized in Blood*, 51–53.

33. Ibid., 25.

34. Calder Loth, *Windows of Grace: A Tribute of Love. The Memorial Windows of St. Paul's Episcopal Church, Richmond, VA* (Norfolk, VA: Teagle and Little, 2004).

35. Luke 2:29–32 (King James Version).

36. John M. Coski, *The Confederate Battle Flag: America's Most Embattled Emblem* (Cambridge, MA: Belknap Press of the Harvard University Press, 2005), 8.

37. Ibid., 9.

38. Ibid., 10.

39. Ibid., 16.

40. Yoni Appelbaum, "Why Is the Flag Still There?," *The Atlantic* online, last modified June 21, 2015, https://www.theatlantic.com/politics/archive/2015/06/why-is-the-flag-still-there/396431.

41. James Foreman Jr., "Driving Dixie Down: Removing the Confederate Flag from Southern State Capitals," *Yale Law Journal* 101, no. 2 (November 1991).

42. Coski, *The Confederate Battle Flag*.

43. "Platform of the States Rights Democratic Party, August 14, 1948." Political Party Platforms, Parties Receiving Electoral Votes: 1840–2004. The American Presidency Project, University of California, Santa Barbara. https://www.presidency.ucsb.edu/documents/platform-the-states-rights-democratic-party#axzzliGn93BZz, accessed December 1, 2019.

44. L. Tuffly Ellis, ed., Texas State Historical Association, *The Southwestern Historical Quarterly 83* (July 1979–April 1980), http://texashistory.unt.edu/ark: /67531/metapth101207/, accessed May 06, 2015, 34–35.

45. Coski, *The Confederate Battle Flag*, 174.

46. Frances Stead Sellers, "The Confederate Flag: A 150-Year Battle," *Washington Post*, October 15, 2018.

47. Coski, *The Confederate Battle Flag*.

48. Ibid.

49. Stead Sellers, "The Confederate Flag."

50. Elliot Kleinberg, "How Confederate Flag Grew Famous—Hint: It Wasn't During Civil War," *Palm Beach (FL) Post*, June 22, 2015, https:www.palm beachpost.com/article/20150622/NEWS/812031630.

51. Brett Bursey, "The Day the Flag Went Up," South Carolina Progressive Network online, accessed July 12, 2019, http:www.scpronet.com/point19909 /p04.html.

52. Nick Corasaniti, Richard Pérez-Peña, and Lizette Alvarez, "Church Massacre Suspect Held as Church Grieves," *New York Times*, June 18, 2015, https://www.nytimes.com/2015/06/19/us/charleston-church-shooting .html?module=inline.

53. Rebecca Hersher, "What Happened When Dylann Roof Asked Google for Information About Race?," *The Two-Way* (blog), NPR online, last modified January 10, 2017, https://www.npr.org/sections/thetwo-way/2017/01/10 /508363607/what-happened-when-dylann-roof-asked-google-for-informa tion-about-race.

54. Frances Robles, "Dylann Roof Photos and a Manifesto Are Posted on Website," *New York Times*, June 20, 2015, https://www.nytimes.com/2015/06/21 /us/dylann-storm-roof-photos-website-charleston-church-shooting.html.

55. Alex Ward, "Charleston Shooting: Dylann Roof's Stepmother Defends 'Smart' Boy 'Drawn in by Internet Evil,'" *Independent* (UK), June 21, 2015, https:// www.independent.co.uk/news/world/americas/the-stepmother-of-dylann -roof-defends-the-smart-boy-she-raised-having-been-affected-by-internet -evil-10334590.html.

56. Dylann Roof, personal journal, cited as government "exhibit 500" in trial. Posted online at Scribd, accessed September 28, 2019, https://www.scribd .com/document/335820753/Dylann-Roof-s-jailhouse-journal#fullscreen &from_embed.

57. Ibid., 5.

58. Ibid., 32.

59. Ibid., 19.

60. Evangelical Lutheran Church in America, "ELCA Presiding Bishop to Attend Funeral in Charleston, S.C.," press release, June 25, 2015, https://elca.org/News -and-Events/7757.

61. Elizabeth A. Eaton, statement issued by Evangelical Lutheran Church in America, June 18, 2015, http://download.elca.org/ELCA%20Resource%20 Repository/long_season_of_disquiet_letter.pdf.

62. Ibid.

63. Lenny Duncan, *Dear Church: A Love Letter from a Black Preacher to the Whitest Denomination in the U.S.* (Minneapolis: Fortress Press, 2019).

64. Ibid., 15.

65. Ibid., 39.

66. Evangelical Lutheran Church in America, "ELCA Presiding Bishop Issues Pastoral Message on Racism and White Supremacy," press release, September 13, 2019, https://www.elca.org/News-and-Events/8005.

67. Ibid.

68. Ibid.

69. Ibid.

70. Abbey Phillip, "Why Bree Newsome Took Down the Confederate Flag in S.C.: 'I Refuse to Be Ruled by Fear,'" *Washington Post*, June 29, 2015, https://www .washingtonpost.com/news/post-nation/wp/2015/06/29/why-bree-new some-took-down-the-confederate-flag-in-s-c-i-refuse-to-be-ruled-by-fear /?utm_term=.cd871de7e0d5.

71. Elahe Izadi and Abbey Phillip, "South Carolina House Votes to Remove Confederate Flag from Statehouse Grounds," *Washington Post*, July 9, 2015, https://www.washingtonpost.com/news/post-nation/wp/2015/07/09 /south-carolina-house-votes-to-remove-confederate-flag-from-statehouse -grounds/?utm_term=.54052d49734d.

72. Stephanie McCrummen and Elahe Izadi, "Confederate Flag Comes Down on South Carolina's Statehouse Grounds," *Washington Post*, July 10, 2015, https://www.washingtonpost.com/news/post-nation/wp/2015/07/10 /watch-live-as-the-confederate-flag-comes-down-in-south-carolina/?utm _term=.150871d7f92b.

73. Marianne Edgar Budde, Randolph Marshall Hollerith, and John Donoghue, "Announcement on the Future of the Lee-Jackson Windows," Washington National Cathedral online, last modified September 6, 2017, https://cathe dral.org/press-room/announcement-future-lee-jackson-windows.

74. C. Michael Hawn, "History of Hymns: 'In Christ There Is No East or West,'" Discipleship Ministries, United Methodist Church online, last modified June 18, 2013, https://www.umcdiscipleship.org/resources/history-of-hymns-in -christ-there-is-no-east-or-west; Emily Cochrane, "National Cathedral to Re- move Windows Honoring Confederate Generals," *New York Times*, September 6, 2017, https://www.nytimes.com/2017/09/06/us/politics/washington -national-cathedral-stained-glass-confederate-lee.html.

75. Ned Oliver, "St. Paul's Episcopal Church Discusses Confederate Imagery," *Richmond (VA) Times-Dispatch*, August 23, 2015, https://www.richmond

.com/news/local/city-of-richmond/st-paul-s-episcopal-church-discusses -confederate-imagery/article_fda4f734-e732-5c7f-bbe3-5f66flf09cb3.html.

76. St. Paul's Episcopal Church online, "History and Reconciliation Initiative (HRI)," accessed July 13, 2019, https://www.stpaulsrva.org/connect/hri.

77. David Paulsen, "Cincinnati Cathedral Drafts Plan to Study Removing Memorials to Confederate Figures," Episcopal News Service, September 13, 2017, https://www.episcopalchurch.org/library/article/cincinnati-cathedral-drafts -plan-study-removing-memorials-confederate-figures.

78. Sheila Vilvens, "A Year After Charlottesville: Confederate Symbols Wear Out Welcome at Ohio Cathedral," *Cincinnati Enquirer*, August 10, 2018, https:// www.wkyc.com/article/news/local/ohio/a-year-after-charlottesville-confed erate-symbols-wear-out-welcome-at-ohio-cathedral/95-58 2469557.

79. Ned Oliver, "Congregation Once Led by Robert E. Lee Votes to Remove His Name from Their Church," *Richmond (VA) Times-Dispatch*, September 18, 2017, https://www.richmond.com/news/virginia/congregation-once -led-by-robert-e-lee-votes-to-remove/article_30d0557f-c3c0-5be2-8a28 -308159dd662c.html.

80. See Boorstein, "Richard Land." The interpretation that the name change was a reluctant shift for the congregation is also supported by the description of the decision on the church's website: "On September 18, 2017, the Vestry voted to restore our name to Grace Episcopal Church. The Vestry is currently exploring meaningful and significant ways to continue to honor Lee." See Grace Episcopal Church online, accessed July 13, 2019, http://www.graceep iscopallexington.org/about.html.

81. Elahe Izadi, "New Orleans to Remove Four Major Confederate Monuments," *Washington Post*, December 15, 2017, https://www.washingtonpost.com/news /post-nation/wp/2015/12/17/new-orleans-to-remove-four-major-confederate -monuments/?utm_term=.a7e945019a6a.

82. Mitch Landrieu, *In the Shadow of Statues: A White Southerner Confronts History* (New York: Viking, 2018), 163.

83. "Confederate Monuments," *Confederate Veteran* 1, no. 1, January 1893.

84. Izadi, "New Orleans."

85. Landrieu, *In the Shadow of Statues*, 191.

86. Ibid., 3.

87. Ibid., 195.

88. Mitch Landrieu, "Mitch Landrieu's Speech on the Removal of Confederate Monuments in New Orleans," *New York Times*, May 23, 2017, 163, https:// www.nytimes.com/2017/05/23/opinion/mitch-landrieus-speech-transcript .html.

89. Landrieu, *In the Shadow of Statues*, 195.

90. SPLC 2019a.

91. Landrieu, *In the Shadow of Statues*, 3.

Chapter 5. Mapping: The White Supremacy Gene in American Christianity

1. See Avidit Acharya, Matthew Blackwell, and Maya Sen, *Deep Roots: How Slavery Still Shapes Southern Politics* (Princeton, NJ: Princeton University Press, 2018), 70. Throughout this chapter, the term *white* refers to white, non-Hispanic respondents. All of the questions used for indexes and modeling in this section come from PRRI's 2018 "American Values Survey."

2. Acharya, Blackwell, and Sen use two questions from the CCES, averaged together, to measure "racial resentment." The wordings of these questions are as follows: (1) "Generations of slavery and discrimination have created conditions that make it difficult for Blacks to work their way out of the lower class;" and (2) "The Irish, Italians, Jews, and many other minorities overcame prejudice and worked their way up. Blacks should do the same without any special favors." See Acharya, Blackwell, and Sen, *Deep Roots*, 59. Both questions were included in PRRI's 2018 "American Values Survey," and I have incorporated both into my own Racism Index analysis.

3. Ibid., 5.

4. Ibid., 52.

5. Ibid., 70.

6. Ibid., 75.

7. Robert P. Jones and Robert Francis, "The Black and White of Moral Values: The Complex Relationships Between Religious Attendance and 'Moral Values' Among White Evangelicals and Black Protestants," in *Faith and Race in American Political Life*, eds. Nancy Wadsworth and Robin Jacobson (Charlottesville: University of Virginia Press), 2012.

8. PRRI 2018a. Public Religion Research Institute (PRRI), "Partisan Polarization Dominates Trump Era: Findings from the 2018 American Values Survey" (October 29, 2018), accessed September 28, 2019, https://www.prri.org/research/partisan-polarization-dominates-trump-era-findings-from-the-2018-american-values-survey/.

9. Ibid.

10. PRRI, 2016b. "The Divide Over America's Future: 1950 or 2050?: Findings from the 2016 American Values Survey" (October 25, 2016), accessed September 28, 2019, https://www.prri.org/research/poll-1950s-2050-divided-nations-direction-post-election/.

11. PRRI 2018a. Public Religion Research Institute (PRRI), "Partisan Polarization Dominates Trump Era."

12. Ibid.

13. PRRI 2018c. "Americans Differ on Participation of Male, Female Athletes in Team Sports: Findings from the 2018 Sports Poll" (January 25, 2018), ac-

cessed September 28, 2019, https://www.prri.org/research/americans-differ
-on-participation-of-male-female-transgender-students-in-team-sports/.

14. PRRI 2018a. Public Religion Research Institute (PRRI), "Partisan Polarization Dominates Trump Era."

15. Ibid.

16. I'm grateful to the following colleagues who gave me feedback and advice
on the analysis in this chapter: Melissa Deckman, professor and chair of the
Department of Political Science at Washington College and author of *Tea
Party Women: Mama Grizzlies, Grassroots Leaders, and the Changing Face
of the American Right* (New York: New York University Press, 2016); Christian Scharen, vice president for applied research at Auburn Seminary and
author of *Fieldwork in Theology: Exploring the Social Context of God's Work
in the World* (Ada, MI: Baker Academic, 2015); Natalie Jackson, director of
research at PRRI; and Jioni Palmer, senior director of communications and
external affairs at PRRI. I am especially grateful for the assistance of two
colleagues, Juhem Navarro-Rivera, political research director and managing partner at Socioanalitica Research, and Paul Djupe, associate professor
of political science at Denison University and coeditor of *The Evangelical
Crackup?: The Future of the Evangelical-Republican Coalition* (Philadelphia: Temple University Press, 2018). Dr. Navarro-Rivera assisted with
overall analysis, the construction of an initial set of regression models, and
final checks of the results. Dr. Djupe helped develop the final set of regression models and charts, made vital contributions to the analysis, and used
his skills in R to create compelling data visualizations. I am deeply grateful
to each of these insightful scholars and professionals for their assistance in
helping me develop a complex analysis into a narrative for a general audience. Of course, I alone take responsibility for the interpretations and conclusions in this chapter.

17. To cope with the difficulty of asking respondents direct questions about sensitive topics such as racism, social scientists have developed techniques—none
of them perfect, to be sure—that capture negative racial or racist attitudes
without labeling them as such. Because these questions are oblique rather
than direct attempts to measure sensitive attitudes, multiple questions are
typically combined into a composite scale, which is more reliable. This is the
technique I have used to develop the Racism Index. In the social scientific
literature this approach is often discussed as measuring a respondent's la-
tent level of "racial resentment" or "symbolic racism." Given the breadth of
the scale here, I have opted for the more straightforward "Racism Index."
For the history of these scales and the challenges of obtaining accurate mea-
surement of racial attitudes among whites, see especially Michael Tesler and
David Sears, *Obama's Race: The 2008 Election and the Dream of a Post-
Racial America* (Chicago: University of Chicago Press, 2010). See also Sears

and Patrick J. Henry, "The Origins of Symbolic Racism," *Journal of Person-ality and Social Psychology* 85, no. 2 (2003): 259–75; Sears and Donald R. Kinder, *Racial Tension and Voting in Los Angeles* (Los Angeles: Institute of Government and Public Affairs, University of California, 1971); and Kinder and Sears, "Prejudice and Politics: Symbolic Racism Versus Racial Threats to the Good Life," *Journal of Personality and Social Psychology* 40, no. 3 (1981): 414–31.

18. Since some questions had different scales, they were all recoded to run from zero to one before combining. The full scale ran from 0 to 1, but effectively cut off at 0.8 (very few people resided in the 0.8–1.0 range). Therefore, the final scale was truncated at 0.8 (respondents with higher scores were recoded) and then recalibrated to run from 0 to 1 for ease of analysis. Cronbach's alpha, a measure of internal consistency that is scaled from 0 to 1, is high (0.91) for the Racism Index, indicating the component questions are closely related as a group. Typically, statisticians look for a Cronbach's alpha score of 0.80 or higher for confirmation that the questions are tapping into an underlying conceptual dimension.

19. See appendix A for the output of all five multivariate regression models.

20. See appendix B for the list of all questions included in the Immigration Index.

21. For the statisticians among my readers, this is my attempt to explain in plain language what statisticians call "marginal effects": the measure of how much the dependent variable (for example, a white Christian identity) shifts ac-cording to a one-unit change in the independent variable (the Racism Index), while holding all other variables in the model constant.

22. The predicted probability for all white Christians is significantly higher than the individual subgroups because it is picking up combined effects for white evangelicals, white mainline Protestants, and white Catholics. As the regional analysis demonstrates, the effects are roughly cumulative for all white Chris-tians because the subgroups are distinct from one another in membership and are dominant in different regions of the country.

23. Note that the statistical significance of the RI impact on white religiously unaffiliated identity ($p < 0.17$) falls below the level of statistical significance that is present for all the other findings in this chart, meaning that we are only roughly 80 percent confident that the six percent difference is distin-guishable from no effect. That estimate should be considered suggestive and interpreted with some caution; the most conservative interpretation would be that the RI has no effect on white religiously unaffiliated identity. By con-trast, all other findings in the chart showing the relationships between the RI and white Christian identities are strongly significant at the 95 percent confidence level.

24. Notably, the addition of statistical controls has a strong effect on the magni-tude of the relationship between the RI and white Christian identities. Before

the model controls are applied, the relationship between the RI and white evangelical Protestants is stronger than the relationship between the RI and white mainline Protestants. But with controls in place, these differences completely disappear; the RI has about the same relationship with both white Christian identities. Increasing the RI to its maximum value makes a respondent nearly one-quarter more likely to be either white mainline Protestant or white evangelical Protestant. In other words, the initial differences observed between white evangelical and white mainline Protestants were almost completely attributable to other attributes, such as political partisanship and regional distribution. But once these differences are accounted for and held constant in the model, it becomes clear that the presence of white supremacist DNA is equally detectable in both.

25. The most serious analysis suggesting that church attendance mitigates racism and anti-immigrant attitudes has been conducted by Emily Ekins. Drawing on data from the Voter Study Group, Ekins argued: "These national surveys find that Donald Trump voters who attend church regularly are more likely than nonreligious Trump voters to have warmer feelings toward racial and religious minorities, to be more supportive of immigration and trade, and to be more concerned about poverty. These data are important because they demonstrate that private institutions in civil society can have a positive effect on social conflict and can reduce polarization." See Emily Ekins, *Religious Trump Voters: How Faith Moderates Attitudes About Immigration, Race, and Identity*, Public Opinion Brief No. 2 (Washington, DC: Cato Institute, February 5, 2019), https://www.cato.org/publications/public-opinion-brief /religious-trump-voters-how-faith-moderates-attitudes-about). While a full analysis of Ekins's argument would be out of place here, one of the biggest missteps in her analysis is her reliance on feeling thermometer scores to measure attitudes toward African Americans. My analysis above shows that feeling thermometers are unreliable as a means of measuring racist attitudes. White evangelicals, for example, simultaneously report warm feeling thermometer scores toward African Americans while scoring high on the Racism Index.

26. More precisely, the error bars denote the range in which the mean of ninety-five out of a hundred samples (given a 95 percent confidence level), drawn from the same population distribution, would be likely to fall.

27. Note that we would not expect the predicted probabilities to be equal in magnitude when the direction of the analysis is reversed. This is principally because each of the white Christian identity variables is dichotomous—a respondent either is or is not a member of that category—while the Racism Index is a continuous scale variable. In the first step in the analysis, we are predicting how much a shift from 0 to 1 on the RI independently increases the likelihood of white Christian affiliation. In the second step, we analyze the

relationship in the other direction; we are predicting how much a particular white Christian affiliation is likely to independently increase a score on the RI.

28. Moreover, even after adding an additional control variable to the model for race (in other words, a switch for white vs. nonwhite), the predictive relationship between white Christian identity and racist attitudes remains significant at the 95 percent confidence level. When a control variable for race is added to the model, the percent increase in racist attitudes associated with white Christian identity drops only modestly, to 5 percent for white evangelical Protestants, 4 percent for white mainline Protestants, and 5 percent for white Catholics.

29. Acharya, Blackwell, and Sen, *Deep Roots*, 7.

30. Michael Ruane, "Slave's Daughter Who Helped Open the African American Museum Dies at 100," *Washington Post*, August 30, 2017, https://www.washingtonpost.com/local/slaves-daughter-who-helped-open-the-african-american-museum-dies-at-100/2017/08/30/2e4bc0ac-8d9d-11e7-91d5-ab4e4bb76a3a_story.html?noredirect=on&utm_term=.aaf0c084e5a9.

31. Acharya, Blackwell, and Sen, *Deep Roots*, 11.

32. Ibid., 214.

33. Ibid.

34. The authors do give brief attention to the establishment of "segregation academies," the all-white schools that quickly sprouted across the South in the wake of federal mandates for school desegregation. But the authors don't strongly tie the "segregation academies" to their sources, which were primarily white Christian churches.

Chapter 6. Telling: Stories of Change

1. DeNeen Brown and Cleeve R. Wootsen Jr., "Trump Ignores Backlash, Visits Mississippi Civil Rights Museum and Praises Civil Rights Leaders," *Washington Post*, December 7, 2017, https://www.washingtonpost.com/news/post-politics/wp/2017/12/09/amid-backlash-trump-set-to-attend-private-gathering-as-civil-rights-museum-opens-in-mississippi/?utm_term=.34f1080cf8f9.

2. Suzi Parker, "African-Americans' Heritage Set in Stone," *Christian Science Monitor*, June 20, 2001; SPLC 2019a.

3. Simon Romero, Manny Fernandez, and Mariel Padilla, "Massacre at a Crowded Walmart in Texas Leaves 20 Dead," *New York Times*, August 3, 2019, https://www.nytimes.com/2019/08/03/us/el-paso-shooting.html.

4. Jackie Rehwald, "On 112-Year Anniversary of Springfield Lynchings, Memorial for Victims Is Planned," *Springfield (IL) News-Leader*, April 12, 2018, https://

www.news-leader.com/story/news/local/2018/04/12/112-year-anniversary
-springfield-lynchings-memorial-victims-planned/504031002.

5. Steve Pokin, "In 1996, Hillcrest Students Decided Two Lynched Men Deserved a Grave Marker," *Springfield (IL) News-Leader*, December 19, 2017,
https://www.news-leader.com/story/news/local/ozarks/2017/12/19/pokin
-around-1996-hillcrest-students-decided-two-lynched-men-deserved-grave
-marker/963085001. There were eighteen indictments, but only one person
was brought to trial and he was acquitted. The impact on the African American community was dramatic. The African American community in Springfield quickly went from approximately 20 percent to 2 percent; today the city
remains 96 percent white.

6. Equal Justice Initiative, "The National Memorial for Peace and Justice," EJI
online (https://eji.org), accessed November 1, 2019.

7. H. Lewis Batts and Rollin S. Armour, *History of the First Baptist Church of
Christ at Macon* (Macon, GA: First Baptist Church of Christ, 1991), 76.

8. Michael Pannell, "Northridge Aims at Grace as It Continues to Serve Those
Around It," *Macon Telegraph*, January 4, 2018, https://www.macon.com
/living/religion/article192900159.html.

9. H. Lewis Batts and Rollin S. Armour, *History of the First Baptist Church of
Christ at Macon* (Macon, GA: First Baptist Church of Christ, 1991).

10. Rosalind Bentley, "Two Churches Began in Slavery; Today They Are Reckoning with That Past," *Atlanta Journal-Constitution*, December 17, 2017,
https://www.ajc.com/news/local/two-churches-began-slavery-today-they
-are-reckoning-with-that-past/myC4MryHYSCazPUQALYmtK.

11. Ibid.

12. Reverend James Goolsby and Reverend Scott Dickison, interview with author, October 17, 2018.

13. Ibid.

14. Ibid.

15. Bentley, "Two Churches Began in Slavery."

16. Goolsby and Dickison, interview, October 17, 2018.

17. Bentley, "Two Churches Began in Slavery."

18. Ibid.

19. Scott Dickison, interview with author, August 12, 2019.

20. Batts and Armour, *History of First Baptist Church, Macon*, 39.

21. Ibid.

22. Scott Dickison, "Learning How to Confess," sermon delivered at First Baptist
Church of Christ, Macon, GA, March 13, 2017.

23. Batts and Armour, *History of First Baptist Church, Macon*, 47.

24. Ibid., 58.

25. Ibid., 48.

26. Ibid.

27. Scott Dickison, "Testimony to the Cooperative Baptist Fellowship, 2019 General Assembly," unpublished sermon, Atlanta, June 19, 2017.

28. Ibid.

29. Dickison, interview, August 12, 2019.

30. Cathy Logue, interview with author, August 22, 2019.

31. Dickison, interview with the author, August 12, 2019.

32. Ibid.

33. See Public Religion Research Institute, "The 2016 American Values Atlas" map for a full breakdown of denominational affiliation, PRRI online, accessed September 28, 2019, http://ava.prri.org/#religious/2016/States/denomination/m/US-MN. PRRI 2016a.

34. United States Department of Commerce, *Statistical Abstract of the United States, 1920* (Washington, DC: US Government Printing Office, 1921), 35; Public Religion Research Institute, "The 2018 American Values Atlas," PRRI online, accessed September 28, 2019, https://www.prri.org//american-values-atlas//#0. PRRI 2018b.

35. Robin Washington, "The Legacy of a Lynching: A Memorial, a Pilgrimage, a Reconciliation," The Marshall Project, last modified May 3, 2018, https://www.themarshallproject.org/2018/05/03/the-legacy-of-a-lynching.

36. Michael Fedo, *The Lynchings in Duluth*, 2nd ed. (Saint Paul, MN: Minnesota Historical Society Press, 2016).

37. James Fallows and Deborah Fallows, *Our Towns: A 100,000-Mile Journey into the Heart of America* (New York: Pantheon Books, 2018).

38. Erika Doss, *Memorial Mania: Public Feeling in America* (Chicago: University of Chicago Press, 2010), 310.

39. Monica Davey, "Letter from Duluth: It Did Happen Here, the Lynching That a City Forgot," *New York Times*, December 4, 2013, https://www.nytimes.com/2003/12/04/us/letter-from-duluth-it-did-happen-here-the-lynching-that-a-city-forgot.html.

40. Clayton Jackson McGhie Memorial Inc. Board of Directors, "Election Day Statement," press release, 2012.

41. Washington, "The Legacy of a Lynching."

42. Ibid.

43. Ibid.

44. James Baldwin, *The Fire Next Time* (New York: Dial Press, 1963), 101–2.

45. William H. Moon is recorded on a payroll that specifies his service under a Virginia militia regiment under the command of Captain William Lang in 1779.

46. By 1805, the Georgia government had completely seized all Creek land east of the Ocmulgee River, which runs through Twiggs and Bibb Counties, the two counties where my family has lived since the late 1790s. The first land

lottery in 1805 featured two-hundred-acre tracts of land. Beginning in 1820, Revolutionary War veterans such as William H. Moon were eligible for two tickets, increasing their odds of winning land.

47. "Parting of Cable Results in Death of Isham Andrews," *Atlanta Constitution*, September 20, 1920.

48. I should note that I have no evidence for this story other than my great-uncle's account. No account of a second accident at the John Sant & Sons Mine appears in the *Atlanta Constitution* through the fall of 1920. It's not unlikely, of course, that the death of an African American worker would have been less newsworthy than the death of a white supervisor.

Chapter 7. Reckoning: Toward Responsibility and Repair

1. Bentley, "Two Churches Began in Slavery."

2. Adelle Banks, "Reparations Fund Announced by Va. Seminary with Buildings Constructed by Slaves," Religion News Service, September 10, 2019, https://religionnews.com/2019/09/10/reparations-fund-announced-by-va-seminary-with-buildings-constructed-by-slaves/, accessed December 1, 2019.

3. Mohler, "The Heresy of Racial Superiority."

4. John McArthur, "The Statement on Social Justice & the Gospel," accessed September 2, 2019, https://statementonsocialjustice.com.

5. Eugene Scott, "Slavery Has Always Been at the Intersection of Race and Politics. Now It's Front and Center in the Political Conversation," *Washington Post*, August 29, 2019, https://beta.washingtonpost.com/politics/2019/08/29/slavery-has-always-been-intersection-race-politics-now-its-front-center-political-conversation.

6. Bob Smietana, "Eric Metaxas on Trump, Bonhoeffer, and the Future of America," Religion News Service, September 27, 2019, https://religionnews.com/2019/09/27/eric-metaxas-on-trump-bonhoeffer-and-the-future-of-america.

7. Bentley, "Two Churches Began in Slavery."

8. Dickison, "Testimony to Cooperative Baptist Fellowship," June 19, 2017.

9. Dickison., interview with author, August 12, 2019.

10. Ibid.

11. Genesis 4:8–9 (King James Version).

12. Genesis 4:10–11 (King James Version).

13. In eighteenth- and nineteenth-century white Christian theology, the "Curse of Cain" and "Curse of Ham" stories were both used to justify the superiority of white Europeans and the enslavement of dark-skinned Africans. In the "Curse of Ham" story in Genesis 9:20–27, there is no reference to a "mark," but Ham is cursed and fated to be "a servant of servants." These stories were sometimes interpreted together, with a claim that Ham married a descendant

of Cain, thereby linking the "curse" of dark skin with servitude, and they were sometimes simply conflated.

14. James Baldwin, "The Price May Be Too High," *New York Times*, February 2, 1968.

15. Baldwin, *The Fire Next Time*, 40, 66.

16. Baldwin., "The Nigger We Invent," in *The Cross of Redemption: Uncollected Writings*, ed. Randall Kenan (New York: Vintage Books, 2010), 113.

17. Baldwin, *The Fire Next Time*, 91.

18. Jones, *The End of White Christian America*; Jones, "Finding a Dignified End for White Protestantism," *Reflections: A Journal of Yale Divinity School* (Fall 2017), https://reflections.yale.edu/article/reformation-writing-next-chapter /finding-dignified-end-white-protestantism-robert-p-jones.

19. James Baldwin, "Speech from the Soledad Rally," in *The Cross of Redemption*, 122.

Bibliography

"A Lynching Memorial Is Unveiled in Duluth." Opinion. *New York Times*, December 5, 2003. https://www.nytimes.com/2003/12/05/opinion/a-lynching-memo rial-unveiled-in-duluth.html.

"A Regional Report: Newspapers of the South." Editorial. *Columbia Journalism Review*, Summer 1967, 26–35.

Acharya, Avidit, Matthew Blackwell, and Maya Sen. *Deep Roots: How Slavery Still Shapes Southern Politics*. Princeton, NJ: Princeton University Press, 2018.

Anti-Defamation League online, "Anti-Semitic Incidents Remained at Near-Historic Levels in 2018; Assaults Against Jews More Than Doubled." Last modified April 30, 2019. https://www.adl.org/news/press-releases/anti-semitic -incidents-remained-at-near-historic-levels-in-2018-assaults.

———. "Hate on Display Hate Symbols Database." Accessed September 28, 2019, https://www.adl.org/hate-symbols?cat_id%5B146%5D=146.

———. *Murder and Extremism in the United States in 2018*. Washington, DC: Anti-Defamation League, 2018. https://www.adl.org/media/12480/download.

Appelbaum, Yoni. "Why Is the Flag Still There?" *The Atlantic* online, last modified June 21, 2015. https://www.theatlantic.com/politics/archive/2015/06/why -is-the-flag-still-there/396431.

Arnold, Edwin T. *What Virtue There Is in Fire: Cultural Memory and the Lynching of Sam Hose*. Athens: University of Georgia Press, 2019.

Associated Press. "Baptist Leader Criticizes Trayvon Martin Support." *Newsday* (Long Island, NY), April 14, 2012. https://www.newsday.com/news/nation /baptist-leader-criticizes-trayvon-martin-support-1.3660945.

Baker, Robert A. "Southern Baptist Beginnings." Baptist History and Heritage Society online. Accessed March 17, 2018. http://www.baptisthistory.org/baptist origins/southernbaptistbeginnings.html.

Baldwin, James. *The Fire Next Time*. New York: Vintage International, 1993. First published 1963 by Dial Press (New York).

———. "On Language, Race, and the Black Writer." In *The Cross of Redemption*: *Uncollected Writings*, ed. Randall Kenan. New York: Vintage Books, 2010.

——. "Speech from the Soledad Rally." In *The Cross of Redemption*.

——. "The Nigger We Invent." In *The Cross of Redemption*.

——. "The Price May Be Too High." *New York Times*, February 2, 1968.

——. "The White Problem." In *The Cross of Redemption*.

Balmer, Randall. "The Real Origins of the Religious Right." *Politico*, May 27, 2014. https://www.politico.com/magazine/story/2014/05/religious-right-real-origins-107133.

Banks, Adelle M. "Southern Baptist Seminary Denies Request for Reparations." Religion News Service online, last modified June 5, 2019. https://religion news.com/2019/06/05/southern-baptist-seminary-denies-request-for-reparations/.

Barnett, Ross. "Ross Barnett, Segregationist, Dies; Governor of Mississippi in 1960's." *New York Times*, November 7, 1987.

Batts, H. Lewis, and Rollin S. Armour, *History of the First Baptist Church of Christ at Macon*. Macon, GA: First Baptist Church of Christ, 1991.

Bentley, Rosalind. "Two Churches Began in Slavery; Today They Are Reckoning with That Past." *Atlanta Journal-Constitution*, December 17, 2017. https://www.ajc.com/news/local/two-churches-began-slavery-today-they-are-reckoning-with-that-past/myC4MryHYSCazPUQALYmtK.

Black, Merle, and Earl Black. *The Rise of Southern Republicans*. Cambridge, MA: Belknap Press, 2003.

Boorstein, Michelle. "Richard Land: A Southern Baptist Warrior Bids Goodbye to Washington." *Washington Post*, August 10, 2012. https://www.washington post.com/local/richard-land-a-southern-baptist-warrior-bids-goodbye-to-washington/2012/08/10/d0f92880-e186-11e1-98e7-89d659f9c106_story.html?utm_term=.260959399a9c.

——. "The Virginia Church of Confederate Gen. Robert E. Lee Has Voted to Drop His Name." *Washington Post*, September 20, 2017. https://www.washing tonpost.com/news/acts-of-faith/wp/2017/09/20/the-virginia-church-of-confederate-gen-robert-e-lee-has-voted-to-dro p-his-name/?utm_term=.faa571f5a9f6.

Brown, DeNeen, and Cleeve R. Wootsen Jr. "Trump Ignores Backlash, Visits Mississippi Civil Rights Museum and Praises Civil Rights Leaders." *Washington Post*, December 7, 2017. https://www.washingtonpost.com /news/post-politics/wp/2017/12/09/amid-backlash-trump-set-to-attend-private-gathering-as-civil-rights-museum-opens-in-mississippi/?utm_term=.34f1080cf8f9.

Budde, Marianne Edgar, Randolph Marshall Hollerith, and John Donoghue. "Announcement on the Future of the Lee-Jackson Windows." Washington National Cathedral online, September 6, 2017. https://cathedral.org/press-room/announcement-future-lee-jackson-windows.

Bursey, Brett. "The Day the Flag Went Up" (Interview with Daniel Hollis). South Carolina Progressive Network online. Accessed July 12, 2019. http://www .scpronet.com/point/9909/p04.html.

Cai, Weiyi, and Simone Landon. "Attacks by White Extremists Are Growing. So Are Their Connections." *New York Times*, April 3, 2019. https://www .nytimes.com/interactive/2019/04/03/world/white-extremist-terrorism -christ church.html.

Charney, Noah. "Critics Call It Evangelical Propaganda. Can the Museum of the Bible Convert Them?" *Washington Post*, September 4, 2015. https://www .washingtonpost.com/opinions/2005/09/04/f145def4-4b59-11e5-bfb9 -9736d04fc8e4U.S._story.html.

Clayton Jackson McGhie Memorial Inc. Board of Directors. "Election Day Statement." Press release, 2012.

Confederate Veteran. "Confederate Monuments." volume 1, no. 1, January 1893.

———. "Chapter Report from Greenville, Virginia." volume 40, no. 5, May 1932.

Cochrane, Emily. "National Cathedral to Remove Windows Honoring Confederate Generals." *New York Times*, September 6, 2017. https://www.nytimes .com/2017/09/06/us/politics/washington-national-cathedral-stained-glass -confederate-lee.html.

Corasaniti, Nick, Richard Pérez-Peña, and Lizette Alvarez. "Church Massacre Suspect Held as Church Grieves." *New York Times*, June 18, 2015. https://www.nytimes.com/2015/06/19/us/charleston-church-shooting .html?module=inline.

Coski, John M. *The Confederate Battle Flag: America's Most Embattled Emblem.* Cambridge, MA: Belknap Press of the Harvard University Press, 2005.

Cote Brilliante Presbyterian Church. "History: The Beginning." Accessed September 16, 2019, http://cbpcstl.org/church/history.

Cotter, Holland. "A New Civil Rights Museum in Mississippi Refuses to Sugarcoat History." *New York Times*, December 18, 2017. https://www.nytimes.com /2017/12/18/arts/design/jackson-mississippi-civil-rights-museum-medgar -evers.html.

Cox, Karen L. *Dixie's Daughters: The United Daughters of the Confederacy and the Preservation of Confederate Culture.* Gainesville: University Press of Florida, 2003.

Dance, Scott, and Michael Dresser. "Senators Pass Bill Stripping 'Maryland, My Maryland' of 'Official' Status." *Baltimore Sun*, March 18, 2018.

Dart, John. "Southern Baptists Vote to Issue Apology for Past Racism." *Los Angeles Times*, June 21, 1995. https://www.latimes.com/archives/la-xpm-1995-06-21 -mn-15534-story.html.

Davey, Monica. "Letter from Duluth: It Did Happen Here, the Lynching That a City Forgot." *New York Times*, December 4, 2003. https://www.nytimes.com

/2003/12/04/us/letter-from-duluth-it-did-happen-here-the-lynching-that-a-city-forgot.html.

Davies, David R. "The Civil Rights Movement and the Closed Society, 1960–1964." Presented to the American Journalism Historians Association, Roanoke, Virginia, October 6–8.

Davis, Cyprian. *The History of Black Catholics in the United States*. New York: Crossroad, 1990.

Deckman, Melissa. *Tea Party Women: Mama Grizzlies, Grassroots Leaders, and the Changing Face of the American Right*. New York: New York University Press, 2016.

Dickison, Scott. Interview with author, August 12, 2019.

———. "Learning How to Remember." Sermon delivered at First Baptist Church of Christ, Macon, GA, March 13, 2017.

———. "Testimony to the Cooperative Baptist Fellowship, 2019 General Assembly." Unpublished sermon, Atlanta, June 19, 2017.

Dillingham, William Paul. *Dictionary of Races or Peoples: Reports of the Immigration Commission*. Washington, DC: United States Printing Office, 1911.

Dittmer, John. *Local People: The Struggle for Civil Rights in Mississippi*. Champaign: University of Illinois Press, 1995.

Djupe, Paul, and Ryan Claasen, eds. *The Evangelical Crackup?: The Future of the Evangelical-Republican Coalition*. Philadelphia: Temple University Press, 2018.

Dorman, Michael. "Who Killed Medgar Evers?" *New York Times*, May 17, 1992. https://www.nytimes.com/1992/05/17/magazine/who-killed-medgar-evers.html.

Doss, Erika. *Memorial Mania: Public Feeling in America*. Chicago: University of Chicago Press, 2010.

Douglass, Frederick. *Narrative of the Life of Frederick Douglass, an American Slave. Written by Himself*. Electronic ed., Chapel Hill: University of North Carolina, 1999. Available at https://docsouth.unc.edu/neh/douglass/douglass.html. First published 1845 by Anti-Slavery Office (Boston).

Dray, Philip. *At the Hands of Persons Unknown: The Lynching of Black America*. New York: Random House, 2002.

DuBois. W. E. B. *Black Reconstruction in America, 1860–1880*. New York: Free Press, 1935.

———. *The Correspondence of W. E. B. DuBois*, Vol. 1. Edited by Herbert Aptheker. Amherst: University of Massachusetts Press, 1997.

———. "W. E. B. DuBois: A Recorded Autobiography, Interview with Moses Asch." Smithsonian Folkways Recordings, 1961. Available at Library of Congress online. https://www.loc.gov/exhibits/civil-rights-act/multimedia/w-e-b-du-bois.html.

Duffy, Michael. "Jerry Falwell: Political Innovator." *Time*, May 15, 2007. http://content.time.com/time/nation/article/0,8599,1621300,00.html.

Duncan, Lenny. *Dear Church: A Love Letter from a Black Preacher to the Whitest Denomination in the U.S.* Minneapolis: Fortress Press, 2019.

Dupont, Carolyn Renée. *Mississippi Praying: Southern White Evangelicals and the Civil Rights Movement, 1945–1975.* New York: New York University Press, 2013.

Eagles, Charles W. *The Price of Defiance: James Meredith and the Integration of Ole Miss.* Chapel Hill: University of North Carolina Press, 2009.

Eaton, Elizabeth A. Statement issued by Evangelical Lutheran Church in America. June 18, 2015. http://download.elca.org/ELCA%20Resource%20Repository/long_season_of_disquiet_letter.pdf.

Eighmy, John Lee. *Churches in Cultural Captivity: A History of the Social Attitudes of Southern Baptists.* Knoxville: University of Tennessee Press, 1972.

Ekins, Emily. *Religious Trump Voters: How Faith Moderates Attitudes About Immigration, Race, and Identity.* Public Opinion Brief No. 2. Washington, DC: Cato Institute, February 5, 2019. https://www.cato.org/publications/public-opinion-brief/religious-trump-voters-how-faith-moderates-attitudes-about.

Eligon, John. "Hate Crimes Increase for the Third Consecutive Year, F.B.I. Reports." *New York Times*, November 13, 2018. https://www.nytimes.com/2018/11/13/us/hate-crimes-fbi-2017.html.

Emerson, Michael O., and James E. Shelton. *Blacks and Whites in Christian America: How Racial Discrimination Shapes Religious Convictions.* New York: New York University Press, 2012.

Emerson, Michael O., and Christian Smith. *Divided by Faith: Evangelical Religion and the Problem of Race in America.* New York: Oxford University Press, 2000.

Equal Justice Initiative. "The National Memorial for Peace and Justice." EJI online, accessed November 1, 2018. https://eji.org.

Evangelical Lutheran Church in America. "ELCA Presiding Bishop Issues Pastoral Message on Racism and White Supremacy." Press release, September 13, 2019. https://www.elca.org/News-and-Events/8005.

——. "ELCA Presiding Bishop to Attend Funeral in Charleston, S.C." Press release, June 25, 2015. https://elca.org/News-and-Events/7757.

Fallows, James, and Deborah Fallows. *Our Towns: A 100,000-Mile Journey into the Heart of America.* New York: Pantheon Books, 2018.

Fedo, Michael. *The Lynchings in Duluth.* 2nd ed. Saint Paul, MN: Minnesota Historical Society Press, 2016.

First Baptist Church. "Church History." 2019. Macon, GA. Accessed August 23, 2019. https://firstbaptistmacon.org/history.php.

Foreman, James, Jr. "Driving Dixie Down: Removing the Confederate Flag from Southern State Capitols." *Yale Law Journal* 101, no. 2 (November 1991).

Fowler, Jason O. "Broadus, John Albert (1827–1895)." Southern Baptist Theological Seminary Archives online. Accessed May 17, 2019. https://archon.sbts.edu/?p=creators/creator&id=7.

Fuller, A. James. *Chaplain to the Confederacy: Basil Manly and Baptist Life in the Old South.* Baton Rouge: Louisiana State University Press, 2000.

Gentry, Jerome. "Roy Coleman." *Jackson (MS) Free Press*, February 25, 2013. http://www.jacksonfreepress.com/news/2013/feb/25/roy-coleman.

Glaude, Eddie S., Jr. *Democracy in Black: How Race Still Enslaves the American Soul.* New York: Crown, 2016.

Gooch, Sheldon C. *I'm Free: The Autobiography of Sheldon Gooch.* CreateSpace Independent Publishing Platform, 2016.

Goolsby, James, and Scott Dickison. Interview with author. October 17, 2018.

Haber, Gordon. "Investigating the Hobby Lobby Family: An Interview with Candida Moss and Joel S. Baden." *Religion & Politics.* Last modified November 8, 2017. https://religionandpolitics.org/2017/11/08/investigating-the-hobby-lobby-family-an-interview-with-candida-moss-and-joel-s-baden.

Harvey, Paul. *Redeeming the South: Religious Cultures and Racial Identities Among Southern Baptists, 1865–1925.* Chapel Hill: University of North Carolina Press, 1997.

Hawn, C. Michael. "History of Hymns: 'In Christ There Is No East or West.'" Discipleship Ministries, United Methodist Church online. Last modified June 18, 2013. https://www.umcdiscipleship.org/resources/history-of-hymns-in-christ-there-is-no-east-or-west.

Held, Amy. "Maryland Gets Closer to Retiring State Song That Calls Northerners 'Scum.'" NPR online, last modified March 18, 2018. https://www.npr.org/sections/thetwo-way/2018/03/16/594305719/maryland-gets-closer-to-retiring-state-song-that-calls-northerners-scum.

Herrnstein, Richard J., and Charles Murray. *The Bell Curve: Intelligence and Class Structure in American Public Life.* New York: Free Press, 1994.

Hersher, Rebecca. "What Happened When Dylann Roof Asked Google for Information About Race?" *The Two-Way* (blog). NPR online, January 10, 2017. https://www.npr.org/sections/thetwo-way/2017/01/10/508363607/what-happened-when-dylann-roof-asked-google-for-information-about-race.

Hill, Samuel S., Jr. *Southern Churches in Crisis.* Boston: Beacon Press, 1966.

Hill, Samuel S., Jr., Edgar T. Thompson, Anne Firor Scott, Charles Hudson, and Edwin S. Gaustad. "The South's Two Cultures." In *Religion and the Solid South.* Nashville: Abingdon, 1972.

Humphreys, Mrs. W. S. "Children at Dedication of Monument," *Confederate Veteran* 17:6 (June 1909), 266.

Izadi, Elahe. "New Orleans to Remove Four Major Confederate Monuments." *Wash-*

ington Post, December 15, 2017. https://www.washingtonpost.com/news /post-nation/wp/2015/12/17/new-orleans-to-remove-four-major-confederate -monuments/?utm_term=.a7e945019a6a.

Izadi, Elahe, and Abbey Phillip. "South Carolina House Votes to Remove Confeder- ate Flag from Statehouse Grounds." *Washington Post*, July 9, 2015. https:// www.washingtonpost.com/news/post-nation/wp/2015/07/09/south-carolina -house-votes-to-remove-confederate-flag-from-statehouse-grounds/?utm _term=.54052d49734d.

Jackson (MS) Daily News. "Greeting for Negro." September 12, 1962.

Johnson, Akilah. "The Forgotten Riot That Sparked Boston's Racial Unrest." *Bos- ton Globe*, June 1, 2017. https://www.bostonglobe.com/metro/2017/06/01 /the-forgotten-protest-that-sparked-city-racial-unrest/0ry39137z87TwdB frqUnTP/story.html.

Jones, Robert P. *The End of White Christian America*. New York: Simon & Schuster, 2016.

——. "Finding a Dignified End for White Protestantism." *Reflections: A Maga- zine of Theological and Ethical Inquiry from Yale Divinity School*, Fall 2017. https://reflections.yale.edu/article/reformation-writing-next-chapter/finding -dignified-end-white-protestantism-robert-p-jones.

——. "White Evangelicals Can't Quit Donald Trump." *The Atlantic* online. Last modified April 20, 2018. https://www.theatlantic.com/politics/archive/2018 /04/white-evangelicals-cant-quit-donald-trump/558461.

Jones, Robert P., and Robert Francis. "The Black and White of Moral Values: The Complex Relationships Between Religious Attendance and 'Moral Values' Among White Evangelicals and Black Protestants." In *Faith and Race in American Political Life*, eds. Nancy Wadsworth and Robin Jacobson. Char- lottesville: University of Virginia Press, 2012.

Jones, Robert P., and Ted Smith, eds. *Spirit and Capital in an Age of Inequality*. London: Routledge, 2018.

Kendi, Ibram X. *Stamped from the Beginning: The Definitive History of Racist Ideas in America*. New York: Nation Books, 2016.

Kinder, Donald R., and David Sears. "Prejudice and Politics: Symbolic Racism Ver- sus Racial Threats to the Good Life." *Journal of Personality and Social Psy- chology* 40, no. 3 (1981): 414–31.

King, Martin Luther, Jr. "The Christian Way of Life in Human Relations, Address Delivered at the General Assembly of the National Council of Churches of Christ in the U.S.A." St. Louis, December 4, 1957. In *The Papers of Martin Luther King, Jr. vol. 6: Advocate of the Social Gospel, September 1948–March 1963*, eds. Clayborne Carson, Susan Carson, Susan Englander, Troy Jackson, and Gerald L. Smith. Berkeley: University of California Press, 2007.

——. "Letter from Birmingham Jail." In *Why We Can't Wait*. Boston: Beacon Press, 2011. Reprinted. First published 1964 by Signet Books (New York).

Kleinberg, Elliot. "How Confederate Flag Grew Famous—Hint: It Wasn't During Civil War." *Palm Beach (FL) Post*, June 22, 2015. https://www.palmbeach post.com/article/20150622/NEWS/812031630.

Lally, Kathy. "A Journey from Racism to Reason." *Baltimore Sun*, January 5, 1997.

Landrieu, Mitch. *In the Shadow of Statues: A White Southerner Confronts History.* New York: Viking, 2018.

——. "Mitch Landrieu's Speech on the Removal of Confederate Monuments in New Orleans." *New York Times*, May 23, 2017. https://www.nytimes.com /2017/05/23/opinion/mitch-landrieus-speech-transcript.html.

Lewis, Danny. "The 1873 Colfax Massacre Crippled the Reconstruction Era." *Smith-sonian*, April 2016. https://www.smithsonianmag.com/smart-news/1873 -colfax-massacre-crippled-reconstruction-180958746.

Linden, Glenn M. *Voices from the Reconstruction Years, 1865–1877.* New York: Har-court Brace/Cengage, 1998.

Logue, Cathy. Interview with author. August 22, 2019.

Loth, Calder. *Windows of Grace: A Tribute of Love—The Memorial Windows of St. Paul's Episcopal Church, Richmond, Virginia.* Norfolk, VA: Teagle and Little, 2004.

Lucas, Lawrence E. *Black Priest, White Church: Catholics and Racism.* Trenton, NJ: First Africa World Press, 1992. First published 1970 by Random House (New York).

Lyon, Carter Dalton. *Sanctuaries of Segregation: The Story of the Jackson Church Visit Campaign.* Jackson: University Press of Mississippi, 2017.

MacArthur, John. "The Statement on Social Justice & the Gospel." 2018. Accessed September 2, 2019, https://statementonsocialjustice.com.

Marsden, George. *Religion and American Culture.* San Diego: Harcourt Brace Jo-vanovich, 1990.

Marsh, Charles. *God's Long Summer: Stories of Faith and Civil Rights.* Princeton, NJ: Princeton University Press, 1997.

Massingale, Bryan N. *Racial Justice and the Catholic Church.* Maryknoll, NY: Orbis Books, 2010.

Matthews, Donald G. *At the Altar of Lynching: Burning Sam Hose in the American South.* Cambridge: Cambridge University Press, 2018.

McBeth, Leon. *The Baptist Heritage: Four Centuries of Baptist Witness.* Nashville: Broadman Press, 1987.

McCrummen, Stephanie, and Elahe Izadi. "Confederate Flag Comes Down on South Carolina's Statehouse Grounds." *Washington Post*, July 10, 2015. https:// www.washingtonpost.com/news/post-nation/wp/2015/07/10/watch-live -as-the-confederate-flag-comes-down-in-south-carolina/?utm_term=.150 871d7f92b.

McKinney, Debra. "Stone Mountain: A Monumental Dilemma." Southern Poverty Law Center *Intelligence Report*, no. 164, Spring 2018, 18–22.

Methodist Episcopal Church. *The Catechism of the Methodist Episcopal Church: Numbers 1, 2, and 3, in One Volume, Designed for Consecutive Study in Sunday Schools and Families*. New York: Carlton and Phillips, 1855.

"Mississippi Mix? Ross Says 'Never!'" Editorial, *Jackson (MS) Daily News*. September 14, 1962.

Mohler, Albert. "The Heresy of Racial Superiority—Confronting the Past, and Confronting the Truth." Albert Mohler online, June 23, 2015. https://albert mohler.com/2015/06/23/the-heresy-of-racial-superiority-confronting-the -past-and-confronting-the-truth.

Moody, Chris, and Kristen Holmes. "Donald Trump's History of Suggesting Obama Is a Muslim." CNN online. Last modified September 18, 2015. https://www .cnn.com/2015/09/18/politics/trump-obama-muslim-birther/index.html.

Morrison, Charles Clayton. *Can Protestantism Win America?* New York: Harper, 1948.

Morrison, Toni. *Playing in the Dark: Whiteness and the Literary Imagination*. New York: Vintage Books, 1993.

National Election Pool. National Exit Polls (2000–2016).

Niebuhr, Gustav. "Baptist Group Votes to Repent Stand on Slaves." *New York Times*, June 21, 1995. https://www.nytimes.com/1995/06/21/us/baptist-group -votes-to-repent-stand-on-slaves.html.

Oliver, Ned. "Congregation Once Led by Robert E. Lee Votes to Remove His Name from Their Church." *Richmond (VA) Times-Dispatch*, September 18, 2017. https://www.richmond.com/news/virginia/congregation-once-led-by-robert -e-lee-votes-to-remove/article_30d0557f-c3c0-5be2-8a28-308159dd662c .html.

———. "St. Paul's Episcopal Church Discusses Confederate Imagery." *Richmond (VA) Times-Dispatch*, August 23, 2015. https://www.richmond.com/news/local/city -of-richmond/st-paul-s-episcopal-church-discusses-confederate-imagery /article_fda4f734-e732-5c7f-bbe3-5f66f1f09cb3.html.

Pannell, Michael. "Northridge Aims at Grace as It Continues to Serve Those Around It." *Macon (GA) Telegraph*, January 4, 2018. https://www.macon.com/living /religion/article192900159.html.

Parker, Suzi. "African-Americans' Heritage Set in Stone." *Christian Science Monitor*, June 20, 2001.

"Parting of Cable Results in Death of Isham Andrews." *Atlanta Constitution*, September 20, 1920.

Paulsen, David. "Cincinnati Cathedral Drafts Plan to Study Removing Memorials to Confederate Figures." Episcopal News Service, September 13, 2017. https:// www.episcopalchurch.org/library/article/cincinnati-cathedral-drafts-plan -study-removing-memorials-confederate-figures.

Pearson, Richard. "Segregationist Governor Ross Barnett Dies at 89." *Washington Post*, November 8, 1987.

Perkiss, Abigail. "Shelley v. Kraemer: Legal Reform for America's Neighborhoods." *Constitution Daily* online. Last modified May 9, 2014. https://constitution center.org/blog/shelley-v-kraemer-legal-reform-for-americas-neighborhoods.

Pew Research Center online. "An Examination of the 2016 electorate, Based on Validated Voters." Last modified August 9, 2018. https://www.people-press.org /2018/08/09/an-examination-of-the-2016-electorate-based-on-validated -voters.

Phillip, Abbey. "Why Bree Newsome Took Down the Confederate Flag in S.C.: 'I Refuse to Be Ruled by Fear.'" *Washington Post*, June 29, 2015. https:// www.washingtonpost.com/news/post-nation/wp/2015/06/29/why-bree -newsome-took-down-the-confederate-flag-in-s-c-i-refuse-to-be-ruled-by -fear/?utm_term=.cd871de7e0d5.

Pokin, Steve. "In 1996, Hillcrest Students Decided Two Lynched Men Deserved a Grave Marker." *Springfield (MO) News-Leader*, December 19, 2017. https:// www.news-leader.com/story/news/local/ozarks/2017/12/19/pokin-around -1996-hillcrest-students-decided-two-lynched-men-deserved-grave-marker /963085001.

Prochnau, Bill. "The Tale of a Pulitzer, a Paper, a Family." *Washington Post*, April 25, 1983. https://www.washingtonpost.com/archive/politics/1983/04/25/the-tale -of-a-pulitzer-a-paper-a-family/2440bfeb-b772-4612-8a10-d0432844673c /?noredirect=on&utm_term=.87bcd4d68461.

Public Religion Research Institute (PRRI). Believers, Sympathizers, and Skeptics: Why Americans are Conflicted about Climate Change, Environmental Policy, and Science (November 21, 2014). PRRI online, accessed September 28, 2019. https://www.prri.org/research/believers-sympathizers-skeptics-amer icans-conflicted-climate-change-environmental-policy-science/.2014.

——. Nearly Half of Americans Worried That They or Their Family Will Be a Victim of Terrorism (December 2015). PRRI online, last modified December 10, 2015. https://www.prri.org/research/survey-nearly-half-of-americans -worried-they-or-their-family-will-be-a-victim-of-terrorism.2015.

——. The 2016 American Values Atlas. PRRI online, accessed November 1, 2019. http://ava.prri.org/#/2016. 2016a.

——. The Divide Over America's Future: 1950 or 2050?: Findings from the 2016 American Values Survey (October 25, 2016). PRRI online, accessed September 28, 2019. https://www.prri.org/research/poll-1950s-2050-divided -nations-direction-post-election/. 2016b.

——. Partisan Polarization Dominates Trump Era: Findings from the 2018 American Values Survey (October 29, 2018). PRRI online, accessed September 28, 2019. https://www.prri.org/research/partisan-polarization-dominates -trump-era-findings-from-the-2018-american-values-survey/. 2018a.

——. The 2018 American Values Atlas. PRRI online, accessed November 1, 2019. http://ava.prri.org/#/2018. 2018b.

———. Americans Differ on Participation of Male, Female Athletes in Team Sports: Findings from the 2018 Sports Poll (Jnauary 25, 2018). PRRI online, accessed September 28, 2019. https://www.prri.org/research/americans-differ-on-participation-of-male-female-transgender-students-in-team-sports/. 2018c.

———. Fractured Nation, Widening Partisan Polarization and Key Issues in 2020 Presidential Elections: Findings from the 2019 American Values Survey (October 20, 2019). PRRI online, accessed September 28, 2019. https://www.prri.org/research/fractured-nation-widening-partisan-polarization-and-key-issues-in-2020-presidential-elections/. 2019a.

———. America's Growing Support for Transgender Rights (June 11, 2019). PRRI online, accessed September 28, 2019. https://www.prri.org/research/americas-growing-support-for-transgender-rights/. 2019b.

Rehwald, Jackie. "On 112-Year Anniversary of Springfield Lynchings, Memorial for Victims Is Planned." *Springfield (MO) News-Leader*, April 12, 2018. https://www.news-leader.com/story/news/local/2018/04/12/112-year-anniversary-springfield-lynchings-memorial-victims-planned/504031002.

Riley, Benjamin F. *History of the Baptists of Alabama*. Birmingham, AL: Roberts and Son, 1895.

Robles, Frances. "Dylann Roof Photos and a Manifesto Are Posted on Website." *New York Times*, June 20, 2015. https://www.nytimes.com/2015/06/21/us/dylann-storm-roof-photos-website-charleston-church-shooting.html.

Romero, Simon, Manny Fernandez, and Mariel Padilla. "Massacre at a Crowded Walmart in Texas Leaves 20 Dead." *New York Times*, August 3, 2019. https://www.nytimes.com/2019/08/03/us/el-paso-shooting.html.

Roof, Dylann. Personal journal. 2015. Cited as government exhibit 500 in trial. Posted online at Scribd. Accessed September 28, 2019. https://www.scribd.com/document/335820753/Dylann-Roof-s-jailhouse-journal#fullscreen&from_embed.

Rothstein, Richard. *The Color of Law: The Forgotten History of How Our Government Segregated America*. New York: Liveright, 2018.

Ruane, Michael. "Slave's Daughter Who Helped Open the African American Museum Dies at 100." *Washington Post*, August 30, 2017. https://www.washingtonpost.com/local/slaves-daughter-who-helped-open-the-african-american-museum-dies-at-100/2017/08/30/2e4bc0ac-8d9d-11e7-91d5-ab4e4bb76a3a_story.html?noredirect=on&utm_term=.aaf0c084e5a9.

Rubin, Richard. "The Colfax Riot." *The Atlantic*, July/August 2003. https://www.theatlantic.com/magazine/archive/2003/07/the-colfax-riot/378556.

Rushing, Jean D. "From Confederate Deserter to Decorated Veteran Bible Scholar: Exploring the Enigmatic Life of C. I. Scofield, 1861–1921." Unpublished master's thesis. East Tennessee State University, 2011.

Sansing, David G. *The University of Mississippi: A Sesquicentennial History*. Oxford: University of Mississippi Press, 1999.

Saxon, Wolfgang. "Obituary: Cardinal O'Boyle of Washington, Liberal Who Espoused Orthodoxy." *New York Times*, August 11, 1987. https://www,nytimes.com/1987/08/11/obituaries/cardinal-o-boyle-of-washington-liberal-who-espoused-orthodoxy.html.

Scharen, Christian. *Fieldwork in Theology: Exploring the Social Context of God's Work in the World.* Ada, MI: Baker Academic, 2015.

Scofield, C. I. *The Old Scofield Study Bible, KJV, Classic Edition.* Oxford: Oxford University Press, 1999.

Scott, Eugene. "Slavery Has Always Been at the Intersection of Race and Politics. Now It's Front and Center in the Political Conversation." *Washington Post*, August 29, 2019. https://beta.washingtonpost.com/politics/2019/08/29/slavery-has-always-been-intersection-race-politics-now-its-front-center-political-conversation.

Sears, David O., and Patrick J. Henry. "The Origins of Symbolic Racism." *Journal of Personality and Social Psychology* 85, no. 2 (2003): 259–75.

Sears, David O., and Donald R. Kinder. *Racial Tension and Voting in Los Angeles.* Los Angeles: Institute of Government and Public Affairs, University of California, 1971.

Shelton, Jason E., and Michael O. Emerson. *Blacks and Whites in Christian America: How Racial Discrimination Shapes Religious Convictions.* New York: New York University Press, 2012.

Shepherd, Josh M. "How a Confederate Memorial Became a Multiracial Worship Site." *Christianity Today*, September 7, 2018.

Shurden, Walter. *Not an Easy Journey: Some Transitions in Baptist Life.* Macon, GA: Mercer University Press, 2005.

Smietana, Bob. "Eric Metaxas on Trump, Bonhoeffer, and the Future of America." Religion News Service, September 27, 2019. https://religionnews.com/2019/09/27/eric-metaxas-on-trump-bonhoeffer-and-the-future-of-america.

Southern Baptist Convention. "Resolution on Racial Reconciliation on the 150th Anniversary of the Southern Baptist Convention." Atlanta, 1995. http://www.sbc.net/resolutions/899/resolution-on-racial-reconciliation-on-the-150th-anniversary-of-the-southern-baptist-convention.

Southern Baptist Theological Seminary. *Report on Slavery and Racism in the History of the Southern Baptist Seminary.* Louisville, KY, 2018. http://www.sbts.edu/wp-content/uploads/2018/12/Racism-and-the-Legacy-of-Slavery-Report-v4.pdf.

Southern Poverty Law Center (SPLC) online, "Hate Groups Reach Record High." Last modified February 19, 2019. https://www.splcenter.org/news/2019/02/19/hate-groups-reach-record-high.

——. "Whose Heritage? Public Symbols of the Confederacy." Last modified February 1, 2019. https://www.splcenter.org/20190201/whose-heritage-public-symbols-confederacy.

Stead Sellers, Frances, "The Confederate Flag: A 150-Year Battle." *Washington Post*, October 15, 2018. http://www.washingtonpost.com/politics/the-confederate -flag-a-150-year-battle/2018/10/23/622ae7e2-d179-11ed-83d6-291fcead2ab1 _story.html.

Stearns, Matt. "Jerry Falwell Brought Religious Conservatives into US Politics." *Mercury News* (San Jose, CA), May 16, 2007. https://www.mercurynews.com /2007/05/16/jerry-falwell-brought-religious-conservatives-into-u-s-politics.

Stone, Caroline Branch. *The UDC Catechism for Children*. Galveston, TX: United Daughters of the Confederacy, 1904.

St. Paul's Episcopal Church online. "History and Reconciliation Initiative (HRI)." Accessed July 13, 2019. https://www.stpaulsrva.org/connect/hri.

Stracqualursi, Veronica. "Museum of the Bible Offers Revelations, Faces Controversy as It Opens." ABC News online. Last modified November 18, 2017. https: //abcnews.go.com/Politics/museum-bible-faces-revelations-controversy -opens/story?id=51194500.

Swidler, Ann. "Culture in Action: Symbols and Strategies." *American Sociological Review* 51 (1986): 273–86.

Tesler, Michael, and David O. Sears. *Obama's Race: The 2008 Election and the Dream of a Post-Racial America*. Chicago: University of Chicago Press, 2010.

Tyler, Alice M. *A Souvenir Book of the Jefferson Davis Memorial Association and the Unveiling of the Monument*. Richmond, VA: Whittet and Shepperson, 1907. https://archive.org/details/cu31924030945020/page/n6.

United Methodist Communications. "Timeline: Methodism in Black and White (1758–2009)." 2009. http://www.umc.org/resources/timeline-methodism-in -black-and-white, accessed March 23, 2019.

United States Catholic Conference. *Pastoral Letters of the United States Catholic Bishops*, vol. 2, 1941–1961. Washington, DC. 1961. Accessed September 16, 2019. http://www.usccb.org/issues-and-action/cultural-diversity/african -american/resources/upload/Discrimination-Christian-Conscience-Nov-14 -1958.pdf.

United States Department of Commerce. *Statistical Abstract of the United States, 1920*. Washington, DC: US Government Printing Office, 1921.

Urofsky, Melvin. "The Virginia Historical Society: The First 175 Years, 1831–2006." *Virginia Magazine of History and Biography* 114, no. 1 (2006).

Vilvens, Sheila. "A Year After Charlottesville: Confederate Symbols Wear Out Welcome at Ohio Cathedral." *Cincinnati Enquirer*, August 10, 2018. https:// www.wkyc.com/article/news/local/ohio/a-year-after-charlottesville-confed erate-symbols-wear-out-welcome-at-ohio-cathedral/95-582469557.

Wallace, Anthony F. C. *Religion: An Anthropological View*. New York: Random House, 1966.

Ward, Alex. "Charleston Shooting: Dylann Roof's Stepmother Defends 'Smart' Boy 'Drawn in by Internet Evil.'" *Independent (UK)*, June 21, 2015. https://www

.independent.co.uk/news/world/americas/the-stepmother-of-dylann-roof
-defends-the-smart-boy-she-raised-having-been-affected-by-internet-evil
-10334590.html.

Washington, Robin. "The Legacy of a Lynching: A Memorial, a Pilgrimage, a Reconciliation." The Marshall Project. Last modified May 3, 2018. https://www
.themarshallproject.org/2018/05/03/the-legacy-of-a-lynching.

Wells-Barnett, Ida B. *Lynch Law in Georgia: A Six-Weeks' Record in the Center of Southern Civilization, as Faithfully Chronicled by the "Atlanta Journal" and the "Atlanta Constitution."* Chicago: Chicago Colored Citizens, 1899. https://www.loc.gov/resource/lcrbmrp.t1612/?sp=1.

Wilkie, Curtis. *Dixie: A Personal Odyssey Through Events That Shaped the Modern South.* New York: Touchstone Books, 2002.

Wilson, Charles Reagan. *Baptized in Blood: The Religion of the Lost Cause, 1865–1920.* Athens: University of Georgia Press, 1980.

Žižek, Slavoj. "A Permanent Economic Emergency." *New Left Review*, no. 64 (July/August 2010), https://newleftreview.org/issues/II64/articles/slavoj-zizek-a
-permanent-economic-emergency.

Index

Page numbers in italics refer to illustrations.
Page numbers beginning with 255 refer to notes.

"**Robert Jones** has established himself as one of the country's most intelligent and fair-minded explorers of the American religious and political minds."

—E. J. DIONNE JR., author of *Why the Right Went Wrong*

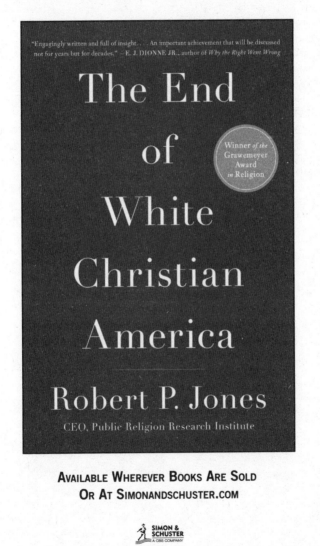

"Engagingly written and full of insight. . . . An important achievement that will be discussed not for years but for decades." —E. J. DIONNE JR., author of *Why the Right Went Wrong*

The End of White Christian America

Winner *of the* Grawemeyer Award *in* Religion

Robert P. Jones

CEO, Public Religion Research Institute

AVAILABLE WHEREVER BOOKS ARE SOLD
OR AT SIMONANDSCHUSTER.COM